FORTY SHADES OF BLUE

FORTY SHADES OF BLUE

Factionalism and Divisions in the Post-war British
Conservative Party from Churchill to Cameron

Vincent McKee

Takahe Publishing Ltd.

This edition published 2017 by:
Takahe Publishing Ltd.
Registered Office:
77 Earlsdon Street, Coventry CV5 6EL

ISBN 978-1-908837-08-0

TAKAHE PUBLISHING LTD.

2017

Dedicated in loving memory to my dear late parents,
Vincent (Senior) and Colette McKee - RIP.

May the Lord God Almighty happily reunite us all on the
Day of Judgement.

Acknowledgements

In researching and writing this book, I was fortunate to be variously assisted by many persons who are gratefully acknowledged here. They include:

All interviewees from the different organisations, groups and walks of Conservative and general political life who made themselves available for lengthy and comprehensive discussions, and often provided useful documentation in addition. (See Bibliography for full list of such persons)

I was further assisted by a number of Coventry Conservatives, past and present, who were kind enough over a period of years to pass over literature from different Tory groups canvassing party conference and other events. Those persons each took time and trouble to discuss with me their impressions of various issues and their impact on the party, which enabled me to acquire a practical feel for the internal culture of the Conservative Party. They included, most prominently, the late party professional agent, now sadly deceased, Mr Gordon Whiting MBE; a successor, Cllr Ken Taylor; Cllr Michael Hammon, former Cllr Andrew Matchett and Mrs Karen Matchett, Cllr Kevin Foster (now MP), the late Mr Alan Tandy, the late Mr Fred Rich, Mr John Farmer, Mr Bernard Capel, the late Cllr Arthur Taylor, Cllr Tim Sawden, Mr Matthew Harris, Mr David Sandy and Mr Nicholas Williams. Additionally, there was Mrs Elizabeth Boswell of Solihull Conservatives, who not only shared with me an informed perspective of her party, but also the warm hospitality of her home. To all those good people, I am truly indebted for their kindness.

On the academic front, Dr Ian Henderson, formerly of Coventry University, kindly read and commented on my earlier scripts. So also did another former undergraduate tutor, Keith Taylor, assist similarly in those early days until his premature death in January 2006 robbed me of a good friend.

Without doubt, the greatest loss was that of my Doctoral external supervisor and dear friend, Professor Tom Nossiter, late of the London School of Economics and Political Science. A consummate and well-published scholar, Tom proved to be the epitome of patience, kindness and encouragement, but always with a firm insistence on maintaining standards. Rather like a decent football manager, Tom knew his protégé's capacity, and accepted nothing less than full delivery. Just as he had got me up to peak level with my Ph.D. thesis in 1996, this was a line he continued to pursue with my book writing thereafter. Every sentence of the early draft scripts came under Tom's hawk-eyed scrutiny, and invariably had to be re-written to achieve better style, balance of content, effective analysis or whatever. For me, it really was a blessing from Heaven to have come under the kindly, caring but determined eye of one of the finest British political scientists of his generation. Alas, it all ended with Tom's tragic death in January 2004, forcing me to manage alone without the support of the old master from whom I had learned so much.

Thereafter, my friend, Professor Peter Hennessy (Queen Mary College, London), proved a positive and consistent encourager, as well as a source of wise counsel. So also did another friend, Professor David Marsland (Emeritus, Brunel University), prove encouraging and helpful, and indeed both those men were impressively loyal to me in the aftermath of a grave misfortune accompanying the collapse of a short-lived business venture over 2011-2012.

Professor Robert Eccleshall, Emeritus Chair of Politics Department, Queens University, Belfast, was kind enough to step in and provide a degree of mentoring over the last couple of years. His time taken in reading and commenting on my evolving script proved invaluable, and without which I would have struggled to bring this book to a successful completion.

Elsewhere, I received much kindly support from a Belfast journalist friend, Mr Martin O'Brien, along with a London-based retired political journalist, Mr Andrew Evans. There was also my Lagan writing services team, of whom my friend and administrative aide, Miss Siobhan Fitzpatrick, and her sister Ann (from my native Co. Down), were beacons of support. Mr John Edwardes, head of Coventry accounting firm, Baldwins Ltd, proved most encouraging and a good business adviser, while my dear daughter, Patricia, my wife, Mary-Jane, and brother, Paul, all proved to be models of commitment and loyalty. So also did I get a first class professional service from my publisher, Mr Steven Hodder, of Takahe Publishing, Coventry, who showed patience and humour at all times.

Finally, and most sincerely, having been granted sound health of mind and body to undertake this work, it falls to me, a committed Catholic and Christian, to bear witness in thanking the Lord God Almighty for his blessings. As unfashionable as it might appear in these secular times, to He who entered the world in poverty, performed many miracles, yet was crucified on Calvary before finally conquering death by his resurrection, I am not ashamed to pay just tribute to that same Jesus Christ for extending me a blessing not given everyone. My prayer now is that He will bless me further to do more writing of the sort that may contribute to legitimate knowledge of this society and its people; His very own creation. I also pray that those kindly persons who helped me, but did not live to see the fruits of their assistance may now be granted a merciful judgement and transition to a peaceful eternity.

Again, with sincerest thanks and God's blessings to everyone.

Dr Vincent McKee

CONTENTS

INTRODUCTION

The idea of writing a book on British Conservatism certainly did not square with my background or natural inclinations. I am not and never have been a Tory by affiliation or affinity; as is equally true of most fellow nationalist people in the rural community from whence I hail in South Down, Northern Ireland. Indeed, fair to say that those peers recalling the younger Vincent as a zealous Gaelic sports player (specifically Hurler), referee, organiser and writer would have regarded me as a most improbable candidate for the role of Tory scribe!

Yet in explaining how things moved to this stage, I am reminded of the caption on a poster advertising a support service at Coventry Polytechnic in 1980:

"Life is something that happens while you are expecting something else".

How true, and throughout the next 37 years I learnt that lesson many times.

My serious interest in Conservative politics began in 1988 when invited by Dr Anthony - now Sir Anthony - Seldon to write an article on Conservative factionalism for his esteemed journal, Contemporary Record. At that time, Anthony, in collaboration with Professor Peter Hennessy, was running the London-based Institute for Contemporary British History (ICBH), and as a Politics/History tutor in a London college I was a big supporter of ICBH conferences, publications and seminars. From the beginning, I developed the highest regard for Anthony and Peter; both scholarly gentlemen in their own right, but each kind enough to reach out to this rough-cut young Irishman working his way up! Thus, Anthony's invitation was one not to be missed.

From that little Oaktree emerged other writing opportunities, leading up to the greater project now put before the reader. The subject of Tory factionalism and divisions was not instantly excitable, but as I got into the research and reading, I found myself entering a twilight world of intrigue, organisational politics, competing personalities and ideological assertiveness. This was a world where in some but by no means all cases, loyalty to the Conservative Party played second fiddle to the group and its agenda. Rivalries were intense, as were the platforms on which Conservative group politics were conducted. There were even cases where certain group zealots had few compunctions about subverting the

xi

party leadership and their principal lieutenants. Outwardly, Tory politics appeared so civil, but in reality was quite barbarous. The groups and personalities whom I encountered were commendably frank and in the manner of their assessments quite fair and proportionate, but that did not hide the fact that their business could be ruthless with high stakes.

Generally, so little seemed to be known about Conservative factionalism or its impact on the party, whereas Labour's internecine conflicts seemed to be the stuff of common knowledge and expectation. Yet Conservatives have occupied government, either alone or as the dominant party for 56 of the last 86 years, therefore leading to the conclusion that what occurred in the party was relevant to public policy making. This rule applied to just about every area of British life ranging from economic and social management to education and the conduct of foreign policy to the winding up of Empire and accession to and subsequent withdrawal from the European Economic Community/Union. It also applied to my native Northern Ireland, where the Tories had historically allied with the Protestant Ascendancy and their Ulster Unionist political force.

Assessments of the modern British state beget the treatises of reputable historians, but those are incomplete without an informed evaluation of the full workings of Britain's most effective political force, the Conservative Party. It was to shed light on the latter that this work was undertaken, and which I have pursued thoroughly with the sole purpose of objective enquiry.

How far I have succeeded is a subject for reviewers and genuine scholars to debate. I make no arrogant claims to having achieved a masterful break-through, definitive text or other such self-adulating indulgences. Moreover, in a spirit of fairness, I have tried to acknowledge the contributions of other writers and scholars by way of copious references to their books, papers, theses and articles. Doubtless, there will be many ways in which subsequent researchers/writers can develop this subject, and to that next stage I look forward. Equally, I am sure there will be those who have fair criticisms of my style and methodology, while others may draw different conclusions. That is a legitimate part of the process, and I genuinely welcome constructive criticism.

Introduction

Yet notwithstanding all the limitations of this work and accepting that others may have different but entirely legitimate ideas about this subject, still I remain hopeful that this book may serve the cause of human knowledge. The short title, '**Forty Shades of Blue**', was actually adapted from the beautiful Irish ballad song titled '*Forty Shades of Green*' as a paradigm to exemplify the breadth and diversity of the modern British Tory Party. It is aimed at the thoughtful, rather than the specialist reader, and to that end I hope will prove just as interesting to the retired teacher and/or civil servant as to the Politics/History student, journalist and/or political activist.

If this book catches the interest of readers and provides some enlightenment, then I shall feel both satisfied and vindicated that a very lengthy and challenging research and writing exercise was finally worthwhile.

Over to you, the readers!

Feast of All Saints, Wednesday 1st November, 2017,

Coventry, United Kingdom.

Dr Vincent McKee

Forty Shades of Blue

PREFACE

Opening this particular angle on post-war British Conservative history, the author anticipates certain key questions in preface about the nature of the work. Not the least of those concerns its aims, scope and parameters. In outlining the latter, it is hoped that the reader will recognise the essence of this enquiry as a proper and long-overdue evaluation of a subject about which others have written in part, but with no study undertaken of its totality.

This author recognises that there are different methods of approach, and his choice of framework for this study in no way excludes the validity of alternative angles. Nor does this effort claim definitive status, far less exclude the likelihood of other, equally useful, perspectives emerging from party observers and a subsequent generation of contemporary historians. There is no such thing as anyone, no matter how learned, having last word on this subject, or indeed others in the world of politics and contemporary history.

This exercise aims to contribute to the limited body of knowledge on a topic frequently aired in media analysis and general literature, but rarely examined by serious academics much beyond a cursory glance at passing activists. As outlined in Chapter 2, in British politics generally factionalism is a subject that rarely excites interest from anywhere. Many view the subject as divisive, while to others it appears abstract and theoretical, rarely connecting to the world of public decision-making or external power competition. Yet so much of public policy-making has been fashioned in the first instance through adoption by influential party groups who either had the ear of leadership or were themselves the bodies from where leadership spawned. One only has to look at Labour's defence and welfare defence lobbies and the Conservatives' pro- and anti-European lobby groups for examples. More on this subject later!

Meanwhile, three questions remain to be addressed herewith.

1. What is this book about?

It seeks to present a comprehensive account and analysis of the post-war British Conservative Party: − its debates, evolution, issues, divisions, leaders and the role of campaign groups, ideological tendencies and trusts. The book is not intended as a straight chronicle of party history −

although in fact it covers much relevant ground for students of post-war Toryism – but rather acts as a reliable account to the character and outcomes of policy and power divisions, and the roles played by groups at Westminster and in the wider party. The original intention was to evaluate the grass roots movement predominantly, but over the course of research and writing the extent to which mainstream Conservative groups were tied to Westminster patrons and political dynamics proved a reality which this study could not ignore.

Along with the party's general features was a recurrent phenomenon that when in Opposition the Conservatives regularly experience an upsurge in factional activity. This trait reflected the party's nervousness with exclusion from office, and fears about how long before it would return. Not that being in office precluded divisions and factional politicking: far from it! Actually, the experiences of Tory reformers, free market liberals, pro-and anti-Europeans during the Heath, Thatcher, Major and Cameron eras testifies to a Tory movement that is just as prone to ideological debate and counter-alignments from within as any and all of its major political opponents. This study will examine those phenomena in some detail over the entire post-war period.

2. Why the Conservative Party?

Any creditable assessment of political trends in twentieth century Britain must acknowledge the party that has dominated government for two thirds of that time. Over the post-war era, Conservatives have held office for 42 of the 72 years since 1945. In that time, the party has stamped its imprimatur on British public policy-making; including imperial wind-up, the constitution, Northern Ireland, the free market economy, state welfare, defence strategy and both European accession and withdrawal ... to name a few key areas. That being so, there is merit in an observation by Professor Dennis Kavanagh: "... that the history of the Conservatives and the British state are synchronised".*(1)

It follows that with Conservatives playing a pivotal role in government, the principal agents of party opinion would inevitably make their mark on the public sphere. Even more poignant was the fact that several of the more cerebral organisations effectively fashioned the ideological components of an agenda for government. Examples included

Tory Reform (in its various guises), One Nation Group, Conservative Group for Europe, Institute for Economic Affairs, Selsdon Group, European Foundation and Conservative Way Forward. Reactionary bodies like the Monday Club, Western Goals Institute and Grass Roots Conservatives were less significant on account of their lengthy distance from leadership, but each of them generated enough heat to ensure the semblance of a democratic debate. Again, more later.

Very significantly, in the early post-war years it was an elite tendency of One Nation policy makers, headed by Rab Butler at the Conservative Research Department, whose lobbying and policy output gradually won the Tories round to accepting a mixed economy, social security, accommodation of the trade unions and a state health service. Indeed the period of so-called 'Butskellism' and the post-war settlement owes much to the persistent efforts of Butler and his influential tendency.*(2) Equally, later Conservative disenchantment with the public sector, trade union power, comprehensive benefits and high taxation was rooted in the ideological campaigns of an influential New Right tendency centred on the Conservatives post-1975 leader, Margaret Thatcher. Subsequent changes to the economy, social security benefits, privatisation and public spending cuts characterised the Thatcher and Major agenda for the 1980s and early/mid-1990s. Moreover, as Kavanagh noted, those changes – composing what the late Peter Jenkins called Mrs Thatcher's 'revolution' – affected every household in1980s Britain.*(3) Again, fundamental transformation of the political and social management of Britain originated in an ideological crusade linked to the policy direction enunciated by Margaret Thatcher. Such testifies to a view that from time to time government can actually make a difference, most especially Conservative government.*(4)

3. Precise Span of this Book

It covers the period 1945-2016, embracing a broad stream of Conservative campaigning, research and Westminster lobbyist groups drawn from almost three quarters of a century. The book does not aim to provide an exhaustive list of all groups operating within the Tory ranks and around the fringe so much as offering an account of all the major organisations, along with their leaders, support base, goals, resources, campaigning strategies and impact. It also seeks to evaluate the ideological leanings, and how such groups operated vis-à-vis leadership of the time, either as supporters and publicists or as a refuge for opponents of the party's official regime.

As earlier indicated, while the primary focus will be directed towards grass roots, the reality of Westminster domination of all mainstream Conservative activity applies to factionalism and debates as much as anything else. That being the case, the study needs to pay attention to the directing groups at Westminster, as well as MPs and peers who acted as sponsors of the various causes propagated. For that reason, readers may understand why so many of my recorded interviews were conducted with parliamentarians; they in many cases being the most reliable custodians of true group capacity and influence over policy, plus leverage with the Westminster leadership.

Another factor concerns a definition of Conservative groups. Many of the organisations listed such as the IEA, Centre for Policy Studies, Western Goals Institute and even the currently eschewed Monday Club, are formally independent of the Conservative Party. They support the Conservative Party, but are not constitutionally affiliated or subject to the party's leadership or discipline. For all practical purposes, I have taken the view that where a body is campaigning within the party's orbit, then it is to be treated as a party group. The same principle will be applied where a campaigning body covers a cross-party platform, such as occurred with both European referendums or indeed the Radical Society which appealed to free market forces inside and outside Mrs Thatcher's party of the late 1980s. Conversely, questions of formal affiliation amount to a fine detail.*(5)

Finally, the study will take as its break-off point David Cameron's defeat in the European Union referendum of 23rd June 2016. Thereafter, the forces bringing Teresa May to the premiership, her subsequent failure to attain a full mandate in the election of May 2017, and follow-up efforts at negotiating a satisfactory Brexit agreement with European leaders, along with its impact on the Conservative Party, amounts to an ongoing fixture. Such an evaluation will have to await a post-script in a future edition of this book.

Meanwhile, it is to be earnestly hoped that the ensuing study will facilitate an objective appreciation of the mechanics of Conservative politics in terms of debates, divisions, alignments and factionalism over the post-war years.

FOOTNOTES and REFERENCES

1. Kavanagh's comment was made in a public lecture on Thatcherism to students organised by the Institute of Contemporary British History (ICBH), Central Methodist Hall, Westminster, London - 7th March, 1989. Author was in attendance at the event.

2. "Butskellism" was an acronym highlighting the triumph of a post-war settlement sustained by a left-leaning Tory Party and centrist-leaning Labour Party - symbolised by the prevalence of Conservative policy guru and One Nationite, Rab Butler, and Labour's revisionist social democrat and second post-war Chancellor, Hugh Gaitskell.

   See: Ian Gilmour, 'Inside Right' (Hutchinson,1977), and David Howell 'British Social Democracy' (Croom Helm,1976).

3. Peter Jenkins 'Mrs Thatcher's Revolution' (J. Cape,1988).

4. Another Kavanagh theme- repeated in his 1989 ICBH lecture.

5. The author remains grateful to Lord/Professor Philip Norton (correspondence 1998) for drawing his attention to this question.

Forty Shades of Blue

CHAPTER 1

OVERVIEW OF POST-WAR EVOLUTION

This first chapter offers a framework for analysing the post-1945 British Conservative Party. Account is taken of the character and culture of British Conservatism, while noting the various changes experienced over the period. An analytical model is offered of recent Conservative history, with particular emphasis given to evolving tendencies that came to dominate the post-war party under different leaders. From the two phases under examination, the question arises as to whether factionalism emerged as an expression of ideological politics or specific policy campaigns being pursued within the party. In order to usefully evaluate the impact of groups operating at the grass roots, first it is necessary to analyse recent party history.

1. Introduction

The British Conservative Party has functioned as a federal entity for over 150 years. At various points since the 1850s tensions have occurred between different bodies, including rank and file, Central Office, the former Conservative Research Department and of course Annual Conference and the leadership at Westminster. Institutional rivalries were and remain inevitable in a large, enduring and – it must be added – successful political movement of the kind that British Tories have long boasted. Yet it is not so much the nature of those strains that concerns this inquiry as more their effects on the party generally and grassroots particularly. Factional activity in the party outside Westminster mirrors the party's general condition in relation to policy debates, "great issues" and leadership questions, all of which have occupied Conservatives over the post-war period.

Assessing Tory development from pre-democratic to modern times is a task best left to the erudite talents of Robert Blake, John Ramsden, John Charmley and other reputable historians.*(1) This study assesses lobby groups from the centre and right wings over the post-war period. While the dividing line between Conservatives at Westminster and in the country is vague and even arbitrary in places, this study is concerned with *groups outside Parliament*. Specifically, it focuses on different group agendas, campaign tactics, leadership and key activists, along with influence achieved at Westminster, Annual Conference and in constituency associations and ancillary groups, e.g. students, trade unionists, women, etc. So also will ideological competition between groups be gauged for the effects on Conservative politics throughout the 71 years from 1945 to 2016.

Initially, a definitive framework for factions is needed, and particularly a model relevant to the changing political tides characterising the post-war party, which shall follow in Chapter 2. To a large extent, factions have been shaped by the party's experience of post-war Britain, inclusive of fundamental changes to its own internal culture over the period. Such was especially true of the post-1960s Conservative generation; they being products of Britain's adjustment to World War 2's ending and peacetime reconstruction.

However, the change process went further than mere evolution. Churchill's party made painful adjustments to the end of empire, and advent of a welfare state and mixed economy... all characterising Attlee's Britain. Later, Anthony Eden's Suez debacle – that ended his premiership – and its aftermath highlighted lingering imperial sentiments prevailing among his generation of Tories. Subsequent debates in the 1960s and '70s over European accession, immigration, race relations, Northern Ireland and economy showed up an increasingly fragmented Conservative Party, which by 1974 lacked a homogenous identity. The nadir of Conservative fortunes occurred in the election of October 1974 when the party registered its then lowest share of the national vote since 1945; but the defeat of 1997 was on a comparable scale. Hence the arrival of Margaret Thatcher at the helm in February 1975, her ensuing policy revisions and subsequent electoral triumphs of 1979, 1983 and 1987 appeared redolent of messianic rescue. Yet in Autumn 1990, with the party's reduced standing in opinion polls and local and Westminster by-election losses mounting, Thatcher's stature had diminished. Then followed her forcible exit from Downing Street in November (1990), to be replaced by a less combative John Major.

Despite negative forecasts, Major's elevation appeared to have been vindicated by the unexpected Conservative victory in the general election of April 1992. Yet it proved to be something of a false dawn. A mediocre performance in office combined with rebellions, divisions – mainly over Europe – and defeats sent Conservatives hurtling towards their greatest election defeat of the twentieth century on 1st May 1997 (30.7% of vote, 165 seats). Thereafter Major's youthful successor, William Hague, leading from the right, sought to stage a recovery by appealing to popular Tory causes, specifically sovereignty and the free market. The exercise yielded only modest gains, and with the party racked by further right-centrist divisions, its showing in the general election of June 2001 showed little improvement from 1997. There followed Hague's resignation and the party's first ever deployment of an electoral college for choosing a successor. From the latter emerged the lesser known, Iain Duncan-Smith, again from the right, but at the expense of ex-ministers Michael Portillo and Kenneth Clark. IDS was charged with leading an unelectable party, with omens that looked distinctly unpromising. Additionally, over an eight-month period from October 2002 until the modest gains of the 2003 English local government elections there occurred a crisis of confidence in Duncan-Smith's (IDS) leadership. Rebel party voices urged his resignation. He weathered that storm, but public doubts resurfaced around the Autumn Annual Conference, with the final inglorious exit of IDS following a no-confidence vote by Tory MPs at Westminster on 31st October 2003.

If Conservatives hoped that by ditching their captain they would be rewarded by the electorate, this calculation proved seriously misplaced. New leader, Michael Howard, proved no more a messiah than his IDS predecessor. The general election of May 2005 saw the Tories, headed by Howard, routed by a Labour Party whose own leader, Tony Blair, lacked the fresh appeal of earlier days as a result of the controversial attack on Iraq. Indeed it was a measure of how grave was the Tories crisis that despite counterpoising a divided and unpopular Labour government, they could not take advantage to reap the electoral rewards that should normally have followed.

In the aftermath of defeat, Conservatives over 2005 and 2006 – repeating experiences of the mid 1970s – grappled with the fear of having permanently lost hold on public office. The suggestion was seriously advanced from various media and academic sources that the party was in terminal decline, forever banished from government and likely to survive only as a reactionary rump in a parliament where other forces, New Labour, Liberal Democrats and Celtic Nationalists prevailed. Of course that speculation turned out to be misplaced. The election of David Cameron as leader in late 2005, the party's slow electoral recovery, and the entry to government as senior coalition partners with the Liberal Democrats in May 2010 told its own story. The durability of the Coalition for its full five year term, and the narrow outright victory for Cameron in the 2015 election spelt the Tories return to power and restoration of confidence. Yet it was a different, more liberal and fractious Conservative Party that Cameron headed from the one that had been led thirty years earlier by Mrs Thatcher. Significantly, Europe continued to divide Cameron's party as it had done forty five years earlier in the Heath era. Those divisions manifested poignantly in the 2016 European referendum, that spelt the UK/EU divorce.

Generally, historical experience shows British Conservatives to be prone to division at times of uncertainty. Whether factionalism is the direct consequence of a leadership vacuum, as occurred in the last twelve months of Edward Heath's tenure, or reflecting a wider power cum ideological struggle, or simply venting honest differences on a policy like Europe is a question to be addressed in the final chapter. Meanwhile, the underlying issues, organisations, troops and generals from over half a century of intra-Conservative battles will be laid bare over the next nine chapters, and conclusions drawn.

2. Character of the Post-war Conservative Party

Accounts of the Tories' evolution in the post-1945 era are many and varied. Several historians of different colours have emerged, ranging from the conventional Blake, Ramsden and Norton to the more polemical Clark and colourful Charmley, with each analysing party development over the 71 years since World War 2.*(2) Conservative group politics

4

fed off a mixture of ideological and policy divisions between rival spokesmen, ideologues and support groups.

The post-war period may be divided into six stages, defined as:

- 1945-56 – Conservative transition from defender of empire and Whig society to embracing social reform and self-determination. – Churchill/Eden

- 1957-65 - Uncertain wandering and managing national decline. Macmillan/Home.

- 1965-75 - Conservatives as a modernising and pro-European vehicle: Heath.

- 1975-90 - Resurgent nationalism and revived Whig economics: Thatcher.

- 1990-2006 - Consolidation of free market and assertion of the nation state: Major, Hague, Duncan-Smith and Howard leadership.

- 2006-16 - Revived era of One Nation-Liberal Toryism: Cameron.

It was against the background of changing policies and leaders, plus alternative periods in office, that party culture adapted over six decades. Those experiences produced the impetus for ideological politics, which in turn generated exponents and reactionaries alike. From this sequence of events, factionalism proved the inevitable result, manifesting in various types across the post-war period.

3. Transition from Imperialism (1945-57)

This period is noteworthy for the manner in which Conservatives responded to their shock humiliation at the polls in July 1945. Among historians there has been debate about the extent of the party's routing, but not its consequences as a catalyst for change and modernisation.*(3) The principal effect of that defeat was a fulsome reappraisal of policy, electoral strategy and party organisation, which in turn led to something approaching a political rebirth of the movement. Moreover, in response to the Attlee government's programme of socio-economic interventionism, public welfare and decolonisation of the British Empire, Conservatives were drawn – albeit reluctantly – into a post-war policy framework that included all the previous ingredients. In return for a de facto recognition of private enterprise, Conservatives were forced to dance to a leftist tune for some thirty years after the war in order to sustain electoral appeal. Plainly, to be effective the Tories had to be relevant, which meant ditching much previous superfluous baggage.

Yet some questioned the genuineness of the Tory conversion. Andrew Gamble argued that perceptions of progressive Toryism were misplaced.*(4) True, the party made concessions over the public utilities and NHS, while embracing expanded public welfare and imperial decolonisation. However, Gamble felt this change to have been tactical rather than principled. In essence, Conservatives had moved away from imperialism and militant anti-Socialism towards a progressive form of capitalism that combined the free market and constitutional defence with tactical concessions to an egalitarian public spirit then permeating British society and the establishment in the aftermath of war.

Gamble contended that the essential purpose of British Conservatives to defend capitalism remained unaltered, which provoked different views among commentators about the Tory Centre and Right. Robert Blake viewed the Conservatives as having been dragged along in the pro-state consensus characterising the post-1945 years.*(5) Blake highlights 'Rab' Butler's role in refashioning Conservatives as a breed of progressive Tories whom he brought to the fore. Also emerging was an acknowledgement among Conservatives over the efficacy of the state. If soundly managed – by Tories – then the belief ran that it could be an effective guardian of free enterprise and manager of public utilities. In any case, winning public office was vital in order to stem the Socialist left.

There was also the priority of keeping the party electable. Tory managers needed no reminding that business sponsors would not indefinitely bankroll a permanent Opposition force. Hence there was something inevitable about the emergence of such forces as the Tory Reform Committee and, later, One Nation Group among younger parliamentarians, researchers, Central Office staff and Tory careerist aspirants.*(6) Prominent advocates included Gilbert Longdon, the youthful Edward Heath, Angus Maude, Viscount Hinchingbroke and – despite attachments to Empire – the cerebral Enoch Powell. All yearned for an early Tory return to office on a social reform programme relevant to post-war conditions. They were embarrassed by the austere records of pre-war Conservative governments. Indeed the 1945 landslide defeat was viewed by many as retribution for digressions by pre-war Whigs, whose free market dogma had contributed to a battered economy and social distress for which Conservatives paid a high electoral price. Accordingly, the changing Conservative character was born of necessity. The influential Tory Reform Committee certainly boosted the centre, but electoral rather than ideological factors determined new strategies. Fresh direction meant declarations of the new centrist faith. The 1945 election manifesto contained ambitious house-building targets, while also endorsing Beveridge's Report on social welfare and the 1944 (Butler) Education Act that established tripartite secondary schools. In Opposition, Tories rowed with, rather than against the prevailing leftist tide. Nationalisation of utilities was barely resisted, save for iron and steel; the Tories' 1947 Industrial Charter accepted trade unions' role in industry, while the National Health Service received qualified approval. In foreign affairs, Indian independence was agreed without a Commons vote, wider decolonisation was accepted, as was, unsurprisingly, Ernest Bevin's pro-Atlantic foreign policy stance.

Tory concurrence in the post-war 'Consensus' was evidenced from the policy continuity characterising Conservative governments running Britain – under Churchill, Eden, Macmillan and Home – from 1951 until 1964. Aside from iron and steel, other public utilities were maintained, as was the social security system. Industrial policy during Walter Monckton's tenure at the Ministry of Labour is recalled by John Charmley and Dennis Kavanagh as a period of union appeasement that horrified New Right advocates a generation later.*(7) Monckton was so anxious to avoid the industrial strife and class antagonisms of pre-war years that his policies reflected those priorities. His conciliatory approach extended so far that he was accused of surrendering vital ground by the historian, Andrew Roberts, and many Thatcherites thirty years on.*(8) It is indicative of political conditions then that Monckton's labour relations epitomised government orthodoxy. The further willingness of Conservative governments from 1951-1964 to even expand social security, while presiding over a growth in secondary schools, colleges and universities during the same period, highlighted two factors.

First was the dominance of a Progressive-One Nation tendency at the higher echelons of the party, with Butler as principal 'guru' in Cabinet and as Chairman of the Conservative Research Department. Other patrons included Harold Macmillan, Iain Macleod, Reginald Maudling, Edward Heath and Quintan Hogg (Junior). The Tory Progressives had their distinctive agenda of 'One Nation' social policies, with a foreign affairs programme that leaned towards Europe, of which more will be said later. Significantly, this tendency peaked during the Macmillan (1957-63) and Home (1963-64) premierships, but was on the ascendant during the Churchill and Eden era (1940-57). Second, by 1953 it was possible to talk about a bipartisan 'Consensus'. Although some writers dispute this concept, the evidence of reputable academics is compelling. Kavanagh showed clear policy frameworks for the conduct of home affairs, labour relations, utilities management, constitutional defence, decolonisation and a pro-Atlantic foreign policy. *(9) Though emphasis depended on the governing party of the day, the broad contours held fast whichever party was in office. This gave continuity to public policy, but also conferred advantage on the centrist wings of both main parties. Thus the Tory Progressives' domination of their party was facilitated by conditions prevailing in the wider British political arena. Plainly this was a creature of its time!

4. Uncertain Journey and Management of National Decline (1957-65)

This era is synonymous with two factors, both contributing to the Conservatives' crisis in the 1970s, notably electoral peaks followed by slow falls and economic decline. How far those problems may be attributed to Conservative governments of the period is an issue hotly debated by historians and political economists. Gamble argued that successive governments of all persuasions managed economic decline, while David Marquand considered Britain to have been left behind by an economically-regenerate Europe.*(10) While details of that debate lie beyond this study's scope, nevertheless a fluctuating economy and electoral consequences impacted heavily on Conservative parliamentarians, policymakers, grass roots activists and factional groups.

The premiership of Harold Macmillan occurred against a background of growing social and economic troubles at home, coupled with imperial wind-up and uncertainty about Britain's future relations with America and Europe. Macmillan's predecessor, Anthony Eden's tenure had been brief (1955-57) due to the Suez debacle. Eden's resignation in January 1957 had – as David Carlton showed – been forced by nefarious intrigues against himself and the other claimant, 'Rab' Butler, thereby leading to Macmillan's arrival at Downing Street.*(11)   His agenda included healing the rift with America after Suez, while winding up the Empire and preparing for UK accession to the European Economic Community. Not all those goals were attained before Macmillan quit office, but he defined the parameters of British domestic and foreign policy over the next two decades.

Accordingly, in economic management, Macmillan's approach was non-dogmatic and aimed at sustaining growth. Contemporaneous data of the late 1950s showed a UK economy with rising living standards, higher incomes, low unemployment, rising home ownership, private investment and optimism about the future.*(12) Such trends accounted in no small way for the Conservatives' third consecutive election victory in 1959. Indeed Macmillan's speech telling the nation that "…you've never had it so good.." typified public optimism while linking his party to the trend. Such sentiments seemed well vindicated, and the travails of Labour after their 1959 election defeat – highlighted by the Rose-Abrams survey – pointed to a continuation of Conservative hegemony throughout the 1960s.*(13) So too was the Prime Minister's personal authority enhanced by electoral and apparent policy success. He was strong enough to continue decolonisation in Africa and Asia, while resisting the right wing Monday Club formed in 1961. Macmillan further defined a new defence initiative that replaced the Blue Streak missile programme with the US-supplied Polaris nuclear submarine fleet.

Yet the Macmillan government's 1960 EEC application indicated an acknowledgement – however tacit – of the Commonwealth's failure as an instrument of British economic and foreign policy. Edward Heath's memoirs recall unease over increasing British dependence on the USA, but moves towards European accession generated assorted tides of Conservative support and hostility.*(14) Yet Charles De Gaulle's veto of the British application in January 1963 threw Macmillan's economic and foreign policy into chaos, thereby compounding an already faltering economy, something two changes of Chancellor from 1958 to 1962 failed to stem. Other difficulties afflicting Macmillan's government included a sex-cum-security scandal implicating the War Minister, John Profumo, which along with adverse opinion polls and by-election defeats, caused a crisis of confidence in the Premier's leadership, thereby forcing his retirement in October 1963.

The emergence of hereditary peer, Alec Douglas-Home, as Macmillan's successor at Downing Street followed from a brief period of intensive hyper-intrigue and venting of personal rivalries.*(15) The succession battle, while devoid of organised factionalism, nevertheless affected Conservatives at Westminster through the refusals of Iain Macleod and Enoch Powell to serve in Home's cabinet. Also, it resulted in the party later choosing future leaders by direct election of MPs, and from 2001 onwards by balloting the membership.

How far the circumstances and fallout from Home's succession damaged his prospects is difficult to gauge. Significantly, the policy continuity carried on between Home and Macmillan over economic management, Atlantic relations, the Commonwealth and attitudes to Europe. Although the narrow Conservative defeat in October 1964 was followed by Home's retirement from the leadership nine months later, neither he nor his policies were repudiated. Moreover, his departure did not boost the Conservative Right as happened ten years later with Edward Heath's election defeat. It is also significant that the manner of Home's departure was entirely voluntary, with no organised groups having forced his hand. Also, policy continuity was maintained with his successor,

Edward Heath. Both Heath and his main rival, Reginald Maudling, were of the same Tory Progressive school, whereas Enoch Powell's derisory 15 votes showed the Right's weakness at Westminster. It also suggested that the Tories were choosing a leader rather than breaking with existing policy boundaries.*(16)

5. Tories as a Vehicle for Modernisation and European Accession: the era of Edward Heath (1965-75)

Edward Heath's leadership tenure raised new challenges of variable worth and durability to his party. Indeed that era is as notable for its failures as achievements. For example, the electoral price paid by Heath for his failed industrial relations and economic strategy, culminating in the two election defeats of 1974, forced Conservatives to review a faltering 'Consensus'. Kavanagh argued that Heath's inability to redeem manifesto pledges or retain office directly paved the way for an internal revolution headed by Margaret Thatcher in 1975.*(17) This thesis appears vindicated by events of the period.

Heath's primary motif was modernisation, a trait defining his leadership. Blake considered Heath's attachment to professional politics distinguished him from predecessors.*(18) Being the first elected Conservative leader, he claimed a mandate for imposing his agenda on the party. Heath's memoirs recalled a desire to replace the obsolete amateurism of the old Tory machine with an efficient right of centre party capable of regaining electoral confidence on a progressive manifesto. Perhaps the policy that defined his era more than all else was U.K. accession to the European Economic Community (EEC). Heath's conviction was that Britain's future lay at the heart of Europe, and the eventual achievement of UK-EEC entry in 1973 ranks as his major crowning achievement.*(19) Yet pursuing that aim divided the Tory Party at Westminster and in the country. It left a legacy impacting on all six of his successors to date, and more so over the past twelve months leading up to the June 2016 E.U. referendum where British voters opted for withdrawal. There was also the gathering economic troubles, including low growth, industrial strife, trade deficits and increasing public spending that frustrated Tory ambitions for tax reductions.

Whatever fair winds favoured Macmillan's tenure, actually Heath was bedevilled by a cocktail of economic stagnation, union militancy, Commonwealth troubles over UDI in Rhodesia and coloured immigration, combined to social and sexual upheavals characterising 1960s Britain.*(20)

In his determination to find responses, Heath resolved that the party should not turn to the Conservative Right for dogmatic solutions that might do further damage. He showed no inhibitions about stamping his imprimatur on the party or shifting rightist critics like Enoch Powell and, later, Nicholas Ridley who challenged his vision.*(21) Actually, Blake and Ramsden both argued that Heath's ruthlessness might have been vindicated by a more successful track record at Downing Street, but such did not happen.*(22) Hence it was inevitable that his enemies would round upon him in the aftermath of two election defeats in 1974. Evaluations of Heath's legacy vary. Gamble viewed him as an expedient manager whose luck ran out when the miners' strike of 1974 and 1973 Arab oil embargo together provoked a crisis in international supply.*(23) While acknowledging Heath's commitments to Europe, the social market economy and progressive social agenda, Gamble also noted his monetarist leanings, and especially the rightist Selsdon Park programme of 1970 fashioning that year's Tory election manifesto.*(24) By contrast, Blake and Ramsden both saw Heath as an updated Butskellite. A Macmillan protégé, under whom he served his apprenticeship, significantly Heath pursued the same goals as his old mentor, notably Keynesian economics, a multi-coloured Commonwealth, smooth relations with the USA through NATO and accession to Europe (EEC).*(25)

Accounts by most contemporary historians suggest Heath's modernising agenda caused strife with his party, hastening his downfall.*(26) Yet it is doubtful whether a more personable style would have saved his leadership after the second election defeat of October 1974. His cold manner and imperious style caused antagonism even among ideological soul mates, several of whom cast negative votes in the vital leadership election of February 1975.*(27) Yet the post-war 'Consensus' was visibly disintegrating under a combination of economic, social and political troubles. At the same time, Labour – then in government – was lurching towards the left, with Industry Minister, Tony Benn, and his Tribune followers openly propagating a new socialist direction.*(28) Thus with the Conservative New Right already mobilised through organisations such as the Monday Club, Centre for Policy Studies, Selsdon Group and Institute of Economic Affairs, it was inevitable that right wingers would bid for party control. Conversely, Heath, defeated and politically depleted, found himself defending a failing system. Against multiple critics who by November 1974 included Powell, Ridley, John Biffen, Keith Joseph, Norman St John-Stevas, Airey Neave and the as yet undeclared Margaret Thatcher, Heath's fortunes sank along with the post-war Settlement.

That Heath fell ingloriously to the challenger, Margaret Thatcher, in February 1975 indicated two factors.*(29) First, that Conservatives were gradually rebuking 'One Nationism' and state-intervention policies of its successor post-war leaders. Second, the end of the post-war Settlement meant the Tory Progressives era had also come to an end.

6. Enter Margaret Thatcher and the New Right (1975-90)

Dennis Kavanagh noted that the rise of Thatcherism in mid-late 1970s indicated sea-changes taking place within the Conservative Party and wider British society.

First, was a growing disenchantment with the post-war Settlement. In place of previous acquiescence in the 1940s and '50s, the new leadership regarded the Settlement as a charter for state-sponsored social democracy. Mrs Thatcher viewed it as a capitulation to the assorted forces of socialism with consequent high taxes that discouraged enterprise. It further channelled wasteful state aid to failing industries, was unproductive and produced over-manned public utilities dominated by over-powerful trade unions, plus a culture of dependence – in welfare payments – which she believed undermined self-dependence and thrift, both vital for revival and national renewal.*(30) All those failings Thatcher blamed on a long running orthodoxy of high taxes, appeasing of trade unions, an unprofitable public sector and a culture of state welfare that discouraged self-reliance. It is significant that her critique was equally scathing about the collusion of past Conservative governments in the post-war Settlement. Hence Thatcher's first major policy document, The Right Approach (1976), signalled a radical break with the past.*(31)

Second, Thatcher's emergence amidst electoral crisis suggests her acceptance was solely related to restoring the Conservatives to government. Such a view is plausible from a long term perspective. Writing just before her accession in 1979, Patrick Seyd assessed the party crisis.*(32) Having lost four out of five previous elections with their lowest share of the post-war vote, Seyd concluded that the party risked being reduced to a voice only for English shires and beleaguered inner city whites. Hindsight shows this thesis to have been overly pessimistic, but there was no doubting the voter crisis underpinning Thatcher plans to restore Conservative electoral appeal by reviving popular Tory causes.*(33)

Third, Mrs Thatcher fell outside the scale of traditional Conservative leaders in that she was both *anti-establishment* and an *ideologue*. While previous Conservative leaders rarely admitted to an ideological direction, Mrs Thatcher unashamedly proclaimed her mission as being to save Britain from Socialism. If that meant embracing causes and symbols viewed in other circles as divisive, so be it! It was a sign of how deep the 'malaise' had gone that there existed an urgent need for reviving nationalism and free enterprise, both causes dear to the Conservative Right. Moreover, because she blamed past Tory leaders for colluding with Socialism, it followed that her reverence for old social elites was minimal. Plainly she held little regard for Socialist mandarins or those Tories who had compromised vital Conservative articles of faith over previous years. Hence Heath people were jettisoned with ruthless efficiency at all levels of the party. One Nation Tories like Ian Gilmour might chafe at Thatcher's New Whiggery, which contrasted with Tory traditions.*(34) However, key Thatcher advocates enunciated their aims with Jesuitical fervour, targeting electoral support for a radical programme of free enterprise, deregulation and national renewal at all levels of British society.

While assessments of Mrs Thatcher's Downing Street years exceed the remit of this study, some consideration of her impact on the party is appropriate. Thatcher was thoroughly comprehensive in scope during her premiership, 1979-90, and the foundations were laid over the four preceding years of Opposition. Indeed Kavanagh's comment that no section of British society escaped her reforms is valid.*(35) So many changes permeated the economy, popular ownership, utilities, law, civil service, industry, local government, welfare and personal taxation that the late Peter Jenkins – writing in 1987 – spoke of her as having forged a revolution.*(36) Jenkins noted Thatcher to have initiated a sea change in social and political attitudes that far transcended her party to embrace new electors with a stake in her reforms, e.g. 3,000,000 new homeowners and 9,000,000 share holders. Many of those new beneficiaries became Tory voters.

Yet there was a negative side. Not least was unemployment, that peaked at 3.6 million in 1983, plus the erosion of heavy industries like steel manufacture, coal mining and ship building ... all on the altar of Whig economics. Perhaps the most visible deficit was an emergent social underclass who were numerous in Northern England and Scotland; hence the much vaunted North/South social divide that Thatcher always denied.*(37)

Thatcher's premiership endured for eleven years and seven months – itself unprecedented – while her Tory leadership lasted almost 16 years. In every sense, she proved a domineering figure, something that contributed to her fall. Yet hers was an era in which British Conservatives embarked on a new ideological crusade, embracing the free market, deregulation, popular capitalism, and as Philip Lynch noted in his 1999 text, renewed British nationalism.*(38) Kavanagh and Skidelsky have each outlined her programme of home, share and business ownership that put popular capitalism clearly in the public domain, sustaining Conservatives in office over four successive elections and silencing internal critics. The latter appeared to have addressed the Conservatives' 1970s crisis of confidence, though research by John Curtice in 1992 re-opens that question.*(39)

Significantly, Mrs Thatcher's departure was forced by the same concern as had brought her the leadership in 1975, electoral defeat. Many Tories had grown anxious at decline over the previous 18 months, inclusive of a biting recession in the late 1980s, blamed on Chancellor, Nigel Lawson, with inflation reaching 15%, housing market depression, negative equity stocks, widespread business bankruptcies and a trade deficit. The Poll Tax flat rate payments – replacing Rates – were widely viewed as unfair, provoking Commons protest – including Tory backbench revolts. Additionally, by-election losses in South Staffordshire, Vale of Glamorgan and Eastbourne, plus poor showings in the 1989 European and local elections, further highlighted the extent of the problem.

Thatcher bequeathed a legacy of popular capitalism, which shifted political parameters to the Right. She had made her party electable again, though whether as a British or English party looked less clear. The persistence of private enterprise in public policy over ensuing years testifies to Thatcherism's durability. Yet she also left a divided party. Her pet causes – Euro-scepticism, Anglo-Americanism and free enterprise – split the party throughout the 1990s, while plaguing John Major's successor government in the process. So also did Thatcher influence rebound during William Hague's tenure, 1997-2001.

Accounts of Conservative politics over the quarter century since Margaret Thatcher's exit are fewer in number. For the purpose of this inquiry, the Tories were affected by similar travails in the years following Thatcher's fall as followed the loss of office in February 1974, through ongoing dissent and factionalism. Together in 1990, an assorted collection of disgruntled ex-ministers, nervous back benchers, Europhiles and One Nationites had taken out a sitting leader/Premier, but therewith their common purpose ceased.

7. Conservatives in the Major Era (1990-1997)

Despite Margaret Thatcher's departure from the Conservative helm, it was inevitable that her persona and legacy would overshadow the party for years ahead. Besides, she tacitly encouraged followers to act as guardians of the free market and nationalism. Throughout John Major's seven year premiership, she pursued pet causes, Euro-scepticism and the free market, with some followers running regular rebellions against Major's government.

In his biography of Major, Anthony Seldon examines the man's intense irritation over his predecessor's disloyalty.*(40) She regarded him as surrendering her legacy through banal concessions to European political leaders. For his part, Major felt Thatcher out of decency might have supported his premiership, and all the more so in view of his slender Commons majority after April 1992. While not holding Thatcher responsible for his general travails or the Conservative Right's wrecking tactics, still he noted her influence being used against rather than for his government. Indeed with the help of a premise provided by Alastair (Lord) MacAlpine, she played the role of a British Barry Goldwater, inveighing against the 'evils' of Socialism and 'threats' from Europe. So also did she become a focus for right wing discontent, thereby devoting retirement to campaigns that undermined her successor's authority at Westminster and party grass roots.

Generally, John Major's premiership (1990-97) might be viewed as among the least successful of the twentieth century. The government he headed was among the most fragmented and directionless ever to have held office in modern Britain. Impediments were many, and despite Thatcherite irritants, there occurred other tribulations. A combination of no mandate at first, then a thin Commons majority of 21 seats from the April 1992 election, followed by defections, by-election defeats, backbench rebellions, a failed 'Back-to-Basics' agenda, plus unwelcome sexual and social scandals involving Conservative ministers and MPs, divisions over Europe and constitutional reform, a leadership challenge in mid-term and multiple policy mishaps ... all contributed to the pathetic spectacle characterising Major's administration.*(41) Even the party's disastrous 1997 election campaign was further plagued by sleaze allegations and dissent over European integration, such as scuttled any lingering prospects of Tory survival in office.

Consequently, it is hardly stretching credibility to suggest that the sleaze allegations, along with Rightist disloyalty, magnified the extent of defeat to a level that capped all previous divisions and defeats experienced by the party in the twentieth century.

Nevertheless, that defeat also masked major attainments. The latter included recovery from recession, reduced unemployment to below 1.5 million, adaption of the economy to digital practice, and inflation reduced below 5%. On other fronts, relations with Europe improved after the Thatcher era, with Major reaching a modus vivendi with fellow E.U. governments at Maastricht exempting Britain from the Social Charter and the impending Euro currency. Elsewhere, the Gulf campaign {first} was successfully completed, albeit under American leadership. Progress was made with the Irish peace process, from which came the Downing Street Declaration (Major/Taoiseach Albert Reynolds) of December 1993, followed by the 1994 paramilitary ceasefires, the 1996/97 Constitutional Convention, peace talks at Stormont and eventual Belfast Peace Accord of Good Friday, April 1998. Though the Irish peace process manifested more fully after the Conservatives left office, Tory N.I. Secretaries, Peter Brooke and Sir Patrick Mayhew, acted as facilitators while John Major was also an encourager.*(42) Yet Major's resilience against the Tory Right – sympathisers with Ulster Unionists – and rebellious Conservatives, highlighted not so much his attainments as more fragmentation levels in his party.

Whether compromise would have pacified the Right on Europe, Northern Ireland or the economy is doubtful. Ongoing dissent fragmented the Conservative fold, which looked increasingly disunited and leaderless. Such was not an edifying spectacle, and taken alongside the Conservatives' longevity in public office, fed public taste for a change of government. Although the defeat of May 1997 was anticipated by learned observers, its scale shocked the Tories.*(43) Negative opinion polls, local election and parliamentary by-elections losses suggested defeat to be imminent, and was indeed forecast by press leaders over preceding months. Doubtless the defeat of four Cabinet ministers – Michael Portillo, Ian Lang, Michael Forsythe and Malcolm Rifkind – along with several junior ministers and backbenchers and the loss of all remaining Welsh and Scottish seats highlighted the extent of that rout. The latter threw Tories into a worse crisis than 1974, and raised the inevitable question of whether the party would ever return to government.

8. Conservatives in Opposition: Hague, IDS and Howard (1997-2005)

John Major's swift retirement precipitated a leadership election. After three ballots of the depleted parliamentary party, former Welsh Secretary, William Hague, was preferred over former Chancellor, Kenneth Clarke. Clearly the Right's dominance of what was a rump party had worked to Hague's advantage. His Thatcherite leanings were openly stated, and support from Right sources was augmented by Baroness Thatcher's personal endorsement. By contrast, Clarke's Europhile beliefs made him anathema to the Right. Also, after the election, Clarke, recognising that Europe would likely divide the Shadow Cabinet, declined a front bench portfolio from the new Leader.

William Hague's leadership marked a return to right wing politics, albeit with tactical modifications for meeting new challenges. No concessions were made to either constitutional reform or the proposed European Social Charter. In the Scottish and Welsh home rule referenda of Autumn 1997, Hague resolutely opposed the Edinburgh Parliament and Cardiff Assembly, and was defeated in both contests. Nor did the absence of Scottish and Welsh MPs, along with an unfavourable image in both countries as an ".. English party .." cause Hague to accommodate even moderate Home Rulers within the Scottish Tories. Yet in the aftermath of defeat, Hague switched tactics, possibly with an eye to regaining credibility among Scottish and Welsh voters. In place of previous opposition to an elected body, Hague subsequently endorsed both national authorities, and later ditched another Thatcher cause by accepting the national minimum wage.

Additionally, Hague's Conservative Party became more inclusive, wooing homosexuals, women and members of ethnic communities, all under-represented in Tory Westminster ranks. His leadership also saw adoption of the first Conservative constitution in the party's 300 year-long history, which provided for a leadership electoral college enfranchising ordinary Tories choosing between two rivals (from a shortlist determined by Conservative MPs) in future contests. The constitution met certain demands of the Tory Charter Movement and Conservative Democracy Campaign, though leaders of both groups regretted the limited concessions on offer.*(44) Yet Hague's 1998

19

constitution made considerable accommodations with democratic tides, thereby quietly dispensing with remnants of the party's centuries-old hierarchical structure that had resisted reform.

Whatever Hague's modernising tactics, his faith in Thatcher economics continued unabated. The programme formulated during his tenure reasserted free market primacy, pledged loyalty to the Union, plus reaffirmation of British sovereignty against further European integration. Hague's further repudiation of a European currency was endorsed by a party plebiscite in October 1998. This agenda, marked by its anti-European posturing, won sturdy support from the Right, while making rather less impact on the British public. Generally, the Hague years were marked by right wing orthodoxy, which won back bench loyalty without the frequent rebellions marking the Major era.

Predictably, rightist allegiance to Hague proved anathema to the party's centre-left. While pledging formal loyalty, in fact Tory Progressives and One Nationites were alienated by Hague's pandering to free market zealots and Euro-sceptics. The latter in particular caused exceptional resentment among centrists at Westminster, with dissent surfacing in occasional letters to *The Times*, *Daily Telegraph* and other journals. Among signatories were such 'grandees' as Geoffrey (Lord) Howe, Sir Edward Heath, Kenneth Clarke, Chris Patten and Ian Gilmour. Also, coded speeches were delivered to appreciative fringe audiences of The Tory Reform Group and Conservative Mainstream. It is interesting to contemplate how Hague hoped for conformity to his European policy among dedicated pro-European ex-Cabinet ministers, many of whom, like Heath and Clarke, placed Europe as their principal guiding cause. Even less obvious was the matter of how Hague felt he could impose a Euro-sceptical line while safeguarding party unity.

In the event, official Euro-scepticism ensured continuing disaffection among Tories that impaired recovery. Also, Ken Clarke's refusal to serve on Hague's shadow team and the subsequent defection of two Tory MEPs, highlighted the degree to which Conservative Europhiles had been alienated by Hague. More defections to Labour of two Westminster Conservatives, Peter Temple-Morris and Sean Woodward, along with the departure of ex-Harrow East MP, Hugh Dykes, to the Liberal

Democrats, further compounded the spectacle of Tory fragmentation. Frankly, Hague's capacity for forging unity after the divisions of the Major years looked seriously in doubt from an early stage. Even taking account of limited Tory gains in the 1999 and 2000 local elections in Wales and England, along with Scottish and Welsh national elections of 1999, progress was patchy. *(45) Those gains were diminished by Hague's poor showings in opinion polls over the period, a trend lasting until the election of June 2001 that finally ended his leadership. *(46)

The Tories failure to improve their position or displace Labour in the 2001 election, forced Hague's exit immediately afterwards.*(47) His failure to head any recovery made resignation inevitable; after all, he had failed the essential test of a Tory leader to deliver his party to office. This view is articulated by Philip Norton, who saw the leader as overall arbiter and driving force within the party.*(48) Andrew Gamble's contention that the Conservatives' primary goal down the ages has been office at virtually any price seems cynical, even harsh, but, on past and recent evidence was the yardstick by which Tory leaders have been measured. Indeed the notion of the Tory leader as a short-term leaseholder rather than secure freeholder – another Norton view – was characterised by Churchill's memorable reflection.*(49)

"The loyalties that centre on Number One (Conservative leader) are enormous. If he trips, he must be sustained. If he makes mistakes, they must be covered. If he sleeps, he must not be disturbed. If he is no good, he must be pole-axed."

Put simply, Hague had failed his party and had to go.

The contest occurring over Summer 2001 to choose Hague's successor was quite unlike anything happening previously. For the first time ever, the Tory leader – determined by election only since 1965 – was chosen not by MPs alone, but instead through a full member vote, at least in its final stage. Embracing democracy might not have accorded with Tory traditions, but by now the party had bent to the winds of change.

In the event, five candidates entered the ring; namely Michael Ancram, David Davis, Michael Portillo, Kenneth Clarke and Iain

Duncan-Smith (IDS). After two eliminating ballots, Clarke and Duncan-Smith emerged in preference to the much-fancied Portillo for the final run-off, held throughout August 2001. Then, grass roots Tories by a 2:1 margin opted for the Right's IDS over his pro-European challenger.*(50) The result, if a disappointment for Clarke, also showed ordinary Tories positioned to the right. It had the further effect of conferring greater legitimacy on IDS than any of his predecessors. Yet, notwithstanding his democratic mandate, in just over two years the first ever elected Tory leader found his position repeatedly undermined to the point of being run out of office.

Frankly, no Tory leader over the course of the twentieth century was ever forced to endure the catastrophic misfortune as that borne by the luckless IDS over his 26 months at the Conservative helm. A combination of hostile press briefings, dissenting parliamentary colleagues, subterfuge, front bench resignations, leaks and outright disloyalty by Tory MPs and peers – especially defeated opponents and their allies – accumulated to undermine the Tory leader's authority. The latter in turn fed negative opinion polls that encouraged critics to seize their chance in October 2003, by pushing a confidence vote at the 1922 Committee. IDS lost; hence his enforced resignation and immediate replacement by former Home Secretary, Michael Howard.*(51)

In his defence, it may be said that IDS assumed charge of a party that by 2001 looked unelectable. The party's prospects looked unpromising, and there was a general air of pessimism among Conservatives about achieving an early recovery.*(52) His modernisation programme ensured there was no place for the right wing Monday Club nor front bench spokeswoman, Anne Winterton, whose joke about Pakistanis – when addressing a constituency rugby dinner – led to dismissal. Also, with Teresa May heading Conservative Central Office, a concerted effort was made at broadening the women and ethnics standing as parliamentary candidates. So too was the crisis of falling membership – as shown by Seyd and Whitely – addressed, albeit with modest results.*(53)

In policy matters, IDS plotted a rightist direction. While a committed British nationalist and hostile to Euro-federalism, he supported the Blair government's Iraq war. IDS also presented new policies to his struggling party, such as Lords reform, endorsing election of all peers in preference to Blair's plan for mixed elections and appointments. This 'born-again' democratic radicalism did not square credibly with several observers, who noted that until recently the Tories had defended the unelected pre-1999 House of Lords where they held an unassailable advantage in terms of hereditary peers over all other parties and crossbenchers. IDS opposed top-up university tuition fees, in response to the Blair government, while also making opposition to homosexual adoptions a three-line whip issue, thereby provoking great unease and a few rebels within his own party. Overall, the Conservative programme was muddled and subject to sharp divisions even among its own faithful, a factor that triggered early doubts about IDS's leadership.

However, the downfall of Iain Duncan-Smith – the first Catholic ever to lead the Tories – was principally attributable to the same problem earlier bedevilling Hague, Major, Thatcher and Heath, namely inability to deliver electoral victory. Although modest gains were made in local council elections of 2002 and 2003 respectively, with Conservatives holding some ground in simultaneous elections for the Scottish Parliament and Welsh Assembly, the pattern did not suggest any likelihood of growth. Moreover, multiple opinion polls placed the Tories behind the Liberal Democrats throughout 2002 and 2003, while Duncan-Smith's personal standing with voters was embarrassingly low. All those factors fuelled media speculation over his future, a position compounded by outbursts of disaffection from rebellious Tory MPs like Crispin Blunt.*(54) A Liberal victory in the parliamentary by-election in Brent East (September 2003) over Labour put the Tories in third place, forcing IDS to promise Annual Conference in October a more combative style. Even that initiative got derailed by media allegations about irregular employment of his wife, Betsy, and together those issues sealed his fate on 31st October 20013.

The IDS debacle highlighted two factors about the Conservatives. First was the enduring need for Tory leaders to deliver office, or be cast aside as failures. Second was the evident difficulty that many Conservatives had with accepting the new democracy operating within their party. When recalling that Edward Heath in 1965 became the first elected Tory leader, the move away from the old system of an 'emergent' leader to election by a full ballot of members throughout the country, involved a democratic transition that was both stark and swift. Given the circumstances of IDS's dismissal, his party's oft-claimed conversion to fulsome democracy looked less than convincing?

Not that the incoming Michael Howard fared better! Over two years of stewardship, Conservatives became entrenched on the Right, making few policy changes from IDS, and addressing the same right wing social constituency. Factionalism remained steady if less overt or influential in terms of policy changes. That said, Elliot & Hanning showed the continuing prevalence of rightists at Central Office and the Research Department. The same climate favoured rightist candidates in constituency selections, as occurred under IDS and Hague previously.*(55) Conservative polls ratings improved, while gains were recorded in council elections of 2004.*(56) Yet the party made little real progress against an incumbent Blair administration or Charles Kennedy's Liberal Democrats.

In the general election of May 2005, Conservatives achieved only a modest rise. From an unmistakable nadir of 165 seats (30.7 of vote) in 2001, the vote share increased just marginally to 32.4 with 33 gains gained to tally at 198 seats. The best that can be said for Howard's performance as leader was that he halted the decline, but the overall picture fell far short of a recovery. Clearly something new and innovative was required. Hence Howard announced he would step down as soon as the party elected a replacement. As one expected to reverse Conservative electoral decline, Howard had proved a disappointment. He failed to impact on an unpopular Blair government, and the party's modest poll showed little progress from four years earlier. Rank and file Tories plainly sought change, and proved receptive to their next leader emerging from a younger generation, something favouring David Cameron and his waiting coterie of supporters.

9. David Cameron: Tories in Office and European Question (2005-2016)

David Cameron's election by Tory rank and file over David Davis in November 2005 proved to be the beginning of a new era. Aged just 39 and in only his second parliament, the youthful Cameron, old Etonian and distant relative of the Queen, projected a patrician manner similar to Harold Macmillan, albeit one adapted to the 21st century. Throughout a lengthy opposition stretch, Cameron revised his One Nation agenda, complete with liberal, secular and European credentials, enough to bolster his party while regaining electoral momentum.*(60) Significantly, Cameron avoided the divisiveness of right wing predecessors, thereby engaging the loyalties of dispirited centrists, not least among them veteran Kenneth Clarke. Cameron proved less interested in ideological politics, as more widening the party's appeal among voters, and continued to prioritise the selection of women, homosexuals and ethnic figures in his party's winnable seats.*(61)

Those traits enabled him to lead a dispirited party back to serious challenger in 2010. The Conservatives were shorn of right wing dogma when winning power, initially in coalition with the Liberals for five years, and subsequently in 2015 gained his own majority mandate. In 2010, the Tories share of the vote rose from 32.4 (2005) to 36.1; gaining an extra 108 MPs, totalling 306; the largest but not majority party in the Commons. Five years later, Cameron led his party to victory with 36.9 vote share (331 seats). It is difficult to imagine the Liberal Democrats entering coalition with a Thatcher or Hague-led party, but Cameron headed a stable and Conservative-Liberal coalition that addressed the UK's financial deficit, while making limited concessions on constitutional reform, specifically fixed term parliaments and retaining Freedom of Information and Human Rights legislation of the previous Labour government.*(62) By so doing, Cameron paved the way for the Tories outright victory of 2015, while his erstwhile Liberal colleagues got reduced to a mere 8 Commons seats and 7.9 vote share.

Whatever about Cameron's mandate, over the course of the next 14 months his party and government got dragged into the mucky and divisive quagmire of Europe. The question of British ties with Brussels that had dogged Heath, Thatcher and Major in different ways proved the same one that finally broke Cameron and ended his premiership prematurely. His failure to get full agreement on revised terms from his colleagues in Cabinet and the subsequent bellicosities characterising the 2016 referendum underlined how the European question had defined the course of progress within the Conservative Party. The British public's rejection of the European Union – a key policy of the Premier – amounted to a public no-confidence vote, making his resignation inevitable. Thereafter, Cameron bequeathed to his successor, Theresa May, a party in turmoil, and different tendencies at war with each other as the terms of European withdrawal raged above all others.

Until his rejection over Europe, Cameron had managed to hold the line for over six years. He had successfully faced down the Scottish nationalists in the independence referendum of September 2014, while honouring a pledge to the Liberal Democrats for a referendum in 2011 over the Alternative Vote, a contest that roundly defeated the reform cause. The party's right wing had been subdued by those attainments, plus the 2015 election victory, and only during the EU campaign and defeat did the Leader lose control. Until then, Cameron's domination of his party was pronounced, as was his policy framework. Over Europe, Coalition relations, same-sex marriages and armed forces reductions, the Right had indicated dissent, but failed to dislodge government policy. However, given the relevance of UK/EU relations to so many key Conservative principles on sovereignty, democratic accountability and economic management, it was entirely predictable that the referendum would ignite multiple tides adding up to an implosion and loss of direction. Europe had divided and damaged Cameron's Conservatives in the early 21st century in similar fashion to Tariff Reform having wreaked a similar toll on Balfour's party over a century earlier.*(63) It remains to be seen how the party will handle electoral fall-out.

It should be noted that the nature of factional activity has changed throughout the Cameron decade. As will be shown in Chapters 9 and 10, the centre of gravity has moved away from campaigning groups to research trusts and specialist bodies whose ranks are headed by MPs, peers and policy experts, and whose funding comes from sympathisers and outside backers. Those groups have the ear of leadership, usually by

26

counting many supporters at Central Office and well presented websites and aspiring parliamentarians in their ranks. Also, by virtue of the quality of their publications and journals, they attract media attention for policy output and publicist functions. Examples include the long running Institute for Economic Affairs, Centre for Policy Studies, Bruges Group and Conservative Home website, all of whom have dominated debates over recent decades. By contrast, single issue groups like Conservative Greens, defence lobbyists and democracy campaigners, while maintaining a profile, have been rendered rather marginal.

Simon Walters's evaluation of recent Tory battles emphasised the role of 'insider' groups, whose leadership and media links enabled them to achieve real influence.*(64) As much as anything else, the emergence of on-line communications and social media fashioned these developments, and in the process consigned previous campaigning styles to the realms of history. David Cameron utilised those instruments to his advantage, and over his 11 leadership years operated with the backing of friendly support groups aided by social media. Only when challenged and defeated by the combined anti-EU lobby did it become clear that social media and on-line communications were the standard means by which current and future battles would be fought within the Tory Party.*(65) The extent of that change offers a future challenge task to an interested political scientist.

10. Summary

The course of post-war Conservative history has been one of adapting and surviving as the country evolved from Empire to Commonwealth to European nation state and on the domestic front from a social democratic mixed economy to a free market social economy. All of those stages produced leaders who were challenged to find policies consistent with the broad Conservative mantra while also winning office. They generated debates about future direction, on which alignments were based and factions emerged. As the party adjusted to changing times, it was forced to ditch obsolete ideological baggage and embrace new causes, as was shown by the cases of Europe and Anglo-Irish relations.

Andrew Gamble and Iain Gilmour have each in different ways identified the pivotal Conservative obsession with statecraft, operating as a party of government.*(66) This guiding theme has enabled the party to adjust policies and appeal even after suffering heavy electoral defeats as in 1945 and 1966. It also provides a litmus test by which Conservative leaders are judged by their brethren. As Gamble noted in 1979, given the predominance of Conservative affinities – overt and/or tacit – among industrialists, lawyers, judges, security chiefs, financiers and even large sections of the academic and art worlds, the Tories do not readily accept lengthy periods in Opposition.*(67) On the contrary, with party still strongly rooted among elite society, the desire to govern rather than merely expound remains steadfast. Hence, regardless of ideology, electoral success is the critical criterion for Tory leaders; a point which Heath, Thatcher, Major, Hague, IDS and Howard all learned to their cost at different times over the past 40 years.

It is therefore arguable that Conservative factionalism is an instrument for the ambitions and authority of successive leaders and their rivals. Significantly, evidence to be presented in this book shows ideological groups to be primarily but not exclusively concentrated on the Right. Organisations like the Monday Club and Tory Reform Group had played their part in raising the profile at grass roots and even among sections of the parliamentary party. Either way, by the mid-1970s the party's character had moved away from a deferential collection of grass roots followers to active participants whose activity had forced some share in choosing the Leadership and holding constituency MPs accountable.*(68) This protracted process reflected the democratic pressures permeating the wider world from which Conservatives were and are not immune.

It may be reasonably concluded that the British Conservative Party has evolved in line with the further democratic development of post-war Britain, a country now deploying referenda and progressive electoral systems … in part at least. Therefore, the nature and scope of party factionalism – on which this inquiry is based – reflects that evolution, as much as the diversity characterising the broad stream Conservative coalition. Armed with that presupposition, this study now proceeds to its next stage.

FOOTNOTES and REFERENCES

1. Robert Blake The Conservative Party from Peel to Thatcher (Fontana, 1985).

    John Ramsden An Appetite for Power: A History of the Conservative Party since 1830 (Harper-Collins, 1988).

    John Charmley A History of Conservative Politics 1900-1996 (Macmillan, 1998)

2. (i) Blake – ibid. (ii) Ramsden – ibid. (iii) Philip Norton eds. The Conservative Party (Harvester/Wheatsheaf & Prentice/Hall, 1996). (iv) Alan Clark The Tories: Conservatives and the Nation State, 1922-1997 (Weidenfield &Nicolson, 1998).

3. Contrast the accounts of Blake, Chap. viii, and Andrew Gamble The Conservative Nation (Routledge & Kegan, 1974) with Ramsden , Chaps. 12 & 13, and A.J. Davies We, The Nation: The Conservative Party and the Pursuit of Power (Little, Brown & Co., 1995).

4. Gamble (1975), Chaps. 2 & 3.

5. Blake (1985) – Chap. viii, pp. 256-263.

6. See V. McKee 'Conservative Factions' in Contemporary Record (Institute of Contemporary History, Vol. 3, 1, Autumn 1989).

7. (i) Dennis Kavanagh Margaret Thatcher and British Politics: The End of Consensus, Chap. 2, pp. 47-49 (Oxford University Press, 1987). (ii) Charmley (1998), Chap. 8, p. 142.

8. Andrew Roberts Eminent Churchillians, Chap. 5, pp. 258-266 (Phoenix, 1995).

9. See Kavanagh, Chap. 2, pp. 40-54.

10. (i) Gamble (1975), Chaps 2-3. (ii) David Marquand The Unprincipled Society: New Demands and Old Politics, Chaps 2-3, pp. 17-91 (J. Cape, 1988).

11. Probably the most scholarly treatise on Eden of recent years was that by David Carlton, with Chap. xi being especially relevant to the Suez aftermath.

    D. Carlton <u>Anthony Eden: A Biography</u> (Allen & Unwin, 1980).

12. See Blake, Charmley, Ramsden and Kavanagh, et al.

13. Cited in David Howell <u>British Social Democracy</u>, Chap. 8, pp. 227-230 (Croom Helm, 1976).

14. See E. Heath <u>The Autobiography of Edward Heath: The Course of My Life</u>, Chap. 8, pp. 203-204. (Hodder and Stoughton, 1998).

15. See Blake, Chaps. viii & ix.

16. See (i) Blake, Chap. x, pp. 299-302 . (ii) Charmley, Chap. 10, pp. 181-87.

    (iii) Alan Clark, Chap. 8, pp. 340-343 .

17. Kavanagh (1987) – Chap. 4, pp. 111-121.

18. Blake – Chap. x, pp. 301-304.

19. Heath autobiography - Chap. 10, pp. 394-395.

20. Kavanagh – Chap. 5, pp. 123-129.

21. Margaret Laing <u>Edward Heath: Prime Minister</u>, Chap. 12, pp. 182-190 (Sidgwick and Jackson, 1972).

22. (i) Blake, Chap. x, pp. 309-317. (ii) Ramsden, Chap. 16, pp. 417-420.

23. Gamble (1975), Chaps 6 & 7.

24. Ibid

25. (i) Blake, Chap. x, pp. 301-303. (ii) Ramsden, Chap. 15, pp. 385-390.

26. (i) Heath's autocratic leadership style and cold manner was a point of agreement among all the contemporary historians – including Ramsden, Clark, Kavanagh, Blake and Charmley.

Even the more sympathetic biography of Laing concedes the point, albeit quite reluctantly.

(ii) For another view of the Heath school and strategy, see:

Robert Behrens <u>The Conservative Party from Edward Heath to Margaret Thatcher</u> (Saxon House, 1980).

27. Interview – Peter Temple-Morris, M.P./V. McKee, 24th October, 2000. Mr Temple-Morris, a One Nation Tory, acknowledged that he had been swayed to the Thatcher camp as a result of Heath's aloofness and cold manner. He added his regrets for that choice. Subsequent clashes with Margaret Thatcher and William Hague had led to his exit from the Conservative Party to Labour in 1998.

28. Se Kogan and Kogan <u>The Battle for the Labour Party</u>, Chaps. 1, 2 & 4 (Koganpage, 1982).

29. Heath withdrew after losing the first ballot to Thatcher by 130 votes to 119, with Hugh Fraser scoring a derisory 16. Thatcher emerged victorious from a run-off ballot.

30. Kavanagh, Chap. 3, pp. 71-76.

31. 'The Right Approach – A Statement of Conservative Aims', Conservative Central Office, 1976.

32. Patrick Seyd 'Factionalism in the 1970s', Chap. 10, p. 234; - <u>Conservative Party Politics</u>, Ed. Zig Layton-Henry (Macmillan, 1980).

33. (i) Kavanagh, Chaps. 5, pp. 143-149. (ii) Kenneth Minogue – 'The Emergence of the New Right', Chap. 7, <u>Thatcherism,</u> Ed. R. Skidelsky (Blackwell, 1989).

34. Ian Gilmour <u>Inside Right,</u> Part iii, Chap 2, pp. 121-144 (Hutchinson, 1977).

35. Kavanagh, Chap. 10, pp. 315-316.

36. Peter Jenkins <u>Mrs Thatcher's Revolution: The Ending of the Socialist Era,</u> Chap. 16, p. 369 (Jonathan Cape, 1987).

37. Jenkins, Chap. 13, pp. 317-319.

38. Philip Lynch The Politics of Nationhood: Sovereignty, Britishness and Conservative Politics; see Chap. 3 (Macmillan, 1999).

39. John Curtice & Holli Semetko 'Does it matter what the Papers Say?' in Labour's Last Chance: The 1992 Election and Beyond (Dartmouth, 1994).

40. Anthony Seldon – with Lewis Baston Major: A Political Life (Phoenix, 1997)

    Note: Major's irritation with Thatcher's disloyalty throughout his premiership is a recurrent theme in successive chapters of the biography. Significantly, John Major shows restraint on that subject when writing his own memoirs

41. Ibid

42. See David McKittrick and Eamon Mallie The Road to Peace (Pan Books, 1996).

43. (i) Seldon, Chap. 39, pp. 729-734. (ii) Clark, Chap. 36, pp. 438-443.

44. Interviews:- (i) V. McKee with Eric Chalker, Chairman- Tory Charter Movement, 23rd February, 2000. (ii) V. McKee with John Strafford, Chairman – Conservative Democracy Campaign, 4th January, 2003.

45. Interestingly, two rightist Conservative MPs admitted to the author that the Right's best interests lay with sustaining Hague's leadership. Interviews- with Teresa Gorman, MP 24th October, 2000 and William Cash, MP 21st November, 2000.

46. Prior to the election, former Tory Health Secretary and prominent One Nationite, Stephen Dorrell, confided to the author his view that anything short of a substantial Conservative gain in the ensuing election would force Hague's exit. He was right.

    Interview – Rt. Hon. Stephen Dorrell, MP/V. McKee, 13th July, 2000.

47. Hague quit the Conservative leadership on 8th June in the immediate aftermath of the Conservatives' dismal showing in the

previous day's general election. At the time, there were many senior voices – e.g. Lord Strathclyde (Shadow Lords leader) and Iain Duncan-Smith (Shadow Defence Spokesman) - who urged him to delay an announcement, but he was determined to quit immediately.

See – Simon Walters – <u>Tory Wars: Conservatives in crisis,</u> Chap. 1, pp. 1-3 (Politicos, 2001).

48. Philip Norton 'The Party Leader', Chap. 9, pp. 142-145, <u>The Conservative Party,</u>

Ed. Philip Norton (Harvester/Wheatsheaf-Prentice/Hall, 1996).

49. Quoted in Norton eds. (1996), p. 142.

50. Iain Duncan-Smith was the first Conservative leader to have been directly elected by a ballot of the full party membership when he emerged from three rounds of voting within the parliamentary party to defeat Kenneth Clarke in a run-off. For an account of this event, see Walters (2001), Chap 18, 'Anyone but Portillo'.

51. Iain Duncan-Smith lost a confidence vote from his own Conservative MPs on 31st October, 2003. See various accounts in Guardian, Times, Daily Telegraph, Independent, Mail and Express, 1st November, 2003.

52. A succession of opinion polls showed the Conservatives trailing by an average of 11 points in the week preceding the leadership confidence vote.

53. Paul Whitely, Patrick Seyd and Jeremy Richardson – <u>True Blues: The Politics of Conservative Party Membership,</u> (Oxford University Press, 1994).

54. On the eve of the local government elections of May 2003 Crispin Blunt called publicly for Iain Duncan-Smith's replacement as Tory Leader. Ironically, the party gained some 300 Council seats up and down the country, although this did not prevent Duncan-Smith's fall later in the year.

55. Francis Elliot & James Hanning   <u>Cameron: The Rise of the New Conservative</u> (Harper, London, 2009), pp 238-298.

56. Opinion polls from November 2003 up to June 2004 showed a modest recovery of Conservative standing under Michael Howard's leadership. Also, in the local elections of June 2004, Conservatives secured 36% of the vote; a modest increase on the party's tally characterising Iain Duncan-Smith's tenure.

57. See Gamble (1975), Chap. 1, pp. 12 & 13; and Ian Gilmour, Part 3, Chap. 1, pp. 109-121, Inside Right: A Study of Conservatism (Hutchinson, 1977).

58. Gamble – Chap. 1, pp. 26-28 – H.M. Drucker (Eds.), Multi-party Britain (Macmillan, 1979).

59. Seyd in Z. Layton-Henry Eds. (1980), Chap 10, pp. 234-235.

60. A growing body of literature has been published on David Cameron's tenure at Downing Street. Until now, my vote for the most comprehensive and factual evaluation goes to Anthony Seldon and Peter Snowdon, Cameron at 10: The Inside Story, 2010-2015. (William Collins, London, 2015) However, that choice may well be overtaken in times ahead as other well-researched titles continue to appear.

61. Elliot and Hanning (2009), pp 328-362.

62. See Seldon and Snowdon (2015), Chap. 39, pp 493-505.

63. Strains emanating from differences over future relations with the European Union revealed themselves at various stages in Opposition, throughout the Coalition and in the 2015 general election. See (i) Selsdon and Snowdon (2015), Chaps 39 & 40. (ii) Elliot and Hanning (2009), pp 262-362. (iii) Tim Ross Why The Tories Won: The Inside Story of the 2015 General Election, (Biteback Press, London, 2015).

64. Walters (2001), Chaps, 9, 10 & 18.

65. Seldon and Snowdon's (2015) comprehensive account of Cameron's relations with his party in opposition and government presents a clear image of the dominance of social media. On-line communications had rapidly come to dominate Tory internal politics over the years after 2005.

66. Gamble (1975), Chaps 1 & 2.
    Gilmour (1977), Chap 2. Also Gilmour's 1997 text.

67. Gamble (Eds. Drucker, 1979). Blake, Charmley, Ramsden and Kavanagh, et al.

Forty Shades of Blue

CHAPTER 2

DEVISING A FRAMEWORK FOR FACTIONAL ANALYSIS

Having examined the evolution and character of the post-war Conservative Party, next it is necessary to consider the nature of factionalism and also offer a framework for analysis. Among political scientists, different perspectives are held on factionalism within political parties. Many studies of this subject relate to the nature of factionalism within specific party systems, e.g. USA, UK and France. Though a limited amount of literature has been produced on British party factionalism by other observers, it is a matter of opinion whether it is suitable for categorising the British Conservative Party, either historically or in its contemporary form. On balance, it is preferable to use the specific framework offered here as the most relevant mechanism for refining the distinctions encountered between various groups arising in this study.

1. Impact of Factionalism

Factionalism is a product of many factors among British Tories. The combination of the party's evolving history, policy revisions, leadership changes, leadership challenges, internal debates, alignments and realignments, plus the ongoing pressures of external electoral competition indicates a few contributory causes.

None of the latter offer a fulsome explanation on their own, nor are they all relevant to every group on the Conservative fringes. Indeed with the slow Tory democratisation over the past forty years, there has occurred a gradual change of culture impacting on the character of factional groups emerging over the period. In general, the decline of deference and more grass roots participation – noted in Chapter 1 – has fed a more assertive type of factional politics. Such is the stuff with which this study is concerned.

Writing over forty years ago, Richard Rose described the Conservatives as "..a party of tendencies..", which he contrasted with Labour's faction-type machine.*(1) Actually, Rose's analysis is heavily dated, both in terms of the two major Westminster parties and the changing British system that spawned them. Even in as far as the assessment dealt with the system of that time, this author feels Professor Rose's analysis to have been flawed by an over-centralised view of each party that failed to take account of culture and regional variations. Nevertheless, Rose was correct in saying that neither of the major parties of 1960s Britain welcomed organised factionalism, and the Conservatives in particular discouraged such activity. Yet Conservative factionalism did manifest through different forms over the post-war period, and it is the character and types of such groups and their impact on the party that forms a dimension to this inquiry.

It will also be instructive to observe how factionalism changed its character at different stages of Conservative post-war history. Specific types of groups emerged in the party during the Churchill and Eden era, when Conservatives wrestled to accommodate the new domestic Britain fashioned by Attlee's government, while keeping alive traditional Tory concerns for the empire and British prestige in international affairs. The party's electoral troubles were nowhere as acute in 1955 as twenty years later, when the Conservatives appeared to have lost a hold on office. Such was what triggered the entry of Mrs Thatcher and her New Right alliance. By then, the assorted 'old guard' of Keynesians, One Nationites and Tory Paternalists – personified by Edward Heath – had been rendered obsolete by social and political change, and the party was now attuned to the fractious conditions of 1970s Britain. A similar spectacle presented itself in the aftermath of the Conservatives' catastrophic election defeat of 1997 and further dismal showing in the election of June 2001. Again, questions emerged about whether the party would return to government or be consigned to long-term opposition, not to mention the threat of replacement by the Liberal Democrats and later, UKIP. Indeed the succession of short-lived leaders of that period highlighted the crisis confronting the Tory party then.

2. Problem of Legitimacy

The term 'faction' gives rise to variable degrees of tolerance and understanding among political scientists and historians. In one context, factionalism is associated with sub-party politics, especially during periods of division. In another, it pertains to intra-party pressure group campaigns, and in a further one focuses on leadership rivalries. Factionalism raises questions about ideology, discipline and group organisation all of which are relevant to a proper understanding of its place in party politics generally and among British Tories particularly. Whether factions have played any serious role in post-war Conservative politics and if so in what forms, remain central questions here.

The question of legitimacy is one that has dogged factions in all British parties, including the Conservatives. There has always been a question mark in the minds of many party stalwarts over the propriety of factions as agents to the organisational culture, while leadership have proved at best grudgingly tolerant and at worst openly hostile. Factions are viewed in some quarters as usurping the proper place of the party organisation in facilitating debates and harnessing members' energies. As for party constitutions, the scarcest recognition is accorded to informal groups, and usually as a method of control.

The American political scientists, Frank P. Belloni and Dennis C. Beller, writing in 1976, highlighted the problem of legitimacy surrounding factions everywhere.*(2) They noted that whereas parties and interest groups are an accepted part of the political process in most democratic countries, conversely factions have not achieved similar credibility.

*"The significance attributed to parties and to a lesser extent to interest groups, is partly due to the greater obviousness of the structure and the activity of these organisations, in contrast to that of factions: as objects of study, interest groups and especially parties are more clearly observed and observable ... And while party has achieved the greater measure of such legitimacy, both party and interest group are now widely regarded as playing positive roles in the political process. It is just such perceived legitimacy that factions .. lack." *(3)*

Interestingly, the Italian political scientist, Giovani Sartori, viewed factionalism as a sign of healthy diversity in democratic parties, provided the competition did not undermine party electoral prospects. Although Sartori viewed factionalism from the angle of party fractionalisation, this study has a different focus. Fractionalisation involves sub-groups – which Italians call 'currents' – whereas factions have minimum degrees of structure, disciplined membership and a clear programme.

"Parties cannot be, nor should they be monoliths. It can be conceded that fractionism might have a positive value, but the vindication of fractionism must be when appropriate, well justified. This is hardly the case with the argument that fractionism testifies to the vitality and authenticity of intra-party democracy. Democracy has a dim future if the word is stretched and abused to this extent. Intra-party democracy bears out how rank and file relate to the party elites; and the magic of a word can hardly regenerate the harsh reality of fractionism – if it can be shown that this is all it is."*(4)

This lack of legitimacy gives factionalism its negative image in Britain. Whereas West European parties like the French Socialists and former Italian Christian Democrats have long tolerated group competition, fashioning their constitutions accordingly, there has been less recognition from mainstream Britain parties. Instead British parties are geared towards electoral politics with priorities placed on leadership authority and policymaking.

Robert McKenzie's thesis on British parties was scornful of participatory democracy, especially that practised by the Labour Party during Hugh Gaitskell's leadership, 1955-63.*(5) He argued that the Conservative model of leadership dominance was more realistic, if not idealistic, and had permeated in practice – if not name – to Labour. McKenzie's scepticism was rooted in the oligarchic theories of Robert Michels, who argued that all parties were dominated by powerful elites of central policymakers and bureaucrats.*(6) Both had surprisingly little to say about the role of intra-party factionalism, which with hindsight – and allowing for different periods of study – leaves a gap. Moreover, despite factionalism on the Labour and Conservative parties, the subject factionalism has generated few tracts among political scientists in Britain.*(7)

Paucity of recognition impairs a conceptual understanding of factionalism, both among British parties and in a comparative context. Therefore in endeavouring to present a suitable framework for assessing factionalism in British Conservative politics, one is hindered by the absence of a consensus on the character and models of factionalism. This gap requires a clear framework as the basis for developing the inquiry.

3. Alternative Models of Factionalism:

In order to devise a suitable framework, first a brief appraisal of relevant literature is required. It is significant that of those models examined, there is merit in more than one, meaning that the framework adopted is eclectic in character. Moreover, as Belloni and Beller noted, factionalism is fashioned more by the political system as parties and their internal power struggles.*(8) What applies in Britain's parliamentary and hitherto centralised culture would not be appropriate to the federalised system of Germany, or the American presidential system where party organisation is relatively weak. This view is supported by the wide range of models presented herewith.

The American political scientist and historian, William N. Chambers, produced a study that focused on the emerging U.S. party system. It viewed factions as pre-party units in an evolutionary process of party development.*(9) Parties take form from:

"..the competition of ideas, interests and personalities, and from ... realisation of the goals deriving from these variables can be achieved by securing control over the decision-making structures of the polity."(10)*

Chambers regarded factions as embryonic parties prefacing the national political elite with programmes, structures, members and leadership. Essentially, he saw factionalism as a stage en-route to full party development with either that outcome or disbandment as the only

41

logical results. The Chambers model is relevant to occasional party types, including David Owen's anti-merger group that became the short-lived 'Continuing SDP' of 1988-90, and equally short-lived pro-European Conservative Party (1998-99) and the Referendum Party (1994-97). Both groups battled vigorously – albeit in different directions – over the extent of British integration in Europe.

Otherwise, the Chambers perspective of factions as proto-parties is more relevant to America with its loose, umbrella type party organisations, as well as pre-1993 Italy and Fourth Republican France (1945-58), both of the latter typifying unstable party systems. It has to be said that the Chambers model does not easily fit with mainstream British parties, which are essentially parliamentary, entrenched and accommodating a range of single issue and wider ideological campaigning groups. Accordingly, while Chambers's observations may be pertinent to a couple of short-lived faction-type parties, otherwise his framework is not one that can be usefully deployed in this inquiry.

Another framework is offered by Ralph Nicholas, who defined factions as ".. leader-follower groups ..".*(11) Their roles are dictated less by ideology and more by bonds of loyalty and common purpose engendered by fraternal links, not the least of which was friendship. Leaders depend on the fidelity of followers in the legislature and within the party, while those same followers can expect to benefit from whatever patronage and party offices fall within their leader's gift. Ultimately, ties between leader and followers are personal, and based on clientele relations and/or mutual self-interest.

It is the leader whose appeal has greatest effect in mobilising a faction according to Nicholas. While recruitment may focus on kinship ties or common economic, ideological or even religious interests, essentially it is the structures of authority along with a dynamic leader and lieutenants that make a group effective. Thus it follows that real political competition is based on factions whose appeal to members' individual interests exceeds that of parties. For that reason factional allegiances assume a priority. Nicholas further contends that factions are a product of conflict, thereby ensuring at least two or more such groups in any political party. However, factions lack the corporate structures of parties, and endure only for as long as there is an effective leader and cause. Thereafter the parent party's wider appeal and popular constituency among voters supersedes the manoeuvrings of narrow-based factions or other kinds of sub-party groupings. Nicholas's general thesis of the factional leader's centrifugal role has much to commend it, both generally and in the context of this inquiry.

There are indeed many groups in different parties operating in different systems across the liberal democratic world whose existence owes much to common political and/or social ties among members of the sort cited by Nicholas. Examples include the Democratic Black Caucus in the American South personified by prominent leader figure, Rev. Jessie Jackson; another was Rev. Gerry Faldwell's Moral Majority movement in the 1980s U.S. Republican Party.*(12) In 1960s Northern Ireland there was Dr Paisley's anti-reformist faction lobbying the governing Ulster Unionist Party against reforms proposed by liberal Unionist Premier, Captain Terence O'Neill. True to the Chambers model, the Paisleyite faction seceded to merge with other Unionist malcontents to form the Protestant – later Democratic Unionist Party.*(13) Later in 1973, another hard-line Unionist faction headed by right wing former Belfast Home Affairs Minister, William Craig, who was disenchanted with the leadership of Brian Faulkner, seceded to form the Vanguard Party. Their numbers included a young lawyer who on Vanguard's return to Unionist ranks in 1978 became an MP, and eventual party leader, David Trimble.*(14)

Equally Southern Ireland's faction-ridden Fianna Fail, as shown by Tom Garvin, was divided throughout the 1970s between the pro-establishment George Colley camp and that of republican grass roots contender, Charles Haughey.*(15) When Haughey won the party leadership and accompanying premiership (after ousting incumbent, Jack Lynch) in late 1979, so fragile was the precarious unit following that a dissident faction quickly established itself around the charismatic leadership of another Haughey rival, Desmond O'Malley – Colley dying in 1983. The result in 1985 was the O'Malley faction breaking with Fianna Fail to form a new party, Progressive Democrats. Of course such innovations viable in a Proportional Voting system (STV) – as has existed in the Irish Republic since its inception in 1922 – that the O'Malley group could feasibly make the progression from faction to party and surviving for over 20 years in a competitive arena.

Fewer such advantages exist for dissident factions in Britain's first-past-the-post voting system for Westminster and local elections. Perhaps the only successful venture of this kind in recent decades was the social democratic secession from Labour in 1981, led by a 'Gang of Four', Shirley Williams, William Rodgers, David Owen and Roy Jenkins.*(16) The creation of the SDP in March 1981 marked a sturdy bid for viability, but after facing two general elections (1983 and 1987) the SDP's seven year life span ended with an enforced merger with the Liberals in March 1988.*(17) Although leader-led factions are often underwritten by some common thread like religion, regionalism, race or socio-political outlook, such is not automatic. Nor does it diminish the importance of leadership in factional politics because the latter provides the charisma and direction necessary for inspiring followers into a purposeful team of campaigners.

Yet neither the Chambers or Nicholas theses are applicable to all or even most instances of factionalism. Factions are not necessarily centred on a leader, far less constructed around "mutual self-interest". Indeed such a view is rather sweeping and inapplicable in many instances. For one thing, Nicholas appears to underestimate the unique loyalty of ideology in binding group loyalties. Also, many ideological factions like the Conservative Monday Club, Labour's Tribune Group and the Liberal Democrats' former Chard Group are all ideological fellowships, but, significantly, all manage without a dominant leader.*(18) Furthermore, Nicholas makes little distinction between the various types of factionalism, overlooking the extent to which cohesion and structure characterise 'tendencies' and 'factions' of the kind so common to Britain's political system.

4. Factions, Tendencies and Cause Groups

Returning to Richard Rose, while his observations appear dated in today's world, still his 1964 model merits a serious examination.*(19)

Rose offers a framework for analysing different factional types, with internal cohesion identified as the primary gauge marking distinctions. His study distinguished between 'factions' and looser units, variously defining tendencies and single issue groups.*(20) While Rose's model is applicable to early 1960s Britain, focusing primarily on Westminster politics, it also provides a useful framework for categorising factionalism more generally. Rose defined a faction as an association with its own programme, strategy, membership, leaders and corporate structures. From this base emerges an intensity of purpose, which generates a communication network and inner discipline. It also follows that factions command first allegiance among their own members, thereby rendering the party a forum, indeed ultimately a prize for the lobbyist energies of group activists. Therefore factions exist either in competition with each other for control of the party, or as refuges for ideological dissenters seeking a base for collective action.*(21)

Few such groups operate within the British system. For one thing, all mainstream parties expressly prohibit "..parties within the party..". Labour's constitution while recognising autonomous associations like the Fabian Society and Cooperative Movement, and registering informal groups like Tribune and various single issue campaigns, otherwise forbids intra-party groups with rival programmes, resources and organisation. The Liberal Democrats' constitution provides for full members ballots in candidate selections and determining key policies as a buffer against group manipulation of the party.

Among Conservatives, the long established practice has been to tolerate a network of informal organisations. This network has included single-issue campaigners like the Conservative Family Campaign and Conservative Action for Electoral Reform, ideological tendencies like Tory Reform and Conservative Way Forward and tighter-knit bodies like the Monday Club (proscribed by Iain Duncan Smith in 2002) and Libertarian Alliance. There have also been Conservative fringe organisations, theoretically independent but committed to some cause or other espoused by the party. They include the former League of Empire Loyalists, National Association for Freedom – later renamed the Freedom Association, Campaign Against Building Industry Nationalisation (CABIN), Institute of Economic Affairs, Centre for Policy Studies and

Lady Olga Maitland's Women and Families for Defence. In other respects, the Conservative attitude towards disciplined factions resembled that of Labour, something that achieved recognition in William Hague's 1999 Conservative constitution.

Essentially, several of the more disciplined party factions have risked the wrath of Conservative Central Office, thereby rendering their appeal marginal. An example of the same was the 1960/70s Conservative Monday Club, who, during Edward Heath's leadership tenure attracted regular censures, along with the Euro-sceptics inside and beyond Westminster who regularly dissented during John Major's Downing Street years.*(22) The Monday Club was – as shown in Patrick Seyd's essay – an example of a highly disciplined campaigning group who facilitated assorted rightist malcontents throughout the Macmillan and Heath era.*(23)

There is also some evidence of similar organisation manifesting in the 1990s Conservative European independence lobby, specifically the Maastricht rebels and their extra-parliamentary acolytes, sufficient to provide a focus for opposition to John Major's premiership. More evidence of those trends will be presented later in this study. Among other parties, Labour's ironically-titled and now debarred, Militant 'Tendency' and David Owen's 1987-88 Campaign for Social Democracy both provide models of organised factions of the type indicated by Rose.*(24) Significantly, each of the groups acted as alternative sub-parties for dissenting ideologues, and all three were detached from mainstream party culture by the intensity of their campaigns.*(25)

A more familiar model to British parties – acknowledged by Rose – is the Tendency. Whereas factions possess firm structures and are ideologically distinctive, conversely the tendency is marked by:

"..a stable set of attitudes, rather than a stable group of politicians. It may be defined as a body of attitudes expressed in Parliament about a range of problems; the attitudes are held together by a more or less coherent political ideology."(26)

Tendencies possess limited structures, but lack the comprehensive organisation and inner discipline of factions. Also, they tend to

46

experience shorter lifetimes and are subject to constant fluctuation and realignment. Until the 1980s, tendencies were normally positioned on a left/right axis in keeping with the ideological parameters of British party politics. Since the early 1990s, ideology has become less important, with the emphasis shifting to issues and interests in a fashion that has become less class-oriented. That said, examples of conventional ideological tendencies include the Tory Reform Group and its predecessor bodies (discussed in Chapter 4) along with the Conservative Charter Movement, both of which were drawn from the centre-left. Rightist tendencies included the Bruges Group and Conservative Way Forward. Labour too has its leftist Tribune and Campaign groups, along with the centre right 1980s Labour Solidarity Group, while Liberal Democrat past tendencies have included the former radical Chard Group, Social Democratic Voice and elitist Jenkinsite 'A1' circle.*(27) Significantly, tendencies are invariably focused on Westminster, relying on sponsorship of parliamentary patrons. They are also affected by cross currents of policy debates, with positions usually shaped by shifting alignments occurring among MPs and peers.

Rose also noted single-issue groups, but it was David Hine's updated framework of 1982 – drawing heavily on Rose's earlier research – that acknowledged their status and role.*(28) Rose viewed single-issue groups as supplementing ideological competition between left and rightist tendencies. That perspective fits groups like the rightist Conservative Family Campaign and leftist Charter Movement. However, it is less appropriate for ideologically non-aligned groups like Conservative Pro-life Campaign and Conservative Action for Electoral Reform, plus comparable groups from the other parties who rarely organise along ideological lines. Also, gender and race groups, along with Tory ecologists, enunciate a cause widely shared by counterparts in other parties.

Both Rose and Hine acknowledge non-alignment as a viable alternative to previous categories of association. This position is based on identification with the whole electoral party and its policies rather than a preference for particular alignments or factions. So too is this a viable option for MPs and activists alike, and their observations are as relevant to the Conservative Party as any of its rivals.

".. Non-alignment may result from an active concern with only the gross differences between electoral parties, from a passive attitude towards policy issues, or from a calculated desire to avoid identification with particular tendencies or factions in order to gain popularity within the whole elected party."*(29)

5. Other Perspectives

Factional classifications can be further sub-divided. Parties are not solely composed of factions, tendencies or non-aligned partisans. Actually, British parties tend towards the pluralist 'broad church' model, whose ranks include various informal organisations approximating to one or other of the frameworks offered. Yet Rose's framework, while useful, is also dated in other respects. To that extent, the ensuing update is required.

First, while all three parties – Labour, Liberal Democrats and Conservatives – are led from Westminster, over recent decades there has occurred a shift away from parliamentary dominance towards rank and file involvement in key decisions over policy and the party leadership. Labour's 1979-81 constitutional changes, as Kogan and Kogan's account indicates, included direct input by the ruling National Executive Committee over the manifesto content, as well as a leadership electoral college, that has since been overtaken by full member ballots within a federal electoral college.*(30) Turning to the Liberal Democrats, previous Liberal leaders were chosen by a full party electoral college, while the former SDP bequeathed to the merged party a 'One member-One vote' system based on postal ballots.*(31) In addition, as Crewe and King noted, the SDP co-founders were strongly inclined to the notion of a members' party, thereby leading to direct membership involvement in policy making and choosing party candidates.*(32) Those practices, as MacIver's edited essay collection highlighted, have since been inherited by the Liberal Democrats and indeed absorbed into that party's emergent culture.*(33)

Yet even the normally hierarchical Tory Party could not remain forever aloof from the changing world of membership democracy, for which its own Charter Movement had long campaigned. It was as recently as 1965 when the Conservatives introduced election by its MPs for choosing the party leader, thereby generating the inevitable, albeit informal, input from the constituencies.*(34) More recently, the party adopted William Hague's new constitution – earlier discussed – that among other things included a mechanism for all members to participate in the final choice of leader. The latter device was utilised to the full by the party membership in August and September 2001 when choosing Iain Duncan-Smith over ex-Chancellor, Kenneth Clarke, as Hague's successor.

Generally, the picture over the past 25 years has been one of slow democratisation of all the British parties, albeit at variable pace. Therefore, Rose's assumption of Westminster primacy in factional affairs looks misplaced in the contemporary climate. This is especially true of Labour and the Liberal Democrats whose constitutions facilitate grass roots initiatives. However, the Tories have also become proactive on the internal democracy front, partly out of a need for credibility and partly to bolster the appeal of recent party leaders – Hague, Duncan-Smith, Howard and Cameron – and their policies.

Second, British intra-party factionalism has been reinvigorated by the success of grass-roots challenges over recent decades, especially where these have contributed to fulsome changes in established orthodoxy and/or alignments. Examples of the latter include the anti-Heath rebellion and subsequent Thatcherisation of the 1970/80s Conservative Party. Elsewhere, there was the Revisionist Social Democratic secession from Labour in 1981 and formation of the SDP, a move that resulted from the Bennite left's success in forcing constitutional change on the post-1979 Labour Party.*(35) In the SDP, there was the success of pro-merger activists who lobbied for two successive 'yes' votes from SDP members for merger in Summer 1987 and Spring 1988 respectively.*(36) Significantly though, in the case of each party, moves were initiated by parliamentarians, in fact grass-roots agitation by activists from the Monday Club, Campaign for Labour Victory, Campaign for Labour Party Democracy, Alliance First ('A 1') and others proved crucial to the success of each initiative.*(37)

Accordingly, in his 1964 framework, Rose's assumption of Westminster dominance of factions and tendencies appears dated and overtaken by events occurring over the past 50 years in British party politics. Yet his framework carries enough merit to warrant adoption for the purpose of this inquiry. In particular, Rose's view of non-aligned activists as necessary allies for any successful campaigning organisation is underlined by the efforts of previously listed groups at wooing uncommitted sections of their parties. We shall see in some detail how Conservative groups in the post-war years set about mobilising the full range of party activists in support of their various causes.

6. A Factional Model for British Conservatives

Having examined various models of intra-party factionalism, now it is necessary to chart a framework appropriate to the British Conservative Party. It is not intended that this model shall have definitive status, save only that it represents an informed view of the place of factionalism in British parties generally and the centre-right particularly.

Although the model adopted approximates broadly to Rose's thesis of factions and tendencies, amendments have been made to the latter. As indicated earlier, Rose was responding to the characteristics of mid-1960s British politics, but yet his thesis was republished a decade later, by which time key changes such as partisan de-alignment and Liberal, Nationalist, UKIP and Green resurgence had occurred.*(38) Yet the second analysis took scarce account of those seminal developments.

It is necessary to deal squarely with Rose's treatise on British party factionalism because in the absence of a wider body of subject literature it has been accorded semi-definitive status by several authors. While respectful of Rose's eminent reputation, this author considers his view of factionalism to be over-simplified and in need of updating. So also has R.T. McKenzie's erudite thesis of political parties been rendered obsolete by developments over recent decades.*(39) While democracy has experienced a slow birth in the Conservative Party, it looks likely to stay. Aside from the Charter Movement's 1980/1990s' lobbies for internal elections and published accounts, such was the momentum generated by leader elections after 1965 that it led to further developments. These included the Thatcher government's statutory imposition on the trades unions of secret ballots for determining strikes and choosing leaders. Accordingly, having pursued democratisation of external bodies, the democracy current was endorsed, albeit with varying degrees of enthusiasm, by the wider Conservative Party in the 1990s. Hence a full member franchise for choosing the Leader – see the 1998 Hague constitution – represents a symbolic shift in Conservative power structures. There is now a tacit recognition of the members' legitimate prerogative in policy making and leader choices, which contrasts starkly with previous assumptions of grass roots as mere infantry for deploying at election times.*(40)

In this atmosphere, the nature of Tory rank and file politics – vis-á-vis leadership and party organisation – has been changed irreversibly. This phenomenon holds out potential for a different, more assertive future, a scenario likely to horrify Tory traditionalists!

Overall, the body of evidence favours Richard Rose's model as an analytical framework. Notwithstanding its dated assumptions, Rose has merit in distinguishing between factions and tendencies, and non-aligned partisans. Also, David Hine's category of single-issue groups fits the framework. However, other models like those of Chambers and Nicholas for all their merits have limited relevance to this inquiry. Accordingly, for this study, the following framework of conclusions will apply:

Factions will be interpreted as tight-knit, disciplined and ideological – or interest – cadres whose membership and leaders are bound together in common cause.

Tendencies are interpreted as loose ideological associations of like-minded fellows, possessing minimal structures, relying on the political camaraderie of shared values and outlook, and generally, though not always, experiencing limited life times.

Single-Issue Groups will be interpreted as cause campaigners operating within the party e.g. Tory abortionists and pro-lifers, pro and anti-hunt campaigners, pro-family lobbyists and environmentalists, etc. Such groups are a conventional feature of democratic political parties everywhere, and in that sense British Conservatives differ little from others.

Additionally, a fourth category has been adopted, namely the *Institutional lobby* or *Party bureaucrats*. This classification is referred to in the writings of the distinguished political scientist, Roberto Michels, but has not been acknowledged by other writers to the degree it deserves.*(41) Essentially, this category may be applied to recognised party organs such as specialist associations, auxiliary, research and staff groups, along with the party press and communications groups. Often, these groups have been used – wittingly and/or unwittingly – by leadership for extending its influence, while pursuing policy crusades. For examples, one only has to look at the extent to which the Conservative machine was used to promote Edward Heath's regime in the 1960s, while after 1975 the same bureaucracy was utilised to expurgate Heath's influence and personnel from the party in favour of his successor, Margaret Thatcher.*(42) In view of the Conservative culture of leadership dominance and Central Office authority, it is essential to present this classification ahead of the substantive chapters, setting the pace for ensuing assessments.

Finally, a fifth category has been created, namely *research trusts*. These bodies represent a growing feature of modern party politics, and particularly among Conservatives where they have mushroomed over the past three decades. Essentially, they are composed of policy 'think-tanks' and journals, and by virtue of their aims, sponsors and literature, the groups have an agenda which usually involves lobbying for a particular direction. Though cerebral rather than activist-led, and often nominally independent of the party, in fact such organisations as the Centre for Policy Studies and Adam Smith Institute have offered intellectual succour to the Conservative Right. A similar purpose has been served by the journal *Tory Reformer* to the now depleted forces on the Tory centre-left. While it might be said that this category constitutes an extension to the tendencies, actually so prolific has been their profile in recent years that a separate categorisation is merited.

7. Summary

A primary goal of this inquiry is to consider the background, nature, causes and types of factionalism emerging in the British Conservative Party over the 71 years since the end of World War 2. To that extent, it aims to be predominantly a work of contemporary history, but also an evaluation of theories on power and leadership structures, partly an analysis of ideological evolution, and partly a consideration of the place of policy and electoral pressures in the constant movement of a long established political party that proudly enunciates its own claims to office. This combination of aims and purpose makes the provision of a suitable analytical framework essential.

Accordingly, the preferred model for this study (i.e. Rose, et al) was adopted because in revised form it represents a relevant framework for assessing different types of intra-party factions emerging at various junctions of post-war Conservative history. This model would not necessarily pertain to parties in other countries, and indeed so many changes have occurred to the British party system over the past 52 years since the paper was first published that clearly it could not have been used in its original form. Therefore, the Rose model has been updated and made applicable to the post-war Tory Party.

In what is plainly an imperfect science, this framework offers suitable contours for dividing and evaluating the various independent groups emerging in the study.

FOOTNOTES and REFERENCES

1. Richard Rose   'Parties, Factions and Tendencies in Britain'; Political Studies (Vol. XII, I, 1964).

2. Frank P. Belloni & Dennis Beller

   'The Study of Party Factions as Competitive Political Organisations'; Western Political Commentary (Vol. 29, 4, 1976).

3. Belloni & Beller   Western Political Quarterly (1976).

4. Giovani Sartori   Parties and Party Systems, Chap. 4, p. 105, (Cambridge University Press, 1976).

5. R.T. McKenzie   British Political Parties (second ed.), Part 111, Chap. XI, (Heinemann, 1963).

6. Robert Michels Political Parties - Int.by S. Lipset (Collier Books, 1962).

7. The limited selection of academic literature on British party factionalism includes:

   • Jack Brand 'Faction in the British Parliament, 1945-1986', Parliamentary Affairs (Vol. 42, 2, 1989)

   • Richard Rose (1964) - as earlier indicated.

   • Eric Shaw   Discipline and Discord in the Labour Party, 1951-87 (MUP, 1988)

   • Patrick Seyd 'Factionalism within the Conservative Party: The Monday Club' Government and Opposition (Vol 7, 4, 1972).

   • Vincent McKee 'Conservative Factions'; Contemporary Record (Vol 3, 1, Autumn 1989).

     'Factions and Tendencies in the Conservative Party since 1945'; Politics Review, (Vol 5, 4, April 1996).

'Factionalism in the SDP, 1981-87'; Parliamentary Affairs (Vol 42, 2, 1989).

'Fragmentation on the Labour Right, 1975-87'; Politics (Vol. 11, 1, 1991).

'Factionalism among the Liberal Democrats'; Chap.7, The Liberal Democrats, Eds. D.J. Maciver (Harvester-Wheatsheaf, 1996).

8. Belloni & Beller (Eds.) Faction Politics, concluding chapter, (ABC-CIO Press, Santa Barbara, USA, 1978).

9. William N. Chambers
    ● Political Parties in a New Nation: The American Experience, 1776-1809 (Oxford University Press, 1963).
    ● 'Parties and Nation-building in America'; Eds. J. La-Polombara & M. Weiner, Political Parties and Political Development (Princetown Univ Press, 1966).

10. Quoted in Belloni & Beller, Western Political Quarterly (1976), p. 535.

11. Ralph W. Nicholas 'Factions: A Comparative Analysis'; Political Systems and the Distribution of Power, Eds. Michael Banton (Tavistock Publications, 1965).

12. Nigel Ashford 'The New American Right'; Social Studies Review (Vol 2, 2, November 1986).

13. Ed Maloney & Andy Pollak Paisley (Poolbeg, 1986).

    Also - John Harbinson The Ulster Unionist Party, 1882-1973 (Blackstaff, 1974).

14. Dean Godson Himself Alone: David Trimble and the Ordeal of Ulster Unionism; Chap 3, pp.25-41 (Harper-Collins, 2004).

15. Tom Garvin 'The growth of faction in the Fianna Fail party, 1966-80'; Parliamentary Affairs (Vol 24, 1, 1981).

16. See Anthony King and Ivor Crewe   The Birth, Life and Death of the Social Democratic Party; Chaps 2 & 3, pp. 27-71 (OUP, 1995).

17. Ibid. - Also, see Maciver (1996), Chap 1, pp 1-21.

18. See Seyd - Government and Opposition(1972)

    - 'Bennism without Benn: Realignment on the Labour Left'; New Socialist (May 1983).

    - V. McKee 'British Liberal Democrats; Structures and Groups'; Contemporary Political Studies, Eds P. Dunleavy & J. Stanyer (UK-PSA, Swansea, 1994), pp 467-470.

19. Rose   Political Studies (1964).

20. Ibid.

21. Ibid.

22. See Seyd - Government and Opposition (1972), pp 467-470. McKee - Contemporary Record (1989) and Politics Review (1996).

23. Seyd (1972).

24. Eric Shaw Parliamentary Affairs (1989), pp 181-184.
    - Vincent McKee - 'British Social Democratic Factionalism, 1981-1996: Case Studies of the SDP, 1981-88, and the Liberal Democrats, 1988-96'. (Unpub. Ph.D. thesis, London Guildhall - now Metropolitan - University, 1996).

25. Ibid.

26. Rose Political Studies (1964), p 37.

27. Shaw (1989); McKee in Maciver eds, (1996) and Social Studies Review (1991) and Politics Review (1991)

28. David Hine 'Factionalism in West European Parties: A Framework for Analysis'; Journal of West European Studies (Vol 5, January 1982).

29. Rose   Political Studies (1964), p 37.

30. D. Kogan and M. Kogan   The Battle for the Labour Party; Chaps 2 & 3, (Kogan Page, 1982).

31. See Stephen Ingle's chapter on party organisation, The Liberal Democrats; Eds. Maciver (1996).

32. Crewe and King (1995), Chaps 12 & 13.

33. Duncan Brack - Chap 4, 'Liberal Democrat Policy', The Liberal Democrats (Macivor eds,1996).

34. Norton in Norton Eds. (1996), Chap 8, pp 127-133.

35. Crewe & King (1995), Chaps 20 & 21.

36. John Stevenson   Third Party Politics since 1945, Chap 6, (Blackwell/ICBH, 1993).

37. McKee - PhD thesis (1996), Chap 6, plus Parliamentary Affairs (1989).

38. Kogan & Kogan (1982);   Seyd, Government & Opposition (1972); Brand, Parliamentary Affairs (1989).

39. Richard Rose The Problem of Party Government; Chap 12, p 45 (Penguin Books, 1974).

40. The evidence of resurgent factionalism in the Conservative Party of the 1970s and '80s produced by Seyd (1972) and McKee (1989), along with Kogan and Kogan's(1982) account of the Labour Party, rather serves to challenge the fundamental predilection contained in McKenzie's celebrated thesis.

41. Michels (1962).

42. Norton in Norton eds. (1996)

CHAPTER 3

RISE OF THE TORY PROGRESSIVES 1945 - 51

Having previously charted the Conservative post-war evolution and offered a framework of analysis for conducting the study, next it is appropriate to pursue the evaluation. The ensuing chapter examines the rising Tory Progressives in the post-1945 Conservative Party, and in particular assesses the war-time legacy of social legislation in response to the 1942 Beveridge Report. There was also the party's accommodation of the mixed economy and reactions to its own heavy election defeat – by Labour – in July 1945. The initiative shown by an assortment of prominent advocates, most notably Rab Butler, also merits assessment, as do responses from the Conservative leadership. Additionally, attention is given to the party trends outside Westminster for evidence of Progressive influence. Also, further attention is paid to the tactics of Conservative right wingers whose reactions proved crucial to the temperature of internal party debates at that time.

It will be apparent to the reader from this narrative that the Conservatives internal culture and power structures in the post 1945 years contrasts sharply with contemporary conditions at the beginning of the 21st century. The prevalence of grass roots deference, along with distaste among activists and parliamentarians alike for factionalism, ensured that independent groups were few and those operating kept a low profile. Yet changes as have occurred, the old deference has gone and in its place has arisen a new, more assertive, climate. This trend has made factionalism a more challenging subject for inquiry than most changes affecting the post-war Tory Party.

1. Election Defeat and its Price:

It was noted in Chapter 2 that factionalism in any political party is a reflection of that party's culture. In the Conservative case, nothing is likely to render greater grief than prolonged exclusion from public office.

Uncertainty over when and if a return will happen renders the pain more acute, especially if there exist doubts over whether Conservatives can win another Westminster election, and at what price?

Defeat and exclusion were the wounds inflicted on the Conservative Party by the Westminster election of July 1945. Such was the extent of Labour's sweeping victory – for which Conservatives had been unprepared – that it prompted many questions about future electoral prospects and which traditional causes should be ditched in order to regain power. The scale of defeat caused grave shock waves as many parliamentarians, including government ministers from Churchill's administration, lost their seats, including Brendan Bracken, Harold Macmillan and Leo Amery, while from the formidable force last elected in 1935 a mere 213 Conservative MPs limped back to the Opposition benches. Election defeat was compounded by the paradox of Churchill's immense personal popularity, which had not saved his party's losses. After 14 years in government, Conservatives had been roundly dismissed by the British electorate, and the time came for taking stock and plotting a new course. New roads might have to be trodden if it was ever to regain power in the post-war world.

The manner of adjustment showed up a key strain in Conservative behaviour, notably the instinct for survival. That could only be achieved by a measure of qualified adjustment. As it happened, ensuing debates highlighted nervous divisions over future direction, not to mention simmering divisions. Patrick Seyd indicated that Conservative deference in the three decades after 1945 meant factionalism was muted.*(1) With the emphasis put on winning elections and supporting the party's Westminster leadership, any divisions emanating from prolonged factionalism risked imperilling electoral appeal and was thus unacceptable to the Tory mainstream.

This changed state of affairs was facilitated by a mixture of rising education, living standards and social mobility. In view of widespread perceptions of national decline, there was a disinclination to accord uncritical trust to the party's Westminster leadership. Robert Blake also observed unsettled traits, specifically a serious worry about how long might be the exclusion from government and the price required for a return.*(2) Yet he also noted how the experience had lurched the party into desperation, plus a mind for accepting post-war reconstruction on a substantial scale. This trend aided the ascendant Tory Progressives whose preferences accorded with the social direction of Clement Attlee's Labour government.

The Tory Progressives benefited from one well-placed and influential patron, Rab Butler. For Butler, who had been education minister in the wartime coalition and afterwards headed the Conservative Research Department, the 1945 election defeat (in which nearly 150 Conservative MPs lost seats) enabled him to refashion the party ready for meeting the challenges of a new state-centred political environment. His biographer, Anthony Howard, noted that Butler felt the dominant inter-war Whigs to have discredited the Conservative cause by a dogmatic insistence on free market hegemony at the expense of social reform and meaningful government intervention in the economy.*(3) This legacy had generated the "..hungry thirties.." which contributed to the election landslide defeat of 1945. Butler's priorities included a full policy review and an overhaul of party organisation at Central Office and in the constituencies. His own memoirs acknowledged that Opposition would facilitate a policy rethink, such as the party needed in order to prepare for a return to government.

"The overwhelming electoral defeat of 1945 shook the Conservative Party out of its lethargy and impelled it to re-think its philosophy and re-form its ranks with a thoroughness unmatched for a century"(4)

Butler was helped by a positive social climate favouring the Progressive Tory cause, and to which his energies were harnessed. He sought to cultivate a new outlook among Conservatives towards the world generally and Britain's place therewith.

Contemporary historians have debated how far the Conservatives were willing partners in the post-war 'Consensus'. Dennis Kavanagh believes the party was forced by the weight of elite and wider public support to conform to the new orthodoxy. Andrew Gamble's more critical view insisted Tory acquiescence in the 'Settlement' to have been a survival strategy for salvaging the institutions and practices of Capitalism in a Socialist dawn.*(5) John Ramsden says that Conservatives were desperate to revive their electoral appeal after the war, while Ian Gilmour and Mark Seddon noted an internal consensus after 1945 that the Tory Progressives' time had come.*(6) This view was based on a notion that the Butler school was ideologically attuned to the realities of post-war reconstruction, which included public welfare, increased taxation, state-owned utilities, a pro-Atlantic foreign policy and orderly wind-up of the British Empire. Butler addressed those challenges squarely.

Two critical developments from that era merit special examination. First was the 1947 Conference's adoption of the Industrial Charter, while the second was the 1949 Woolton/Maxwell-Fyfe reforms of Conservative organisation. Both innovations ranked as prime reforms. They signified a modernising influence at work within the party, while registering a positive appeal with Tory voters across the country and among progressive sections of the Conservative membership.

The 1947 Industrial Charter marked a turning point in respect of Tory reactions to the post-war world. Details of the Charter's articles are less important than its symbolic value, most notably Conservative acceptance of the legitimacy of trade unions in the industrial and political life of the nation.*(7) Such was the magnitude of election defeat that among many Conservative campaigners and policy specialists there was a desire to avoid the bitter class confrontations of the 1930s. The Charter affirmed union legitimacy, along with negotiation rights, wage bargaining, legitimate strike action and pickets.*(8) Given the history of Taff Vale, the General Strike and the ensuing Trade Union and Trade Disputes Act, this new course showed Conservatives tacitly accepting the changing parameters of a leftist political climate. It also included vague references to a more corporatist approach to economic management. This was a world in which Conservatives had to be pro-active defenders of the constitution and property in order to effectively serve their cause. Ramsden describes the Charter as ".... *a public relations success of the first order...*".*(9) Even the opposition of Lord Beaverbrook's Daily Express was turned to advantage. Given the latter's pre-war advocacy of free market economics, the Charter suggested Tories to be mending bridges with the unions while moving away from Beaverbrook's divisive school.

The 1948/49 overhaul of party organisation accelerated the reform pace. Being inextricably linked to the initiatives of Lord Woolton, the party's post-war national chairman, they aimed to refashion Conservative practices in line with the democratic tides touching most other areas of British political life. Woolton sought to broaden the pool of parliamentary talent by curbing the old practice of wealthy individuals effectively 'buying' safe seats and thus controlling party affairs in several areas. The new rules barred candidates from making anything beyond nominal donations to their election expenses while limiting sitting MPs annual donations to their local parties to £50 maximum. Other related reforms were carried, resulting in increased selection prospects for talented but non-privileged Conservatives like Edward Heath, Enoch Powell and Iain Macleod who could realistically aspire to a career at Westminster.

At the same time, the reforms increased the difficulties for Catholics, Jews and other minority candidates in being selected as parliamentary standard bearers, due to constituency committees being empowered to choose candidates free from financial concerns. However, aspirants had to walk the gauntlet of familiar racial and religious prejudices governing party activists. Such a system worked to the better advantage of some over others. Overall, it appears to have increased the numbers of grammar school-educated Tories at the expense of their counterparts in the public schools.

Indeed evidence by David Butler and Michael Pinto-Duschinsky showed that within 20 years of the Woolton/Maxwell-Fyfe reforms the Conservative Party remained dominated in parliamentary candidates and constituency chairmen by business men and professionals.*(10) Less than 3% of constituency chairmen and 1% of parliamentary candidates came of the manual working classes. Yet university 'meritocrats' were active throughout the party, and frequently gained selection in winnable seats. This trend represented real progress for Butler's reformist vision.

The latter reforms are significant in two respects. First, each indicated a new policy direction for the Conservatives. This was especially true of the Industrial Charter which prioritised a workable relationship with the trade unions, itself a contrast to the confrontational track record of inter-war Conservative governments. It further signified the willingness of Conservatives to work within the new parameters of the post-war 'Settlement', thereby boosting electoral appeal. Second, the Woolton/Maxwell-Fyfe organisational reforms had the effect of modernising party organisation and opening up candidate ranks to middle class talent. Though not extending the party's internal democracy, nevertheless the numbers of middle ranking Tory 'meritocrats' emerging in Parliament and Tory cabinets substantially increased over the ensuing 70 years with implications for policy making and leadership choices.

Such was the climate in which Tory Progressives first found their feet, prospered and eventually reached high watermark. The process began in the immediate post-war years, and thus it is to that period that this inquiry is initially directed, embracing electoral defeat, opposition, policy review and organisational reforms, all of which combined to chart a new Conservative direction. This was a task beckoning the Tory Progressives whose agenda and advocates were best qualified to push forward the reformist agenda in the unfolding social conditions of post-war Britain.

2. Tory Progressives: Character and Patrons

From the beginning it is self-evident that the crisis afflicting post-war Conservatives was brought about by the party's election defeat of July 1945. The latter having been widely blamed on the party's 1920/30s track record in government, it thus fell to Tory Progressives to provide impetus and policy reforms necessary for electoral recovery. Thus Tory Progressives – who included Butler, Macleod, Macmillan, Heath and Reginald Maudling – were appositely positioned for discharging their historic task.

Anthony Howard's biography of Butler shows him to have been an energetic patron, shrewdly cultivating a plethora of like-minded colleagues including Heath, Macleod, Boyle, Derek Heathcote-Amery, Oliver Stanley and Gilbert Langdon.*(11) In that sense, two key traits of the broad fellowship were evident from the beginning. First, was an internal coherence based on Oxbridge education, which fashioned a common outlook as well as political and social camaraderie. Second, was the tendency of Tory Progressives to focus on Westminster, Central Office, the Conservative Research Department and other national institutions of the Conservative Party. There was a clear lack of involvement and roots in the various committees of the National Union and Conservative grass roots. This deficiency meant Tory Progressives faring less effectively among rank and file activists at Annual Conference than at Westminster.

Fundamental questions arise about the nature of Tory Progressives. Specifically: Who were they? Where were their supporters? Who were their leaders? What was their agenda and which were their principal causes? How were they organised in strategy and from the inside? Most importantly, what was their impact? Those issues need to be addressed by this study, and to them the ensuing section is addressed.

3. Tory Progressives: General Character

It has to be acknowledged that Tory Progressives were a broad-based tendency from the outset. Ensuing evidence points to this fraternity lacking the rigorous internal discipline and enduring organisation normally associated with pure factions. Instead Progressives acted in the fashion of an amorphous tendency. They sought to influence policy making rather than seize control of party organisation, targeting parliamentary leadership, Central Office and the Conservative Research Department, then headed by Butler. Progressives further lobbied ancillary bodies like the Conservative Students, women, trade unionists and, later, the Bow Group.*(12)

A particular feature of Tory Progressives was the scarcity of formal structures. There were some bodies like the Tory Reform Committee and – after 1951 – the One Nation Group, along with successor organisations like the 1970s Pressure for Social and Economic Toryism, Macleod Group and Tory Reform Group; the latter having functioned since 1975. (More in Chapters 4-6) However, those 1970s groups served as, first, publicists and second, advocates rather than agents of change. The need for co-ordinating like-minded brethren pursuing a common course was self-evident. The pre-war Tory Reform Committee offered a platform at

Annual Conference, a few Westminster patrons and recruiting standard for supporters. However, beyond a publicist role, little else of lasting significance was achieved in a party still consumed by the twin causes of defending the British Empire and stemming Communism.

Given that the post-war climate favoured modernisation and concessions to the new left-wing climate in the country, significantly it was the Conservative Right who organised into dissident groups over the next decade. The groups – most of whom have long since disappeared – aimed to resist the socialist embrace. Accordingly, rightist campaigners operated as publicists for traditional Conservative causes, e.g. Empire, free enterprise, employers' rights and in opposition to extended state welfare, etc. Their prime supporters included Lord Beaverbrook, whose Daily Express became the Right's principal Fleet Street organ; Churchill's "Irish wolfhound", Brendan Bracken, and his fellow minister from the war-time coalition, Leo Amery, along with old-style Chamberlainites, Sir Waldron Smithers and Sir Douglas Hacking, and the pro-Conservative pressure groups, Aims of Industry (founded 1942) and the National League for Freedom (founded 1943). Although something of a motley crew by the late 1940s, clearly the Conservative Right was far from being a spent force.

Tory Progressives were clearly creatures of a rising 'Settlement' that was a product of its time. This factor is borne out by the climate of the post-1945 Conservative Party and reactions to the party's ejection from office. The willingness to embrace a progressive agenda endorsing universal welfare, a mixed economy and orderly wind-up of the Empire was clearly linked to a desire for electoral recovery. Progressives were agents of that process. Yet, as Andrew Gamble's comprehensive account of the post-war party outlined, the Progressives star seems to have risen and fallen with the varying fortunes of the peacetime 'Consensus' or post-war Settlement.

4. Agenda and Causes

Having identified the Tory Progressives, next it is necessary to chart a policy agenda for this diverse fellowship. Progressives subscribed to a broad set of principles rather than fixed dogma. Such proved to be both their strength and weakness at different times over the next three decades. Its ingredients included the following:

First was the belief in a consolidated welfare state characterised by targeted benefits to those in need. The latter included social services and effective management of the welfare system. Ideological justification could be found in Disraeli's 'One Nation' legacy with its emphasis on ensuring a safety net for the weak and vulnerable of society. The latter, along with pragmatic considerations, acquired a resonance among Progressives in the immediate post-1945 years that lasted over the ensuing three decades. Moreover, that same theme was addressed by the 1950s One Nation Group in their prime publications.*(13) Robert Behrens emphasised the priority that One Nationites attached to public welfare when appraising the Heathites in the 1970s, as well as examining the nature and output of the original One Nation Group.*(14) This legacy has been a consistent feature of the Tory Progressives throughout the post-war era and marked a key clash point with the Conservative Right in the 1970s.

Second was de facto acceptance – if not endorsement – of public sector utilities, indicating recognition of the mixed economy. This position recognised a valid role for trade unions in the workplace and in wider society, something already symbolised by the 1947 Tory Industrial Charter. While the reasoning was mainly pragmatic, the same strategy set in motion the wheels for defining a crucial characteristic of Tory Progressives, notably a belief in the capacity for public intervention in select social and economic issues. Again, the contrast with the Right's unbridled free market credo was stark, as became poignantly clear during the Thatcher years three decades later.

Yet Tory Progressives had long felt embarrassment at the perceived irresponsibility and crude self-interest exhibited by owners of coalmines, railways and other key utilities. Those surviving remnants of the pre-war economic order had rendered the party unelectable in a radical climate as prevailed in July 1945. Any return to power depended on Conservatives demonstrating adherence to a new order of well-managed public utilities and legitimate trade unions. Butler viewed his agenda as essential for party modernisation.*(15)Yet, aside from the not-inconsiderable difficulty of getting leadership and Conference approval, the principal test would be whether the public sector would reap electoral benefits. Only ensuing electoral contests held the answer.

Third was a belief in effective guardianship of free enterprise. The calculation was made that acceptance of the publicly-owned utilities (the Conservatives 1945 manifesto plans envisaged public control of utilities) allowed the party to effectively defend the bulk of private industry. In essence this meant that Conservatives having conceded utilities to state ownership – i.e. railways, coal, gas, electricity, buses, civil aviation and the Bank of England – they could champion the free market status of pharmaceuticals, the building industry, oil, aircraft manufacture and other industries whose prosperity was deemed essential to the national economy. Interestingly, in the bitter debates ensuing over iron and steel nationalisation, those arguments surfaced.

In that way, Tory Progressives viewed their agenda as conducive towards boosting free enterprise while also preserving the essential features of the British state. Among notable exponents of this line was Quintan Hogg in his text, *The Conservative Case.**(16) Like so many One Nationites, Hogg wanted to be part of a campaign that would wrestle control away from those reactionary Whigs whom he blamed for inter-war social neglect that had caused the 1945 election defeat. Moreover, he feared the consequences of a failure to reform, and had little hesitation about encouraging full scale policy transformation and modernisation of the party structures.*(17) As for Butler, his priorities were articulated by this extract from his memoirs.

"I called for a total reorganisation of the social structure on which our party rested, an acceptance of redistributive taxation to reduce the extremes of poverty and wealth, and the repudiation of laissez-faire economics in favour of a system in which the State acted as 'a trustee for the interests of the community and a balancing force between the different interests'... I envisaged codes of behaviour for industry, with sanctions as a last resort, which would expose anti-social monopolistic and restrictive practices, lay down standards of quality for the consumer,

*and above all create a spirit of partnership between management and
workers as the real link between political and economic democracy".**(18)

It was within the latter disciplines of a 'responsible' social agenda
that Butler felt the cause of free enterprise was best protected over the
decades lying ahead.

Fourth, was a perceived need to reach an accommodation with the
trade unions. The Progressives had long been embarrassed by the failure
of inter-war Conservative governments to achieve any positive dialogue
with the unions, as well as reactionary posturing of former Conservative
ministers and their supporters in industry. Such had contributed to the
social polarisation characterising 1930s Britain, and was deemed
non-conducive towards social harmony and economic growth on which
Conservative electoral revival depended. Predictably, among Tory
Progressives there was general rejoicing at adoption of the 1947
Industrial Charter, which was viewed as a reconciling gesture towards
the trade union movement. It is also significant that Walter Monckton,
Labour Minister in Churchill's 1951-55 administration, was considered
by rightist historian, Andrew Roberts, to be an appeasing figure who
shamelessly capitulated to the unions to a degree unbecoming of a
Conservative minister.*(19) Notwithstanding Roberts' judgement, the
policies of successive Conservative governments 1951-74 included
substantial autonomy for the unions.

Fifth was a commitment to social justice. This view reflected
Progressives' distaste for the market hegemony outlook of the
Conservative Right, as much as genuine concern for the weak and
defenceless. Butler's impatience with the failures of free market
capitalism in the inter-war years was augmented by his belief in the need
for cautious intervention by the state in social affairs.*(20) Additionally,
there was a moral dimension to correct what were seen as the worst
excesses of unbridled capitalism, something that earlier inspired the
youthful Harold Macmillan to write his radical pre-war text, *The Middle
Way*. The latter pleaded for government assistance to resuscitate the
depressed North East. Nevertheless, viewed through the eyes of the
Right, this was the mentality that had contributed to an excess of state
power in post-war Britain. Indeed so profound was the Right's

condemnation that three decades later the Thatcher crusade sought to fashion a new consensus around the contrasting orthodoxy of state abstention from the economy and social affairs.

Sixth was a reformist outlook on the constitution and British system of government. Though far from being state reformers, actually Tory Progressives proved less dogmatic about maintaining institutions and practices that had outlived their usefulness. While this penchant manifested after, rather than during the Butler era, nevertheless the markers were laid during earlier times. It was during the Macmillan era that Britain's first EEC application was made, and concluded successfully by Edward Heath. The latter figure also terminated Belfast's Unionist regime in March 1972, introduced elections by proportional representation and reorganised the structure of government for Northern Ireland, while further contemplating devolution for Scotland and Wales in response to the 1973 Kilbrandon Commission report. All those factors showed decisive trends in the reform direction.

The willingness to revise solemn Conservative beliefs in response to changing tides showed a flexibility that highlighted the progressive nature of this school of opinion. Among certain sections of the Tory Progressives there was sympathy for electoral reform, especially after 1974 and also for reforming the House of Lords. Overall, the Tory Progressives viewed many articles of Conservative faith – e.g. sovereignty, the Union and traditional institutions – as amounting to inflexible dogma that hindered imaginative government. So too did they look askance at later reactionary campaigns mounted by die-hard unionists and anti-Europeans like Enoch Powell, Teddy Taylor and Julian Amery under the auspices of defending Conservative beliefs. Generally, it was in such areas as Europe, constitutionalism and reforming the representative process that Tory Progressives showed their colours. Equally significant was the fact that Conservative groups like the European lobby and the 1980/90s Charter movement were led and dominated by Progressives. So also was the Pro-Remain lobby group of Tory MPs in the 2016 European Referendum led by updated One Nationites like Prime Minister, David Cameron, and veteran Europhile, Ken Clarke.

Seventh was the Progressives distaste for privilege, a trait that stood awkwardly in contrast to the wealthy antecedents of so many leading Tory Progressives e.g. Butler and Macmillan. This outlook was prompted by two factors. First was a genuine desire to enable social mobility as had occurred with access to secondary and university education after 1945 in the aftermath of Butler's own 1944 Education Act. The latter, as observed by A.H. Halsey et al, profoundly enhanced opportunities and social mobility for a generation of talented working and middle class children.*(21) Yet that same educationalist also noted that it was middle – rather than working class – children who were principal beneficiaries. This trend – as Anthony Sampson's celebrated study acknowledged – was in line with the scale of changes characterising Britain as in the three post-war decades.*(22) The Tory Progressives were resolved that their party should adapt to such changes while avoiding the reactionary image that might linger from being suspected of defending privilege.

The second factor is that Progressives were both supporters and beneficiaries of the extended democratic culture characterising post-war Britain. They had little sentiment with hereditary peers and disliked plural voting by both business men and graduates, as well as other privileges of the old order. So too were Progressives more enthusiastic about womens' entry to politics, while broadening the social ranks of Conservative parliamentary candidates. Small wonder that during these years a new breed of Progressive Tory 'meritocrats' emerged, including Heath, Maudling and Macleod; middle rather than upper class, grammar rather than public school educated, professionals rather than aristocrats, and career politicians rather than "public service minded" patricians. Progressives were dedicated to a new Conservatism based on opportunity, and the principal thrust of their political agenda was aimed at widening opportunity for the disadvantaged while defending the institutions of free enterprise and the British state against major change.

At the same time, it would be wrong to overlook the impact of aristocratic paternalism on the Progressive school. Butler and Macmillan each held such connections, as did several others, while Kavanagh wondered whether Tory paternalism really sprang from guilt over wealth or a sense of 'noblesse oblige'? Moreover, not all middle class 'meritocrats' sustained the Progressive faith. Examples included Enoch

Powell and Angus Maude; both 1950s 'One Nationites', who became disillusioned with the failings of Keynesianism, and in the mid-1960s re-embraced the free market and reinvigorated nationalism, moving to what became known by 1975 as the New Right.

Eighth was a distinctive preference for party modernisation. Progressives were concerned about the archaic state of Conservative organisation and absence of internal democracy; weighing heavily against the advancement of able, unconnected persons. Reform was essential, and Maxwell Fyfe/Woolton's reforms were welcomed. After all, reform made the party amenable to the talented 'meritocrats' whom Butler patronised. Also, modernisation meant the party keeping step with the post-war political tide which sustained credibility with voters and observers alike.

Finally, Progressives favoured an orderly wind-up of the Empire and building bridges with post-war Europe. Among Macmillan and Butler, and their protégés, Heath and Macleod, there was an understanding that the Empire had reached its demise, and it remained only for Britain to undertake a dignified withdrawal.*(23) In common with many forward-looking Liberals of that time, Tory Progressives hoped Britain might salvage some influence through development of the Commonwealth, but otherwise preferred a pro-Atlantic foreign policy tempered by involvement with the tentative steps being taken from 1950 onwards towards European co-operation.

This retreat from Empire mapped out clear ideological distinctions between Progressives and the Conservative Right. The Right in the late 1940s viewed defence of the Empire as an article of faith, and over ensuing decades provoked intensive debates prefaced by accusations of treachery at Tory Progressives. Significantly, various issues had imperial roots, such as colonial administration, Rhodesian UDI, coloured immigration and race relations questions, all of which saw the Right take a familiar reactionary position in contrast to reform-minded Progressives. European accession did not gather momentum until after Macmillan's failed bid for EEC entry in 1963.*(24) Nor did Europe appeal to all Progressives in equal measure in the early years, and did not greatly occupy Butler in the immediate post-war decade.*(25)

Generally, Tory Progressives viewed themselves as heirs to the Disraeli tradition of One Nation Toryism. Issues of social justice, democratic reform, imperial wind-up, acceptance of a mixed economy and the welfare safety net all ranked paramount with this tendency. Yet Tory Progressives were – as Behrens observed – interventionist and corporate-minded, preferring to shed an old image of Whiggery.*(26) Their principal strategy was to effect party reforms and also to wrestle control from Whigs, imperialists and other reactionaries who had so damaged the party's electoral appeal.

In essence, Tory Progressives reacted to the election defeat by supporting an 'in-house' revolution that transformed the party from reactionaries to what Gamble viewed as social capitalists.*(27) While Progressives were never committed to any formal definition of aims, the agenda listed previously corresponds to the programmes pursued by successive Conservative governments from 1945 to 1974. Some causes like Europe acquired further momentum as circumstances changed in the 1960s and '70s, while others like trade union power and public welfare received a consistently cautious approach from successive Conservative leaders. It is on this basis that Tory Progressives have a reasonable claim to having fashioned public policy for 30 years.

5. Features and Spheres of Influence

The Tory Progressives represented a distinctive fellowship for their time. Like other tendencies, they were bound together by a shared set of policy goals, headed by an acknowledged lead figure – if not straightforward leader – in Rab Butler, and with specific political and social traits characterising their ranks.

Those traits have already been noted earlier, but require clarification. Yet, because Tory Progressives avoided developing formal organisations, available evidence is largely impressionistic. However, the various histories of the period, along with occasional primary sources, give telling evidence of social and political features. It is not possible to be any more precise but the picture, if not scientifically generated, at least conforms to an image that was true of that breed of Tory moderates and 'modernisers' who took the lead in reshaping the party after 1945 under Butler's lead.

One indelible trait of the Progressives in post-war years was their centralised character. They were London-centred, very middle class and with most key figures possessing an Oxbridge university base. This flavour served to maintain their coherence as a loose fellowship. Significantly, many younger talents had worked in and around either Westminster and/or the Conservative Research Department, headed by Butler, and it naturally followed that youthful Progressives like Heath, Maudling, Hogg and Macleod all held parliamentary ambitions. This taste for Westminster, on a reformist policy review combined to show a metropolitan elite whose bonds achieved coherence but whose principal limitation was a lack of grass roots appeal.

The common threads of social class, university education, the experience of war and military service, and parliamentary ambition, all moulded a similar political outlook and strategy. Such bonds offered coherence to an ideologically homogenous collection of upwardly mobile young Tories whose talents were more recognised by senior party figures than Churchill or Eden. As for Butler and Macmillan, they were both chief mentors and indeed the ideological gurus to whom the fellowship looked up. Actually, they offered more than just leadership; they offered preferment for the likes of Heath, Maudling, Macleod and an as-then conforming Enoch Powell.*(28)

Tory Progressives were restricted in influence to those areas where their writ ran deep. In practice, that excluded a great majority of the constituency associations where traditional Conservative causes were greatly valued and the Tory Progressives viewed with suspicion. Significantly, it was at constituency level that rank and file influence was strongest and from there parliamentary candidates and most Annual Conference representatives emerged. This factor affected dynamics over the ensuing three decades when leadership and grass roots experienced strains in their rapport.

At the same time, Progressives enjoyed scope for lobbying. After 1951 there was the influential Bow Group whose appeal to talented, liberal-minded Tories of the younger generation was comprehensively described by James Barr. This organisation being something of a 'brains trust', it was well placed to facilitate the lobbying of Butler's people. Barr recounts a proliferation of university graduates and young professionals emerging among the Bow membership. This ensured that the Group offered an appropriate lobbyist base for One Nationites, Tory Reformers, fiscal reformers and others of the Progressive tendency.*(29)

Another sphere of influence was the universities, where student organisation provided a ready-made clientele for Tory Progressives. Among the late 1940s generation, the modernising purpose of Butler appealed to the progressive instincts of many youthful Conservatives. It is also noteworthy that with the Empire on notice of dismemberment and extended state welfare a reality by 1948, political ground was visibly changing. Also, increased numbers of middle – rather than upper class – students were pursuing university degrees due to the extension of secondary education and scholarships that had begun in the inter-war years. The latter mushroomed in the three decades following the 1944 Butler Education Act.*(30) As a result, the new Conservative emphases were placed on opportunity and mobility, rather than defending Empire, privilege and employers, as previously. This climate was spearheaded by the Tory Progressives whose campaign to restore their party to government was augmented by the backing given by students and graduates to the new direction and advocates.

The press proved a more diverse estate for the Butler school. On one hand, pro-Conservative newspapers like the Times and Daily Telegraph held little sympathy for the ideological aims of the Attlee government, but were equally anxious to avoid the travails and impotence of prolonged opposition. Hence the Times found itself welcoming the emergent bipartisan 'Settlement', inclusive of modernisation and the policy review. Further support came from Conservative 'provincial' papers like the Birmingham Post, Yorkshire Post and Glasgow Herald, along with the influential Economist journal. All desired to see the party regroup, modernise and achieve a swift return to government on a programme relevant to the state of post-war Britain.

The Conservative Party's political mutation was self-evident well before the 1950 general election. Acceptance of the NHS principle (if not its final layout), the 1947 Industrial Charter and Woolton/Maxwell-Fyfe organisational reforms all showed the extent to which Conservatives had adapted to changing conditions in the post-war era. Very significantly, the changes were all made in a centrist direction, which squared with the Tory Progressive ethos. In large part, they were the product of the party leadership's anxiety for a return to public office. Yet they also underlined the degree to which the Progressives time had come, and with Butler as chief mentor they were making the most of this appeal. So too did Tory Progressives take full advantage of the demoralised state of the Conservative Right. Depleted and discredited, the Right during the 1945-50 Parliament were in no state to offer a credible alternative.*(31)

6. Overview and Conclusions

Electoral devastation for the Conservatives in 1945 ushered in a period of reform and retrenchment. That change was necessitated by the scale of defeat is self-evident, but the process went further. Peace time reconstruction, social building and economic planning were all determined by the programme of Attlee's Labour government. It therefore followed that if the Conservatives were to exercise any influence on future political redirection, their party itself had to be redefined as a progressive movement.

Conservatives could no longer bear the charge of reactionaries or 'Colonel Blimps', because such an image might have impeded their electoral recovery. Instead their new mission was to be vigorous in defence of the constitution and free enterprise, accepting the imperial demise and at peace with the expanded welfare state, trade unions and public utilities. So prolific were changes to the political domain that the party had to undergo several fundamental changes in order to remain competitive.

The task of transforming the Conservative Party into a credible, alternative government proved helpful to the Tory Progressives. This school had the good fortune to be well placed with influential leadership at a time when national currents favoured their cause. The Conservatives under Churchill had headed a war-time coalition with Labour and the

Liberals on terms that produced progressive home policies on health, education, housing and labour practices. Butler was among the key Conservative home ministers, and in a position to influence post-war social policy development. His Progressive ideological school – who included the war-time Tory Reform Committee, later the One Nationites, later still Pressure for Economic and Social Toryism, and their united successor, Tory Reform Group – were all resolved that the Conservatives should not fall under dominance by the old Right again. Accordingly, they lobbied for the adoption of progressive social and economic policies such as would meet the needs of post-war recovery. Also, they sought to curb rightist influence at the higher levels – both at Westminster and Central Office – so as to guard against them regaining a hold on the leadership after the coalition's demise.

Essentially the Tory Progressives were products of a political generation inspired by the Coalition social policy and planning. Their great strength lay in the esteem of leading patrons as Butler, Macmillan and Walter Monckton, plus younger advocates like Heath, Maudling and Macleod. High level patronage ensured that the Progressives influenced policy and strategy in the party's most influential quarters, including Central Office, Conservative Research Department, Executive Committee of the National Union and the Parliamentary Party. During the War, a total of 37 Conservative MPs were declared supporters of the Tory Reform Committee, and lobbied for leadership endorsement of the Beveridge Report.*(32) After the 1945 election defeat, the party proved more amenable to Butler's social reform line, and his chairmanship of the Conservative Research Department provided a pivotal opportunity for influencing post-war policy making. The willingness of Churchill and his deputy, Anthony Eden, to accept the Industrial Charter and Woolton/Maxwell-Fyfe reforms to party organisation indicated a new direction. This climate of change was further underlined by the ease with which the Settlement – including imperial demise, welfare state, public utilities and the N.H.S. – were accepted by the Conservatives.

Another advantage to the Tory Progressives was the relatively weakened state of the Conservative Right. As shown earlier, the Right's credibility had been damaged by popular memories of the inter-war years when the previous orthodoxy had been non-interventionist, for which the Conservatives had paid a high price at the polls in 1945.

The free market and Empire lobbies remained, but with little potency in the post-war years. One former Conservative MP recalled the Empire lobby as amounting to an army of *"..quaint, right wing old ladies.."* whose major tactic was to hector centrist speakers at Annual Conference and provide speakers for pro-colonial motions.*(33)

More generally, the right were always an assured presence at Annual Conference and on the fringe, but the shrill tone and lack of front bench patrons showed up their weakness more than strength. Occasional dissidents like Sir Waldron Smithers – who produced a polemical paper titled 'Save England' – joined forces with Lord Beaverbrook's Daily Express and the Daily Mail to oppose the Industrial Charter and nationalisation of utilities. There were also such pressure groups as Aims of Industry and the National League for Freedom (both previously mentioned) lobbying on the fringes of Conservative Conference and the National Union with patronage from right wing MPs like Smithers and Sir Douglas Hacker; they being among the few right wingers to have survived the 'clean-out' of July 1945. Also, as Andrew Roberts documented, there was an old Chamberlain rump surviving into the post-war era.*(34) However, the Right posed no threat then, if only because their stock was low with both leadership and the wider electorate. Even Churchill and Eden viewed rightist causes – e.g. opposing the NHS and social services – as outdated.

Overall, Tory Progressives were a phenomenon of the post-war era. They comprised a broad school of like-minded individuals whose organisation was limited to a small number of loose tendencies, including the Tory Reform Committee, the 1950s One Nation Group and the various successor bodies. There was also the post 1950 Bow Group which provided a sympathetic base and focal point for Tory Progressives of that generation. It also needs to be stated that Progressives did not lay much emphasis on developing disciplined organisations at that time because of patrons' prominence at senior party levels. The Progressives avoided organising activists into rank and file campaigning groups, and indeed maintained a profile that was rather elitist and cerebral. Those few Progressive organisations were either policy-orientated 'brains trusts' or publicists. This situation proved a stark contrast to the Thatcher era – over three decades later – when organisations like the Tory Reform Group and Tory Charter Movement provided a haven for centrist dissidents alienated by a rightist leadership.

Ultimately, the Tory Progressives were products of a generation that reached its peak during the Churchill-Eden-Macmillan years, 1951-63. The foundations were laid in the opposition years following World War 2, drawing upon a favourable political climate when the party struggled to recover from catastrophic defeat. As times changed, so did the political climate, raising new issues and challenges. The task of assessing the actors, trends and events from that period – which Conservatives spent in government – belongs to another chapter in this inquiry.

FOOTNOTES and REFERENCES

1. Seyd in Layton-Henry, Eds. (1980) - Chap. 10, p.p. 234-236.

2. Blake (1985) - Chap. Viii, p.p. 257-262.

3. Anthony Howard - RAB: The Life of R.A. Butler, Chap. 11, p.p. 143-154, (Macmillan, 1988).

4. R.A. Butler - The Art of the Possible: The Memoirs of Lord Butler, Chap. 27, p. 126 (Hamish Hamilton, 1971).

5. Dennis Kavanagh - Thatcherism and British Politics: The End of Consensus Chap. 2, p.p. 34-39 (Oxford University Press, 1987).

    Andrew Gamble - The Conservative Nation, Chaps 1 & 2 (Kegan-Paul, 1974).

6. Ramsden (1998) - Chap. 12, p.p. 316-324.

    Gilmour and Seddon (1997) - Chap. 2.

7. See Ramsden (1998) - Chap. 12, p.p. 321-324.

8. Ibid.

9. Ramsden (1998), Chap. 12, p. 323.

10. For evidence of Conservative candidates and the party machine contesting the 1970 election, see D. Butler and M. Pinto-Duschinsky-The British General Election of 1970, (Macmillan, 1971).

11. Howard (1987), Chap. 11, p.p. 143-145.

12. James Barr On the Make: The Bow Group, 1950-2000, (2001) Chap.1, p.p. 6-7. This author is grateful to Mr Barr for kindly granting access to his pre-publication draft, as well as discussing his work in a recorded interview on 13th July, 2000 at the Palace of Westminster.

13. See Robert Behrens 'The One Nation Group, 1951-55', PSA Paper, 1988.

14. Behrens (1980), see Chap. 2.

15. Howard (1987), see Chap. 11, p.p. 140-145; also Butler Memoirs (1971), Chap. 7, pp. 150-153.

16. Quintan Hogg <u>The Case for Conservatism</u>, Chaps 1 & 2 (Penguin, 1947).

17. Ibid.

18. Butler Memoirs (1971) - Chap. 7, p.p. 133 & 134.

19. Andrew Roberts - <u>Eminent Churchillians</u>, see Chap. 5, p.p. 282-285 (Phoenix 1995).

20. Howard (1987), Chap. 11, p.p. 150-155.

21. A.H. Halsey, A.F. Heath & J.M. Ridge - <u>Origins and Destinations: Family, Class and Education in Modern Britain</u>, Chap. 2, p.p. 27-29 (O.U.P., 1980).

    A.H. Halsey eds. <u>Trends in British Society Since 1900</u>, chap. 7, p.p. 192-200, (Macmillan,1972).

22. Anthony Sampson, <u>Anatomy of Britain Today</u>, see Chap. 13, (Hodder & Stoughton, 1965).

23. See:
    (i)   Nigel Fisher - Iain Macleod, Chap. 8, (Andre Deutsch, 1973).
    (ii) Harold Macmillan - <u>Memoirs - At the End of the Day</u>, 1961-63, Chap. 5 (Macmillan, 1973).
    (iii) Howard (1987), Chap.11.

24. Nigel Ashford in Conservative Party Politics, ed. by Zig Layton-Henry, Chap. 5, p.p. 102-108 (Macmillan, 1980).

25. Information was imparted in interviews with Giles Marshall, Editor of Tory Reformer, 25th March, 2000 and Rt Hon. Stephen Dorrell, MP, 13th July, 2000.

26. Behrens (1980), see Chaps 2 & 3.

27. This view of the Progressive Tories – referred to as 'Right Progressives' – is recurrent in Professor Gamble's two major published works on Conservative post-war history, Conservative Nation (Kegan Paul, 1974) and The Free Economy and the Strong State (Macmillan, 1988).

28. See:
    (i)   Heath memoirs (1998), Chaps. 5 & 6.
    (ii) Howard (1987), Chap. 11.
    (iii) Fisher (1973), Chaps. 3 & 4.

29. Barr (2001), Chaps 2-3.

30. Halsey ed. (1972), Chap. 7, p.p. 192-200.

31. This view seems to have produced a consensus among various historians; for example, see J.D. Hoffman The Conservative Party in Opposition, 1945-51 (MacGibbon & Kee, 1964). Also, Ramsden (1998), Chap. 13.

32. Interview with Giles Marshall, 25th March, 2000.

33. Interview with Peter Temple-Morris, MP – 25th October, 2000.

34. See Roberts (1995), Chap. 3 – Roberts comprehensively demonstrated the existence of an influential Right wing group, loyal to the former leader, who persistently undermined Churchill's authority within the party throughout the war years.

CHAPTER 4

HIGH NOON FOR THE TORY PROGRESSIVES 1951 - 65

This chapter will chart the character and progress of Tory Progressives throughout the years of Winston Churchill's peace-time premiership and subsequent Downing Street tenures of Anthony Eden, Harold Macmillan and Alec Douglas-Home. It will also identify the emergence of the One Nation policy group, while further analysing its impact on the Conservative Party at Westminster and beyond. So too will the chapter explore the various causes and advocates whose devotion to building a modernised and progressive Conservative political movement provided impetus for the party's transformation throughout that period. Further issues to be considered will include the impact of being in government over three consecutive electoral terms from 1951 until 1964, as well as the style and policies of different Conservative leaders. It will also evaluate the influence of the Tory Progressives in defining the party's direction, while asking if Progressives thrived or went into long term decline. What strategy did the Progressives deploy? Did they engage in overt factional politicking, or was their main thrust directed at winning influence among at Westminster and among party 'think tanks'? How did Progressives fare among Conservative rank and file, in constituencies, at Annual Conference and organisations of the National Union?

Significantly, 1958-65 was a period of slow revival on the Conservative Right. A combination of conducive causes, including lingering imperialism, anti-Europeanism, anti-Americanism (especially after Suez), free market ardour and support for white settler communities in Africa … all combined to feed the Right's agenda while swelling its ranks with assorted malcontents. Later, hostility to non-white immigration from the New Commonwealth became something of a defining cause for the Right. Yet it was the perception of national decline that encouraged disaffection towards the Macmillan and Home administrations, thereby swelling the ranks of dissenters. The process gathered pace with the onset of economic troubles in the early 1960s, and thereafter acquired further momentum with Enoch Powell's crusade against Europe and immigration in 1968. This chapter will evaluate the Right as a fragmented school of dissenters represented by organised groups like the Monday Club and Anti-Common Market League, plus such extra-party organisations as the National Association for Freedom, Aims of Industry and the League of Empire Loyalists.

Evidence presented is instructive about the party generally, along with power structures and the gathering left/right divisions that surfaced in the 1970s and beyond.

1. New Parameters

It is a belief of historians everywhere that important lessons are understood with the benefit of hindsight, a point appropriate to analyses of the post-war Conservative Party. The party's dismissal to Opposition in the election of July 1945 has been agreed by most contemporary historians and Tory writers to have provided relief from the burdens of office. It further facilitated a reappraisal of policy, organisational affairs and campaigning strategy such as aided Churchill's return to government in the election of October 1951. As shown in the previous chapter, the principal justification for intensive changes was cast as "modernisation", with the priority being the party's survival, enabling it to compete in a post-war world whose foundations had been fashioned by rival forces.

Various studies of post-1945 British Conservatism point to the movement having absorbed a crisis of direction, itself born of electoral uncertainty. Conservatives were nothing if not a party of power; hence in the first instance recovery of public office provided the principal impetus for policy and ideological reappraisal such as characterised the post-war years. That goal challenged Butler's progressive reformers and the traditional, empire-minded Winston Churchill and his deputy, Anthony Eden. Although Churchill and Eden remained less interested in internal party affairs, they had not obstructed Butler's social reforms or Woolton/Maxwell-Fyfe's organisational reforms. Accordingly, by the time of the Conservatives' partial recovery in 1950 and ensuing victory the following year, the party's transformation was wholescale.

By 1951 Butler's influence was reaching peak point.*(1) Evidence presented in Chapter 3 showed his Progressive tendency to have made much running among younger generation MPs, party researchers, policy specialists and aspiring parliamentarians. Additionally, there was the lobbyist campaign waged by the semi-organised Tory Reformers outside Parliament, aided by Westminster sponsors. Tory Progressives proved especially influential among the new generation of emergent Conservative leaders like Heath, Macleod and Hogg, as well as the older stalwarts like Macmillan and Gilbert Langdon. Ideology exerted an appeal, but there was also the momentum of change that by 1950 had swept all but the most resolute die-hards of the Conservative Right in its pathway. Plainly, the earlier discrediting of the Right after 1945 and subsequent Progressive ascendancy was linked to a belief that the latter represented an appealing face of British Conservatism to an electorate radicalised by war and the austerities of peacetime reconstruction. Hence for the sake of electoral recovery, the party followed the Churchill/Eden lead in endorsing major policy changes that anchored Conservatives to the post-war Settlement ... but were later so detested by the 'New Right'.

Several contemporary historians observed that post-war governments from 1945 until 1975 were managing continuous British national decline. The end of empire did not produce a dynamic Commonwealth, nor was foreign affairs influence easily transferred to other areas. Also, 1950s economic prosperity gave way to fiscal problems that eventually produced stagnation in the 1970s, fed by constant inflation and semi-permanent trade deficits. While the pool of scholars – including Minogue, Gamble, Kavanagh and Marquand – provide alternative assessments of cause and impact, there is no escaping the reality of a nation and political system in turmoil by 1975.*(2) Those circumstances generated the New Right and Margaret Thatcher, a phenomena examined in later chapters. What is relevant here is the reality – again more obvious to Mrs Thatcher than her predecessors – that Conservative governments of those years had played a not-inconsequential part in managing the country's affairs to that state. Hence Tory Progressives as the dominant force within the party 1945-75 became synonymous with national decline. This charge of collusion with a Socialist-led socio-economic system was used by Thatcherites after 1975 to discredit Edward Heath's leadership tenure.

Yet some twenty years ahead of Margaret Thatcher's accession, there was evidence of a slow revival on the Conservative Right. As far back as the mid-1950s an amorphous collection of reactionary tendencies emerged to challenge leadership orthodoxy in key policies. This category included die-hard imperialists, anti-Europeans, free-market militants, anti-Socialists and anti-Communist stalwarts, along with old-style Conservative traditionalists. It is significant that most such groups fed off reactionary causes, counterpoising policies of the Macmillan and Home governments. Loss of empire, the Suez debacle and concomitant surrender to American pressure, along with Common Market accession, debates about trade union power, public spending, taxation and nationalisation initiated by 'Consensus' post-war public policymakers .... all raised hackles on the Conservative Right. Each issue generated implacable opponents on the Right within the party and challenging the party leadership. Such was the record of organisations like Lord Salisbury's Anti-Common Market League, the Westminster-based Suez Group and ultra-disciplined Monday Club, along with Aims of Industry, National Association for Freedom and the League of Empire Loyalists on the outside.

Some groups subsequently found a role permanently beyond the Conservative Party e.g. League of Empire Loyalists, while others maintained an independent association e.g. National Association for Freedom.*(3) However, short of endorsing one of the extreme right parties, there was really nowhere else for right-wingers to go but the Conservative Party. Hence policy concerns were directed at the party leadership, while their campaigns impacted on the Conservative movement as a whole. In fact, as subsequent evidence will show, rightist groups of that period lacked strength to seriously challenge party leaders, but instead provided a conduit for dissent. During the Heath era, those groups offered a haven for rebels of the Right. Insignificant though they were, their populist causes provided a portent of things to come after the Right captured the leadership in 1975.

2. Why the Progressives?

Assessments of Tory Progressives over the period 1950-65 beg two main questions.

First, how far were they fashioned by Conservative electoral successes over the period? After all, three victories in four contests over fifteen years was a reasonable showing for a party whose main ethos was government. Second, how were Progressives affected by the closeness of Conservative ministers like Butler, Boyle, Macleod and Macmillan to Progressive groups like the Tory Reform Committee, Butler's cadre at the CPC and the One Nation Group? Were they truly independent or publicists for successive Conservative governments of the period? The latter question is significant in respect of the type of factionalism generated by governing parties generally and British Conservatives particularly. It is also indicative about the influence which 'in-favour' ideological tendencies can expect from Conservative leaders in government. The marginalisation of the Conservative Right over that period highlights the role of factions as refuges for out-of-favour ideologues, while maintaining some cohesion in adversity.

Addressing the two principal issues highlights an essential purpose of this inquiry. The Tory Progressives constituted an 'insider' elite operating during critical times. Essentially the question repeats itself about whether Tory Progressives were ever really campaigning visionaries or publicists for the Macmillan and Home governments. Preliminary evidence points to them being 'elite publicists' because assessments of the Tory Reform Committee and its sister bodies show little evidence of authentic organisation or grassroots functionaries.*(4) Also the evidence shows a close connection to leadership figures and their policy agendas. In particular, there was the continuing focus of TRC activists around ambitious politicians like Butler, Macmillan, Macleod and Heath. The trend effectively hitched Tory Progressives to successive Conservative governments in policy and direction, which proved advantageous for as long as the post-war Settlement held firm among Conservatives. Yet after 1970, national decline was palpable. This emergence curbed Tory Progressive influence, which was widely synonymous with a failed orthodoxy, and later displaced in favour of the New Right.

Meanwhile, it is useful to examine the small range of Progressive organisations functioning over the period 1951-65. While assessments of influence are difficult to quantify, some relevant observations may be made of the active groups.

3. Progressive Organisations

Perhaps the most influential Progressive lobby of the 1950s was the One Nation Group. It was composed of a collection of reform-minded backbenchers and policy researchers, most of whom later progressed to Westminster. Prominent 'One Nationites' included Angus Maude, Enoch Powell, Edward Heath, Iain Macleod, Gilbert Langdon, Lord Hitchinbroke, Robert Carr and Quintin Hogg, with ideological alignments later changing in some cases.*(5) Their primary role was as a 'brains-trust' for influential Tory Progressives to develop policy for refashioning the party in tune with post-1945 Britain. As with so many Conservative initiatives, this one was driven by electoral concerns. Responding to the emergent consensus, 'One Nationites' sought to tackle the remaining ideological barriers hindering Conservative participation. Essentially, 'One Nationites' were home missionaries, advocating a benign Conservatism for managing public sector industries and social services. This ongoing introspection characterised Conservative responses to their party's uncertain direction in the post-war world.*(6)

It is important to understand that 'One Nationites' operated as a policymaking forum, not a campaigning group. They produced books and pamphlets for influencing the climate of opinion among Conservative leaders and policymakers in the direction of accepting the welfare state and public utilities. The group never contemplated corporate lobbying or large scale membership recruitment, nor did it seek party offices, far less countering other groups, confronting leadership or other such tactics. Instead their output was a number of influential publications that caught the Tory mood at a crucial point of its post-war development. Throughout a nine-year lifetime, four important texts were published namely: One

Nation (1950), The Social Services, Needs and Means (1952), Change is Our Ally (1954) and The Responsible Society (1959). From this literature emerged three principal – if occasionally confused – themes which went to the heart of Progressive Tory thinking. First was an acceptance of the principle of a social security safety net. Second was a commitment to individualism and capital accumulation. Thirdly, a revised view of society was adopted, balancing individual rights with those of the whole nation.*(7)

Aside from a preference not to involve internal campaigning, 'One Nationites' influenced events from other angles. The place of Butler as head of the Conservative Political Centre and Conservative Research Department meant there was an assured role for this group and its ideas at the party's higher levels. He acknowledged the reality of his position and the advantages that it conferred on his supporters.*(8) Hence it succeeded in attracting Tory intellectuals and impacting on leadership, beginning during Churchill's peacetime premiership and continuing into Anthony Eden's brief term. Progressive influence reached high peak during the premiership of Harold Macmillan (1957-63), and indeed held the party's intellectual high ground right up until Edward Heath's fall in 1975.

Tory Reform was perhaps the most enduring and established of all the Tory Progressive campaigning organisations. Its origins go back to the war-time coalition. Taking their cue from Rab Butler's 'modernising' initiatives, this band of socially-conscious Tories formed the Tory Reform Committee as a vanguard for the party's One Nation traditions of reform and social justice. Over the next half-century this school operated through various guises, notably Tory Reform Committee (1940s), Pressure for Social and Economic Toryism (1963-75), before being re-launched in 1975 as the Tory Reform Group. To an extent, the same people lent their support and campaigning energies to each of these bodies, whose causes were promoted and updated to their time. The Progressive outlook has already been explored in Chapter 3, but it needs adding that the emphasis was adapted to new challenges arising throughout later decades. Accordingly, post-war Progressives - under Butler's influence - lobbied for a social economy, while their colleagues in Pressure for Social and Economic Toryism focused on the legacy of social capitalism and growth under the administrations of Macmillan, Home and Heath. *(9)

As will later be shown, the Tory Reform Group provided a refuge for dissident 'One Nationites' and 'Heathmen' throughout the Thatcher years. So too did the primary purpose of each Tory reform lobby vary in line with the changing fortunes of the Progressive tendency and its proximity to the party helm. Plainly, for as long as the Conservative leadership articulated domestic social policies consistent with One Nation principles – as happened under Churchill, Eden, Macmillan, Home and Heath – then Progressive groups acted as government publicists. However, when threatened by the New Right after 1975, the Tory Reform Group became a focus for centrists, Europhiles, 'Heathmen' and social reformers opposing the dogma and style of Margaret Thatcher.

4. Importance of the Bow Group

Another important group of Progressives was to be found in the Bow Group. This body was a 'brains trust'; it being small, cerebral, elitist and composed of policy researchers and ambitious young parliamentary candidates, mostly with common university backgrounds at Oxford, Cambridge and London. The Bow Group's official historian, James Barr, commented on the organisation's early purpose during the 1950s:

"They formed the Bow Group to counter the Tories' image as the 'stupid party'. Only recently graduated. The Left was intellectual, exciting and eclectic; the Right hobbled by constant reference to an image of pre-War Conservative Government 'a paradise for profiteers and hell for everyone else'.+[a] J.M. Keynes' political economics dominated both Conservative and Labour thinking, but it was the Left which harnessed his message more effectively, and portrayed nationalisation as picking up where the wartime communal spirit left off". *(10)

Note +[a] - quote attributed to Herbert Morrison.

Barr noted that the Bow Group had ambitions to match the Fabian Society as a vehicle of ideas, policy research and planning, and – like the Fabians – learned specialists would dominate the process.

Accordingly, Bow interests were articulated by way of pamphlets, a periodical journal, *Encounter*, that began in 1957, along with booklets and major publications on topical policy issues. Barr further noted that Bow Group publications were studied by Central Office and successive leaders at Downing Street alike. Moreover, establishment connections were highlighted by the willingness of grandees like Lord Windlesham to patronise the Group's Conference meetings and write forewords for its publications.*(11) The Group playing host to Prime Minister, Harold Macmillan, for the launching of Crossbow at the Constitutional Club, London in October 1957.*(12)

It is not the business of this inquiry to regurgitate Barr's worthy study, but rather to identify the link between the Bow Group and the fortunes and policies of Progressive Tories of that time. Also noteworthy is the degree to which the Bow Group trained a generation of up-coming Tory Progressive politicians, of whom John Selwyn-Gummer, Peter Walker, Christopher Brocklebank-Fowler, Hugh Rossi and Julian Critchley are examples.*(13) Yet the Bow Group was not a Butler coterie, far less bastion of Tory 'One Nationites'. In fact the Bow Group contained a diversity of political views, including individuals who later became prominent on the right. They included Geoffrey Howe (who combined Bar duties with pamphlet writing), Keith Joseph, Norman Lamont, Peter Lilley, Kenneth Baker and Michael Howard, all of whom – according to Barr – played key roles in their time.*(14)

At the same time, such was the political climate that Tory Progressivism was boosted by the prevalence of Keynesian economics and welfare social planning in public policymaking – so-called Butskellism. The latter in turn gave a degree of orthodoxy to Progressive advocates. Right wingers of the 1950s and early '60s were left to grumble about taxation levels, universal welfare provision, an excessive public industry sector and imperial withdrawal. Not until the 1970s did they come into prominence, and even then many New Right advocates, such as Keith Joseph, claimed to having been "converted" by an alleged failure of One Nation Conservatism over the previous decade.*(15) However, in the 1950s and 60s', Joseph, Howe and Howard articulated a centrist ideological chord not evident in their subsequent political careers.

Notwithstanding the Bow Group's ideological non-alignments, evidence shows that throughout its first 25 years the organisation leaned towards Progressivism. Indeed to all practical intents the Bow Group, with its growing array of pamphlets, policy documents and a periodical served as a 'brains trust' for that school. Three areas marked out those leanings:

First was the emphasis on planning contained in its documents. The 1953 pamphlet, *The Non-Specialist Graduate in Industry*, (Author: Anthea Tinker, and produced by the Birmingham Bow Group) which argued for an increase in the provision of university places for science and technology and a reduction in Arts places was typical of Progressive thinking. Another was the 1952 Bow pamphlet, *Coloured Peoples in Britain*, which argued for integration of non-white immigrants in British society by a combination of education, media and greater social contact. However well-intended may have been this pamphlet, in fact as Barr acknowledges, it was flawed by two misplaced assumptions.*(15) First was an expectation of continued full employment; a picture that changed over ensuing decades. Second, it failed to foresee proliferating immigration characterising the 1960s and '70s. Such planning was based on evidence available then. After 1965, planning and professionalism became hallmarks of the Heath leadership, and acquired status in what Progressives considered the promotion of social capitalism.*(16)

Second was a propensity for Bow pamphlets to articulate a humanitarian dimension. This line was dictated by the One Nation view that social justice had its place in the free market; hence the advocacy of workers' rights, protection for immigrants and support for widows and deserving social welfare claimants. Almost all pamphlets of the 1950-75 period reflected this ethic, and thus did the Bow Group maintain a specific identity of purpose. Writing in 1961, Richard Rose viewed the Group as a Tory modernising force and policy-making elite, associated with the prevailing orthodoxy of the Macmillan leadership like previous post-war leaders.*(17) Rose's view was based on the Group's economic and technological penchant without similarly acknowledging its social ethics. Nevertheless, given that the rise of the New Right was still some way off, Rose lacked an alternative model to counterpoise the prevalent One Nation orthodoxy of that time.

Third was the Bow Group's endorsement of the Macmillan government's 1960 application for United Kingdom accession to the European Economic Community.*(18) The Brussels debate had by then engrossed the broader Conservative Party, and thus the Group's enthusiastic pro-Europeanism placed it firmly in the Progressive orbit. Moreover, by aligning with the European lobby, and promoting the government's key foreign policy, the Bow Group had made its thinking clear to allies and opponents alike. Only later – indeed much later – when the New Right had taken control of the Party did attitudes to Europe change, by which time pro-Europeanism had become a defining issue for Tory Progressives who by 1978 represented a displaced ascendancy.

As for the Group's impact, this is more difficult to quantify. That it exercised influence at the higher echelons is evident from numerous establishment contacts, previously described. There was also a widespread view of the Bow influence permeating government (an over-generous calculation), hence the occasional grant from British United Industrialists and other such bodies.*(19) The willingness of leading Tory figures like Prime Minister Harold Macmillan to address its events and the journalist, T.E. Utley, to become its president served to underline its growing stature. Moreover, Bow pamphlets facilitated debates among party intellectuals, MPs, and activists alike, while it provided an extra cerebral dimension to Conservative politics from the 1950s onwards.

Bow events were well patronised, and the Group's ranks provided a training ground for Conservative parliamentarians, ministers and writers of the future. Yet such was the degree of specialist talent available that its publications attracted government interest, while *Crossbow* retained a discerning readership and variable list of contributors.*(20) The Group proved an influential cerebral elite, but made little attempt to woo grass roots or Conservative voters. Nor did it engage in internal organisational battles or seek controlling positions in constituency associations. Generally, the Bow Group propagated a battle of ideals, for which its means, connections and elite manpower equipped it well.

5. Growth of Dissent on the Conservative Right

Contemporary historians differ in their interpretations of how and when the Conservative Right were re-galvanised. For some, it marked a reaction to British national decline, while for others it counterpoised the over-weaning growth of state authority in the economy and society. Almost all trace the Right's re-emergence to the late 1950s, but gained extra reaction from the party's electoral defeats under Edward Heath in 1974.*(21) For the purposes of this inquiry, it is appropriate to identify the symptoms of dissent, such as unsettled the party and led to a slow revival of the Right.

The Conservative Right is a remarkably heterogeneous force, being no more coherent than rivals on the left or centre. It is a broad school that articulates those many concerns felt by an assortment of British nationalists, old-style imperialists, social disciplinarians, anti-statists, free market devotees, economic libertarians, anti-Communist zealots, 'little Englanders', Scottish, Irish and Welsh unionists, monarchists, Protestant constitutionalists and others. The success of the Right in the 1970s and '80s in first, capturing control of the party, and then winning and retaining public office for eighteen years (1979-97) was a phenomenon facilitated by events occurring over the previous 20 years. Accordingly, when noting the dissenting signs manifesting from the 1950s onwards, and accentuated by a perceived malaise over the ensuing two decades, plainly there emerged an accumulation of rightist hostility towards the Post-war Settlement. The latter looked increasingly worn and alien to Conservative core beliefs.

Indeed during the Thatcher era, it became common parlance in rightist quarters to denounce past Tory leaders as "compromisers", "traitors" and "closet socialists" etc.*(22) Such demonising of previous Tory Progressives served to highlight the degree of difference separating the two rival forces. The gulf was part-ideological, part-social, part-policy and part-strategic. It ran deep enough to ensure the prevalence of factional rivalry such as has rarely been experienced in the Conservative Party in the twentieth century. Significantly, tensions and divisions emerging during the Macmillan era came to fruition in the Heath years following the electoral crisis of 1974.

The causes of the rightist revival that began in the late 1950s and continued throughout the 1960s were many and varied.

First was a growing public perception of national decline. The latter did not reach the public until the mid-1960s, but the reality was already embedded in the minds of Tory activists and the political establishment long before then. There had been a growing balance of payments deficit from the late 1950s onwards, followed by Chancellor Selwyn Lloyd's 'Stop-Go' economic strategy of 1960-62. Yet, as contemporary historians recall, despite having had three Chancellors, Macmillan and his successor, Alec Douglas-Home, failed to arrest the decline.*(23) The process was further accentuated by adverse inflation figures and low economic growth throughout the 1960s. All this evidence served to make Macmillan's earlier boast "... You've never had it so good ..." look hollow and smug. It also nurtured growing dissatisfaction with the workings of the post-war Settlement.

Second, the loss of Empire had wreaked emotional toil on more than just the Conservatives' Neo-imperialist/Nationalist wing. In fact by 1959, with India and Malaysia gone, and other Afro-Asian territories being prepared for independence, the reality of Britain's decline from world power to a European middle ranker caused more than a little soul-searching among the party elites and hierarchy. For the Right there was the unpleasant fact of successive Conservative governments from 1950-65 having overseen independence for many colonies including Ghana, Nigeria, Sudan, Kenya and Malaysia. So also had the party leadership given tacit backing to Indian independence under Attlee's government, a factor that caused Enoch Powell to literally "... walk the streets in disbelief". The pain that such changes wreaked among a generation of imperialists – reared on the "White Man's burden" – found expression in the right-wing Monday Club, inaugurated in 1961, to defend European interests in Africa.

Third, was replacement of British hegemony in world affairs by the USA. Aside from the withdrawals from Palestine and Greece, there had been other developments that confirmed British decline and US ascendancy. The emergence of super-power organisations like GATT, NATO and SEATO – all US dominated – along with its atomic/nuclear weapons arsenal, commercial might and dynamic economy all served to underline the growth of American economic, military and political authority in the post-war world. Nor did the Commonwealth prove a successful vehicle for maintaining British international influence, far less produce the economic or diplomatic channels envisaged by some visionary statesmen. Indeed it turned out to be something of a white elephant as far as rebuilding British international prestige was concerned.

Fourth, never was the reality of UK decline more poignantly demonstrated than by the humiliating retreat of British and French armed forces from Egypt – under pressure from Washington – in October 1956 following the Suez invasion.*(24) David Carlton's biography of Anthony Eden recounted the humbling spectacle of the Prime Minister's enforced exit from office in January 1957.*(25) This insult rankled deeply with many Conservatives, who observed the UK becoming ever more dependent on a country that prioritised its own national interests under the guise of an alliance. Interestingly, much anti-Americanism on the Conservative Right lingered into ensuing decades and manifested through demands for revived national sovereignty and Powellism.

Fifth, was the emergence of the European Economic Community, and the depressing experience of the Macmillan government's failed application. To many on the Right, applying for EEC membership highlighted the unpalatable fact of British weakness, as well as placing Britain in a regional organisation alongside former enemies. Yet there was also the reality of Britain's trade position being increasingly focused on North America and Western Europe rather than the Commonwealth. Pitching for a place in Europe was a desperate move aimed at lessening British dependence on America, while offering growth prospects for the British economy through belonging to a vibrant free trade area likely to develop further over times ahead. Yet as was noted by Nigel Ashford, the European Community did not evoke much enthusiasm, either on the Conservative Right nor indeed among the broad party membership.*(26) Moreover, French blocking of the first application in January 1963 did little to enhance the EEC reputation in British eyes or among sceptics in the Conservative Party.

Plainly, the 1963 rejection torpedoed Macmillan's already faltering economic policy, thereby hastening his downfall later that year.*(27) Although the pursuit of Community membership eventually succeeded in the following decade, Europe was for long synonymous in Conservative eyes with British weakness. It also drew opposition from the Right, who found its workings, culture and constitutional incursions unacceptable. Therewith lay a prime ingredient of what became in the 1960s/70s Powellism.

Sixth was a general sense of withering stature and limited sovereignty that had taken root in Britain by the early 1960s. With the Empire now all but gone, the international stage dominated by the Americans, Britain was barely even NATO's principal secondary power. Also, by 1965 UK economic capacity had been overtaken by West Germany and Japan, thus feeding depression over where this decline would lead. Significantly, national newspapers and journals (e.g. Times, Guardian, Daily Telegraph, Spectator, etc.) abounded with supporters contributions throughout the decade, while political debates focused on arresting the decline. It was this decline that played into the hands of right wingers. Their criticisms were directed at post-war Conservative as much as Labour governments, whose policies, they argued, had relegated the UK from the premier stage of world powers to a second division of European middle-rankers. Such a drop proved painful for what after all was an establishment party of the British upper middle class.

Seventh was the emergence of white reactionary issues in 1950s/60s Africa. There had been the Mau Mau rebellion in Kenya, with its ramifications for white and Anglo-Asian settler communities. Later came the attempt at preserving white influence in Central Africa through the ill-fated Federation. However, it was Ian Smith and his Rhodesian Front's stand against black majority rule in Southern Rhodesia, inclusive of the 1965 UDI, that galvanised the Conservative Right both inside and outside the party. Their preference was for backing Smith in Salisbury, as much as Vorwoerd's white nationalist regime in Pretoria, and the indecisiveness of Conservatives at Westminster (who split three ways in a parliamentary vote) served to highlight the substantial support for this band of colonial reactionaries. The party leadership was embarrassed over right-wing polemics, but support garnered by the Monday Club pointed to a residual sympathy for the Settlers cause, a cause so dear to the Conservative heart.

Eighth was immigration, which had not yet reared its head as a prime issue in 1960. Although Cabinet papers released from 1953 indicated discussions about restricting coloured immigration from New Commonwealth countries, labour shortages in UK, plus post-independence troubles in some countries, dictated a pragmatic open door policy.*(28) However, the emergence of racial tensions e.g. 1958 Notting Hill riots, effectively linked both issues in the public mind and it was the Conservative Right's defence of a white, Anglo-Saxon Britain that surfaced poignantly in ensuing public debates. As Zig Layton-Henry's research shows, post-1968 Powellism with its explicit anti-immigration tones fed off a residual current of Anglo-Saxon xenophobia that chimed with popular trends in the wider electorate.*(29) The Right's campaigns were given added impetus by popular unease over immigration, which manifested in colour bars operating in pubs and clubs, and among many landladies, hotels and even employers. So also were impromptu marches staged by malcontents, including London dock workers and Birmingham car workers, in support of Enoch Powell in 1968.*(30)

It was indicative of the Right's growing appeal that the Monday Club thrived from the popular discontent emerging then over the issues of race and immigration. Although in the early 1960s the Monday Club had not adopted the hard line rightist strategy for which it became known later in that decade, nevertheless its right wing agenda was gathering momentum.*(31) Such was a portent of things to follow.

Finally, by 1965 the economy's performance had become at best, sluggish and at worst retarded. Inflation had returned, with limited economic growth, recurrent trade deficits, fiscal uncertainties and a revival of industrial relations troubles, such as haunted the economy over later decades. Andrew Gamble viewed the thirteen Conservative years in government, 1951-64, as a monumental Capitalist failure, while elsewhere Conservative writer, Alan Clark, saw the period as dictated by policies of the left.*(31) Nowhere was this more apparent than in economic and social policy where the state was keeper, fiscal regulator, copious welfare and employment provider and punitive tax collector.

Actually, Clark's disaffection then found an echo among assorted right wing fellowships.

The years 1950-65 featured gathering storms on several fronts. Although it is difficult to see how a right-wing Conservative government could have shielded Britain against the effects of shrinking markets and diminished international stature in the 1960s, the New Right maintained that Tory Progressives had betrayed Conservative core values while in office. As a result, the party paid a high electoral price in the 1970s. Given that a comparable theory was previously mooted against the Right to explain the party's 1945 defeat, evidently such polemics are not exclusive to either side of the party!

6. Tendencies and Schools of the Conservative Right

The many rightist tendencies emerging since the 1940s divided into two broad schools, notably Nationalists/Neo-imperialists and Whigs. Although writers like Seyd and Kavanagh have devised their own models (which are not challenged), the model offered here seems suited to this inquiry.*(33) While different issues emerged at various junctures, and power politics within the party altered to indicate changing circumstances, there was a certain consistency of causes and manpower. The Conservative Right has a lengthy pedigree, and its ideological character has some continuity that merits further examination. This framework takes account of the degree to which the Right has been shaped by events inside and outside the party over some 50 years.

7. Nationalists/Neo-imperialists

This school had a long legacy among Conservatives dating back to the days of Disraeli, Joseph Chamberlain and Lord Randolph Churchill. Its emphasis on the acquisition of territory and subjugate peoples chimed with a key Conservative belief in the propriety of Britain's imperial missions to the African and Asian continents. Such demonstrated the alleged superiority of British political, administrative, cultural, commercial and military means, and imperialists insisted on an "obligation" to share those achievements with "... the less developed peoples of Africa and Asia". This "... white man's burden ..." was, as historians like Thomson and Wood recount, by no means limited to the British establishment, but the durability and scale of the British Empire meant its impact was particularly marked among colonies elites, including military officers, administrators, colonial servants, migrants, Protestant missionary clergy etc.*(34) Accordingly, from those quarters much residual support for the Empire was drawn, as also were campaigning imperialists. Aside from self-interest, national pride played some part.

By the early 1960s, events had rendered the imperialist cause anachronistic. The Empire was being dismembered, UK/American links had been consolidated through GATT and NATO, and even the Commonwealth looked an unlikely sphere for rebuilding trade links, far less international stature. Accordingly, after 1945 neo-Imperialists mounted a reactionary school fighting one lost cause after another; decolonisation, GATT, Suez withdrawal, and the independent - Blue Streak - British nuclear deterrent. Later, during the Heath tenure, there was the fall of the Ulster Unionist regime at Belfast, plus UK accession to the European Economic Community. There was also rising immigration, the growing race debate and anti-Rhodesian sanctions that split the party. Previously, Churchill and Eden, though Imperialists at heart, were pragmatic enough to operate the post-war 'Settlement' in domestic and foreign policy. Suez was an aberration, and Eden's departure ended lingering Imperialist sentiment at the Tory helm. Yet from this tendency emerged parliamentary champions like Leo Amery and Lord Salisbury, later Julian Amery, Enoch Powell, Teddy Taylor, William Cash and Alan Clark.

All those figures have commanded big followings at Conservative conferences, and several have exploited this popularity to drive changes in party policy. In the case of Cash and the late Alan Clark, with the Empire having passed into history, their nationalism has asserted Westminster sovereignty against interventions by European Union commissioners.*(35) Hence the 1990s Euro-sceptical crusade by the Conservative Right! Taylor has also been a stern critic of European "encroachments" and equally prominent supporter of the Union in his native Scotland. In that sense, Unionism and Constitutional campaigns in defence of monarchy and pre-1999 House of Lords (both Taylor causes) served to augment the neo-imperialist programme.

Imperialists and nationalists spoke the language of national greatness, which was always a guaranteed success with traditional-minded Conservatives, especially during periods of decline or recession. Predictably, the inflationary 1960s proved conducive to agitation by the Monday Club and Anti-Common Market League. Both those organisations directed their ire at the Tory Progressives whom they accused of compromising the imperial legacy and national sovereignty. Indeed the Right's campaign assumed an aura of intense hostility. It acquired a populist dimension when endorsed by Enoch Powell (a former One Nationite!) after his enforced exit from the Shadow Cabinet in 1968. Powell's mixture of nationalism and free market economics added extra spice to the assertive right wing campaigns plaguing Heath's Shadow Cabinet 1968-70 and beleaguered administration of 1970-74. Although by no means the only force on the Conservative Right, nevertheless neo-imperialists and nationalists played an important role in shaping the Thatcherite New Right that eventually displaced Edward Heath and the Tory Progressives from their control of the Conservative Party by 1975.*(36)

8. Whigs

There are several inter-changeable names denoting the Conservative Right's free market lobby including libertarians, economic liberals, free-marketeers, anti-statists, Whigs, and - post-1975 - Thatcherites, etc, while Robert Behrens in his appraisal of post-war Conservatives labels the right "Diehards".*(37) The author has chosen the Whig label because its historical meaning adequately summarises that school's purpose. Whigs were essentially concerned with curbing state regulation of commerce and voicing the interests of business and property-owners. They resented high taxes, and expected Parliament to legislate for conditions conducive to the growth of enterprise, while safeguarding the national interest against perceived enemies, external and internal. The historic defection of erstwhile Whigs from the Liberals to Conservatives during Victorian/Edwardian times confirmed the new alignments, as did the politics of the economic liberals from the 1950s onwards. Yet just as the nationalist/neo-imperialist school represented a concentration of assorted strands of unionism, imperialism and British nationalism, so did the diverse free market tendencies make up the broad Whig school that came to fruition after 1975.

The Whigs had previously held high ground in the inter-War years during the leader tenures of Stanley Baldwin and Neville Chamberlain. However, their dogged defence of the coalmine owners, while reluctant to either tax or spend on welfare had ensured their unpopularity with the Butler-led Progressives. They were widely blamed for the election defeat of 1945, and fell out of popularity among the Churchill/Eden leadership as well as younger sections of the party. A few Whig voices remained in the post-war party, such as Aims of Industry and surviving Chamberlainites, but otherwise this school had been discredited by the legacy of the austere thirties. In the post 1945 Butskellite world there was no place for reactionaries from another era. Whatever may have been the residual sympathy for the free market, previous Whig dominance had proved an electoral embarrassment to the Conservatives; hence their estrangement from party mainstream!

However, by the late 1950s concerned voices questioned Conservative collusion in the mixed economy. In his biography of Enoch Powell, Robert Shepherd indicates Suez withdrawal to have caused Powell's review of his fundamental outlook.*(38) Moving away from erstwhile confidence in the social market and benign power of government intervention, Powell gradually moved to a preference for curbing the state sector. So did Suez highlight Britain's decline as an international power; hence his growing contempt for the Commonwealth, hostility to the USA and dislike of the nascent EEC. The Commonwealth he viewed as a device for maintaining 'great power' delusions, while the EEC he considered to be an American-backed instrument for dominating West European states. Also, for Powell there was the matter of the EEC's unacceptable infringement of constitutional British sovereignty. Further ire was added by certain EEC states whose armies he had literally faced in battle 30 years earlier. The significance of Powell lies not just with his post-1968 battles over Europe, the economy, foreign affairs, immigration and Northern Ireland. His 1958 resignation from the Treasury, with Peter Thorneycroft and Nigel Birch, signalled growing unease about UK direction.*(39) There then followed Powell's advocacy of so many rightist causes over the three ensuing decades. This strategy, according to another biographer, Patrick Cosgrave, was fashioned by his self-chosen exile as South Down's MP (1974-87) and consummate advocate of the Ulster Unionist cause, while similarly estranged from the Tory mainstream.*(40)

Concern about taxation, union power and public spending levels was expressed from other quarters, including the newly-founded Monday Club after 1961, National Association for Freedom and Aims of Industry throughout the 1951-65 period.*(41) However, not until the economy visibly faltered in the late 1960s and early '70s did the free-market become a revitalised cause. It was then that the array of Whig lobbyist and study groups – like the Centre for Policy Studies, Institute for Economic Affairs, 92 Committee, Selsdon Group, Libertarian Alliance etc. – so closely linked to Margaret Thatcher and the New Right re-grouped with a new-found confidence.*(42)

Significantly, from 1960 onwards a broad stream of rightist lobbies began to articulate Whig concerns about the 'imbalance' of state and private enterprise boundaries, along with taxation and trade union powers. Patrick Seyd's essay on the early years of the Monday Club noted their scathing criticisms of the nationalised industries' poor performance, plus large welfare payments.*(43) The National Association for Freedom viewed trade union powers with grave concern, and argued for substantial curbs, along with lower taxes and reduced public spending. Equally, many Whig groups in the 1970s and '80s actively campaigned for greater police powers and a more traditional – authoritarian – approach to defence, education and foreign affairs, as indeed happened during Margaret Thatcher's premiership, 1979-90. From there came the convergence of Whigs and Nationalists/Neo-imperialists in the New Right of the mid-1970s and beyond. Their common agenda of national revitalisation and a return to market forces and enterprise owed much to a harmonisation of different priorities propagated by those two schools. There was also the advantage of leadership that made all the difference for 'capturing' the party and re-defining policies to those preferred by the New Right. The roots of that change may be traced back to Macmillan's era at Downing Street.

9. Impact of the Right?

An inevitable question arises about the effectiveness of Conservative right wing groups during those years of Tory Progressive ascendancy, 1950-65. Did they achieve any lasting results? Were the Right influential or merely conduits for dissent by imperialists and free market zealots? Given that the Right became more garnered as a result of the Macmillan and Home governments' failings, it follows that their organisations facilitated dissenters throughout this phase in Conservative history.

The Conservative Party's history shows Tory Progressives to have been a dominant force throughout this period. Their leader, Rab Butler, sat in Cabinet and twice bid for the party leadership, while his rival, Harold Macmillan, was distinguished more by ambition than separate ideology. Additionally, Butler and his protégés headed the Conservative Research Department, while many ideological fellow travellers e.g. Heath, Macleod, Hogg and Maudling all sat in Parliament, thereby giving the Progressive school some strength of numbers at Westminster, plus a substantial role in defining the manifesto. All those factors kept the Right on the outside, counterpoising leadership and subtly challenging party strategy. Given the Conservatives' convention of leadership deference, it was inevitable that the Monday Club and Anti-Common Market League were battling against a government that enjoyed widespread support from its party rank and file. Only after 1962 did the leadership visibly falter, leaving the Right to challenge a party establishment that appeared unsure of its own ideological and policy direction.

Conclusively, it may be assumed that the Right acted as both agents and publicists for dissent during the high noon era of domination by Tory Progressives. Those various incidents ranging from post-1956 protests against the US by the Suez Group, the 1958 Thorneycroft/Powell/Birch Treasury resignations, the Monday Club's 1961 formation, Lord Salisbury's campaigns against EEC accession and the Right's declarations of support for Ian Smith etc. are all attributable to unease over the existing framework of government policy. Ineffectual though their protests may have been, groups like the Monday Club, Suez Group and Anti-Common Market League provided forums for right-wing protestors, plus a banner for ideological kinsfolk within the party.

Another distinguishing feature of the period was the initial indifference followed by hostility of Conservative leaders, Macmillan, Home and Heath towards reactionaries of the Right. To a large degree, this reflected political realities of those years. Plainly, the Monday Club and Anti-Common Market League and their ilk represented an obstruction to leadership, and could prove dangerous nuisances at Annual Conference plus some constituencies. Later hostility showed up leadership unease over the damaging electoral impact Rightist tactics rendered to the Conservatives public image. This point was conceded to the author in interviews with individuals as politically diverse as Peter Temple-Morris and Norman Tebbit.*(45) It was as though they were fighting battles on behalf of an empire that by 1964 was all but gone, and in the process inhibiting the efforts of leadership at achieving modernisation of policies and voter appeal. Heath in particular displayed serious contempt for the antediluvian tactics of the Monday Club and post-1968 Powellites, a factor of which he makes little secret in his memoirs.*(45) Predictable leadership practice was to encourage supportive organisations like the Tory Europeans, Tory Reformers, One Nationites and even Bow Groupers.

Robert Mackenzie's thesis on British political parties demonstrated the minor impact available to dissenting groups of the Right during the Tory Progressive era.*(46) Such were the realities of Conservative politics throughout the twentieth century, and conversely the same limits of influence by Tory Reformers applied during the Thatcher era. It is arguable that the party is geared to supporting its leaders, and only during times of crisis and uncertainty -as happened twice between 1945 and 1975 - do factions of any kind have a real role to play in fashioning the party's power politics.

10. General Conclusion

Following Harold Macmillan's resignation in October 1963 and the brief interregnum of Alec Douglas-Home, Edward Heath's election by fellow MPs in 1965 marked the first democratic leadership choice. However, by then the Tory Progressives' high noon had passed, as had the Butskellite hegemony. Indeed Butskellism was in decline, a fact highlighted by Hugh Gaitskell's premature death in January 1963 and Rab Butler's political retirement in 1965 to become Master of Trinity College, Cambridge.

Although not obvious then, in fact the Tory Progressives decline was guided by the adverse conditions afflicting the British state and economy – inclusive of limited growth, ongoing inflation, lost markets, continuous trade deficits and fiscal uncertainties, crowned by the failed EEC application. Additionally, there was a widespread perception of national decline, a factor highlighted by the previous Suez debacle and concomitant loss of Empire. All those factors augmented growing suspicion on the Conservative Right of Macmillan and his cohorts as agents of national decline. This perceived abrogation of the basic Conservative aim of strengthening Britain was exploited by the Right to undermine the authority of Progressive Tories as represented by party leaders of the period 1950-1965. Indeed the line propagated by Margaret Thatcher and her New Right was that the Macmillan/Home/Heath era was one of self-induced decline.

No allowances were made for prevailing conditions of the time; instead the accusation of "betrayal" was repeated with fervent insistence, and proved a defining polemic of the New Right throughout the Thatcher era. Yet conditions were slowly playing into the Right's hands throughout the 1960s. Indeed ensuing social upheavals that followed immigration debates, the Vietnam War and sexual upheaval further encouraged growing fractiousness within the Conservative Party that rumbled on throughout the decade.

A principal consequence of socio-economic and political decline was the growing challenge to established orthodoxy from the Conservative Right. The Tory Progressives had been in charge of the party and government for a generation, and thus their credibility was assailed as

Britain entered troubled waters. Factionalism became a proliferating symptom of a party increasingly fractionalised by challenges to leadership and its policies. Yet this was a challenge for which the Tory Progressives were singularly unprepared. From 1963 onwards, their case was conducted under the guise of official lobbying and publicising of leadership, none of which exuded conviction or appeal.

Progressive lobbyist groups tended to be leadership-focused, lacking independence and the essential grass roots presence so vital for political effect. Moreover, organisations like the Conservative Europeans, One Nationites, Tory Reformers and Bow Groupers were essentially 'brains trusts' rather than campaigning groups and thus dependent on patronage from parliamentarians. For as long as Butler, Macmillan, Heath, Macleod, Maudling, Gilmour and other senior patrons held control, and Conservatives continued their electoral successes, then Progressive hegemony was assured. However, after the 1964 election defeat, despite Heath's election as Leader, the party in Opposition showed increasingly nervous symptoms that bade ill for his Progressive school. More generally, the Conservative ideology, fluid as ever, was nevertheless undergoing a major revision, something reflected in its continual evolution over the ensuing 40 years according to Robert Eccleshall's thoughtful reflection on Tory thinking.*(47)

Nevertheless from 1965 onwards, it was the Right who made the running. Fighting from the outside, their case was made stridently and with ever greater potency. The growing ranks of Westminster right-wingers were augmented by the Monday Club and Anti-Common Market League on the outside and loose allies of Enoch Powell on the inside. Though not a defeated force, still Tory Progressives were forced onto the defensive. The nature and character of the Conservatives' internal ideological, policy and leadership battles over the ensuing ten years provides the basis for the account and analysis contained in Chapter 5. Meanwhile, it is fair to conclude that by the time of Edward Heath's accession to the party captaincy, his ideological fellowship had most definitely passed their high noon.

FOOTNOTES and REFERENCES

1. Howard (1987) - see Chap. 11.

2. (i) Kenneth Minogue 'Europe in Hubris: The Tempting of Modern Conservatism': D. Anderson - Centre for Policy Studies (1992).

   (ii) Gamble (1988), Chaps. 2 & 3.

   (iii) Kavanagh (1987), chaps 3-5.

   (iv) Marquand (1988), Chaps. 2 & 3.

3. The League of Empire Loyalists after many internal dissensions was subsequently reconstituted in the early 1970s as the National Front, while the National Association for Freedom was renamed the Freedom Association. While the League/National Front operated as a separate party on the militant right, conversely NAF/Freedom Association continued its role as an independent pressure group espousing nationalist and free market ideals which were primarily directed at influencing the Conservative Party.

4. This view came across firmly the following interviews:

   (i) Peter Temple-Morris MP/V. McKee - 24th October, 2000.

   (ii) Giles Marshall, Editor - Tory Reformer /V. McKee 25th March, 2000.

5. Robert Behrens 'The One Nation Group, 1950-59' - Paper presented to PSA-UK, Annual Conference, Plymouth Polytechnic, April 1988.

6. (i) John Ramsden 'A Part for Owners or a Party for Earners? How Far did the British Conservative Party really change in Opposition?' Transactions of the Royal Historical Society (1987), pp.49-63.

   (ii) Ramsden (1988); pp. 340 & 53.

7. Behrens (1988) - PSA paper, p.p. 4-5.

8. Howard (1987), Chap. 11, p.p. 149-155; Butler Memoirs (1971), Chap. V11, p.p.138-140.

9. Discussions Temple-Morris/McKee and Marshall/McKee, and is reflected in the various pamphlets published by different Progressive Tory groups of the period.

10. James Barr 'On the Make: The Bow Group, 1950-2000' - Chap. 1, p. 10; unpublished draft, April 2000.

    Notes (i) Mr Barr was commissioned by the Bow Group to write the official history of the organisation.

    (ii) Mr Barr, an active Conservative, served as aide to Francis Maude, MP.

    (iii) Mr Barr's history of the Bow Group was published in 2001 by Politicos.

    (iv) The author is grateful to Mr James Barr for kind permission to examine his pre-published script as well as the ensuing interview.

11. Barr, Chap.2.

12. Ibid.

13. Barr, Chap 2, pp. 33-35.

14. Barr, Chap.1, pp. 8 & 9.

15. See two published collections of Sir/Lord Keith Joseph's speeches include:

    'Reversing the Trend' (Barry Rose, 1975) and 'Stranded on the Middle Ground' (Centre for Policy Studies, 1976)

16. The prime Heath characteristics were identified by a range of contemporary historians including Blake (1985), Kavanagh

(1987), Gamble (1988), Charmley (1998), Ramsden (1998) and Clark (1998).

17. The Bow Group acquired a political identity allied to the Progressive leadership of Macmillan and Heath throughout the 1950s, 60s and early '70s, something that Barr acknowledges in his account. Only after the Thatcher accession in 1975 did the Bow Group tacitly realign, but not at the point of becoming pro-Thatcherite.

18. Richard Rose 'The Bow Group's Role in British Politics' Western Political Quarterly, 1961.

19. Barr (2000) - Chap. 2, pp. 43-48.

20. Barr (2000) - Chaps 2, 3 & 4 indicate a list of contributors.

21. Patrick Seyd 'Factionalism in the 1970s', Chap. 10, Conservative Party Politics, Ed. Zig Layton Henry (1980).

22. See for example:

   (i) Margaret Thatcher 'The Path to Power', Chaps vii, viii & ix, (Harper-Collins, 1995).

   (ii) Norman Tebbit 'Upwardly Mobile: An Autobiography', Chap. 6, (Weidenfield & Nicolson, 1988).

23. See Kavanagh (1987) Chap. 2; Blake (1985), Chap. ix; Charmley (1998), Chap. 7.

24. Robert Shepherd 'Enoch Powell: A Biography', Chap. 5, p. 64 (Hutchinson, 1996).

25. Charmley (1998), Chap. 8, p.p. 152-156.

26. David Carlton 'Anthony Eden', Chap. xi, p.p. 458-465 (Allen & Unwin, 1986).

27. Nigel Ashford 'The European Economic Community', Chap. 5, Eds. Layton-Henry (Macmillan, 1980).

28. Philip Lynch 'The Politics of Nationhood: Sovereignty, Britishness and Conservative Politics', Chap. 2, p.p. 27-28 (Macmillan, 1999).

29. Zig Layton-Henry's chapter on Conservatives and Immigration provides a useful background account to the ensuing debate. - Chap. 3, Conservative Party Politics (1980), Eds. Layton-Henry.

30. (i) Zig Layton-Henry (1980), Eds. - pp. 61-65.

    (ii) Zig Layton-Henry 'Race, Electoral Strategy and the Major Parties'; Parliamentary Affairs, xxxi, 3, (1978) p.p. 268-281.

31. Patrick Seyd - 'Factionalism within the Conservative Party: The Monday Club', Government and Opposition, Vol. 7, 4, Autumn 1972 - see particularly p.p. 467-472.

32. Clark (1998); the "Surrender to Socialism" view is recurrent throughout Chaps 25-27.

33. (i) Patrick Seyd 'Factionalism in the Conservative Party: The Monday Club; Government and Opposition,' Vol. 7, 4, Autumn 1972. Seyd - Chap. 10, Layton-Henry (1980), Chap. 10.

    (ii) Kavanagh (1987), Chap. 3, pp. 80-94.

34. David Thompson 'Europe Since Napoleon', Chap. 20, pp. 489-508; (Pelican, 1957).

    Anthony Wood 'Great Britain 1900-1965', Chap. 18, pp. 190-199 (Longman, 1978).

35. Cash co-founded the pro-sovereignty European Foundation, whose journal argued a fervent case against European integration.

36. See (i) Seyd in Layton-Henry Eds. (1980) - (ii) McKee, Contemporary Record (1989) and Politics Review (1996).

37. Robert Behrens (1980), Chaps. 2 & 3.

38. Shepherd (1996), Chap. 8, pp. 152-156.

39. Shepherd, Chap. 8, pp. 172-179.

40. Patrick Cosgrave, 'The Lives of Enoch Powell', Chaps, 6-9 (Bodley Head, 1989).

41. The National Association for Freedom was founded in 1975 by Norris MacWhirter.

42. See McKee - Contemporary Record (1989) and Politics Review (1996); also Kavanagh (1987), Chap. 3, p.p. 80-98.

43. Seyd 'Government and Opposition' (1972), pp. 478-481.

44. Interviews - with Rt. Hon. Lord Tebbit, 9th July, 2001; and Peter Temple-Morris, MP - 24th October, 2000.

45. Edward Heath - The Autobiography of Edward Heath: 'The Course of My Life', Chaps. 12 & 13 (Hodder & Stoughton, 1998).

46. R.T. McKenzie 'British Political Parties', Parts 1 & 111 (Heineman, 1955).

47. Robert Eccleshall 'English Conservatism as Ideology'; Political Studies; 25: 62-83, 2006.

CHAPTER 5

REVIVAL OF THE CONSERVATIVE RIGHT

THE HEATH YEARS 1965-73

This chapter will evaluate factionalism on the Conservative Right throughout the mid-late 1960s and early 1970s. That phenomenon manifested primarily, if not exclusively, in opposition to the policies and style of Edward Heath's leadership. It fed off a mixture of ideological and strategic malcontents, and was boosted – albeit indirectly – by the Powell rebellion of 1968. The Right enjoyed a growing number of patrons, but experienced a set-back with the unexpected Conservative election victory of June 1970. Thereafter, the Right's campaign was revived by 1972, partly as a result of policy U-turns by Heath's government, partly by divisions over European (EEC) accession and public spending, and partly electoral disappointments for the Conservative Party. This confidence crisis generated an assorted collection of campaigning and research groups whose main purpose was to provide a focus for ideological dissenters of the Right, along with alternative policies and direction. From that ideological fringe, the New Right was born in the early 1970s. Significantly, by capitalising on discontent brewing at Westminster and among Conservative grass roots from 1972 onwards, eventually they contributed to Heath's fall from power and subsequent loss of the party leadership.

The chapter also looks to analyse organisations on the Conservative Right for evidence of activities, influence and impact. It will also examine the struggling Tory Progressives, whose party domination was undermined and eventually terminated by the fall of Edward Heath in 1975. Evidence presented here shows their organisation's woeful inadequacy for fighting an effective counter-campaign in defence of Heath's leadership and key policies when it really mattered, and thus how low had their stock fallen within the party.

1. Introduction

In 1964 Richard Rose's seminal commentary on factionalism in the two major British parties categorised the Conservatives as comprising a collection of tendencies, a perspective from which he never subsequently demurred.*(1) His essay carried several examples of ideological and single cause groups whose campaigning vigour proved crucial in determining power balances. This thesis had much to commend it, and for many years Rose's view went unchallenged. Yet but whatever may have been its merits then, there is a need for reviewing the type of factionalism characterising the Tory Party since and following Heath's day. That task forms a major task of this chapter.

Another issue of interest is whether the Conservative Right's political challenge that gathered force in the late 1960s and assumed serious proportions in the last two years of Edward Heath's beleaguered administration, was based on strategy or momentum. It is also worthwhile inquiring as to how far Heath's fall was self induced, and how much occurred as a result of pressure levied by factional lobbyists and their parliamentary patrons. Put simply, how effective was the Conservative Right as a political force, and how far did their factions fashion that process? Also, why did Tory Progressives make such a poor defence of Heath's leadership when that battle also involved their own survival?

Those questions need to be addressed in order to assess the party's direction over that period. In the process, doubtless the observer will see the post-war Settlement strained to breaking point. Indeed the lingering death agony of that Settlement accounts in no small way for the public ideological debates and power struggles within the 1970s Conservative Party in government and Opposition, at Westminster and across the country.

2. State of the Conservative Party in 1965

When Alec Douglas-Home quit the Conservative leadership in July 1965, he paved the way for Edward Heath. Emerging from a contest with

114

Reginald Maudling and Enoch Powell in the party's first-ever election, Heath's inheritance was a questionable asset.*(2)

The previous October, Tories narrowly lost power to Labour, and after 13 years in office were returned to Opposition, Therewith lay room for soul searching, but also uncertainty. Moreover, as happened before, leadership was traditionally weakest in the aftermath of election defeat. Although Heath was a new face on the captain's bridge, he had played a prominent part in previous Macmillan and Douglas-Home governments; enough to be viewed with suspicion by the Right. Also, as chief propagator of European accession, his election was not welcomed on the Right, many of whose leading ideologues like Lord Salisbury staunchly opposed British accession to the European Economic Community.

In 1965, the narrowness of Harold Wilson's Labour government majority made a fresh election inevitable. Yet it was widely assumed that Conservatives would be spending the next two to three years in Opposition. Hence there was a desire to get the leadership issue settled ahead of the next poll and draft a policy programme. The Tory Progressives remained the dominant ideological school at Westminster and Central Office, a factor borne out by the magnitude of Heath and Maudling's combined vote of 283 MPs, as against the derisory 15 MPs backing Powell. Still, as shown in Chapter 4, by 1964 there were signs of a resurgent Conservative Right, spearheaded by the Monday Club who stirred opposition to leadership on issues like imperial decolonisation, EEC accession, public spending and immigration. Rightists were largely found outside Westminster, but throughout the late 1960s key figures emerged to augment their profile. Most important among the latter was the cerebral Enoch Powell, who broke with his leader in April 1968 over immigration, and formally with the Tory party over EEC accession, six years later.

The new leader was drawn from the same political school as his predecessors, and as he readily acknowledges in his memoirs, his aims were specific.*(3) Heath wanted to prepare his party for a return to office by prioritising modernisation and professionalism, while putting the party squarely behind European accession. So also did he view the Empire as outdated and unworthy of further defence, hence the scaling down of

British commitments in Suez, the Gulf and South East Asia Alliance. While as pro-NATO as other Conservatives, Heath had become concerned at British dependence on USA in trade and defence. This inclination to avoid US dependence underpinned his ardent enthusiasm for British entry to the European Economic Community.*(4)

Plainly the party had undergone considerable evolution over the two decades after 1945. Professionalism had been incorporated to the party culture by a combination of the Maxwell-Fyfe reforms, plus policy modernisation pursued by RAB Butler. It was a sentiment which found much favour with the new leader, whose election – rather than "emergence" through the 'charmed circle' – was novel, but testified to how democracy was slowly fashioning Conservative politics. At the same time, deference was on the wane, both in the party and across wider British society. Clearly, 1960s Tory grass roots activists interacted with their leaders in a new culture of assertiveness and occasional confrontation. This climate encouraged extra-parliamentary groups like the Monday Club and later National Association for Freedom to challenge the Conservative leadership over policy, thereby facilitating further developments over the ensuing decade.

Perhaps the most significant reason for the Conservative Right's rise was the decline of the post-war Settlement – the so-called 'Consensus' – in the early-mid 1970s. The latter was visibly faltering under the combined weight of inflation, economic stagnation, trade deficits and industrial unrest. There was also widespread public dissatisfaction with high taxation and the propriety of universal welfare benefits, along with cost and effects of government subsidies to ailing industries. The Conservative Right, especially the Monday Club, proved an effective conduit for articulating those concerns among rank and file. The latter trend eventually resulted in an undermining of the party leadership.

Significantly, with the 'Consensus' slowly waning, there followed a concomitant decline in Tory Progressive political hegemony. Also, it was during the leadership tenure of Edward Heath that this process took its full course. The One Nation programme of Tory Progressives gradually lost appeal, and throughout the late 1960s its corporatist character was gradually overturned by a more radical agenda based on

116

curbing union power, ending state subsidies, cutting taxes and public spending and reviewing the general direction of education. This approach was highlighted by the Selsdon Park manifesto – so called from the London hotel where senior Conservatives planned election strategy – on which Heath led the Conservatives to unexpected victory and back to office in June 1970.

3. Tory Progressives under Siege

Observers of the Heath years will be struck by how two election defeats (1964 and 1966), plus the leadership succession, affected power struggles within the party.

Loss of office meant Conservatives struggled for ideas and policies that would lead them back to power. Such was an inevitable corollary of defeat, with Tory confidence having been dented in the process. Actually Heath inherited a captain's post with a clear briefing to steer the party back to office. Fulfilment of that goal or otherwise would be the yardstick by which he would be judged by fellow Tories. Yet it was in the wake of defeat that there followed a questioning of parameters of the so-called 'Consensus'. Issues like taxation, public spending, trade unions, industrial policy, welfare, immigration, education and race relations all entered the pool. As Gamble observed, after 1968 it was the Right who made the running, with the Powell rebellion serving to augment that challenge.*(5)

Notwithstanding the growing right wing profile, Tory Progressives remained dominant at Westminster, and from their ranks key figures were appointed to Central Office and the party's key positions. Heath's leadership style was definite, indeed intransigent; he made few concessions to the Right in strategy or policy. Although Gamble argued Heath's record was one of continual capitulation to the Right, highlighted by the 1970 Selsdon Park manifesto, other evidence casts the Conservative leader as a pugnacious reformer. He was determined to fashion a progressive force, with European accession dictating domestic and foreign policy. Heath's memoirs contain undisguised contempt for the Right, whom he regarded as antediluvian, divisive and an electoral liability. Conversely he saw his own appeal as progressive, relevant, and likely to win the voters.

The issues on which left/right battles were fought were familiar, but assumed a new poignancy by virtue of Powell's challenge. Race relations and immigration were raised by Powell in his 'Rivers of Blood' speech of April 1968 in Birmingham (leading to his sacking from the Shadow Cabinet), but had been earlier raised by the Monday Club. The debate about British EEC entry was gathering momentum and although Nigel Ashford highlighted how Europe crossed party left/right divisions – as with Labour – it was among the Right that anti-Europeanism was strongest.*(6) The latter was bound up with a sense of nationhood and, to many right wingers, the EEC represented a downward spiral for the British state. Conversely, to Tory Progressives Europe represented a positive future for British enterprise and the direction of foreign policy, and they regarded objectors as ill-informed and outdated jingoists. So did they view right-wing attacks on state welfare, unions and public enterprises as predictable reactionary carping.*(7)

The endemic ailments of Britain's troubled economy and restless society of the late 1960s gave the Conservative Right clear focus for dissent. In those areas, a dichotomy emerged between the Westminster leadership and wider party grass roots. Given the uncertainty of Conservative electoral appeal throughout the 1960s and challenges to Edward Heath's leadership from dissenting right wingers, it was inevitable that rightist factionalism would manifest on a wider scale. Yet not until the mid-1970s, with the Conservatives agonising from the effects of two election defeats in one year, did the Right triumph in a coup born of desperation at the party's electoral slide, which eventually led to their taking over the party. By that stage, the scene had been firmly set for the defeat of the Tory Progressives and subsequent rise of the New Right.

4. Impact of Edward Heath on Factionalism

It is generally agreed among historian and commentators that the leadership years of Edward Heath, 1965-75, were synonymous with certain characteristics. Moreover, Heath was judged as much for his personal style as his key policies. Heath was widely considered autocratic, intolerant and given to making policy as he went along. Those traits proved to be a serious liability in the months following election defeats of 1974 when his leadership was under attack.*(8) This inquiry must consider how far those characteristics provoked internal divisions both at Westminster and throughout the party, thus begging examination of the principal characteristics of Heath's tenure.

First, was Heath's inimitable professionalism that balanced discipline and coherence with a preference for full-time politics. He prioritised modern methods of management at all levels starting with his own party, while jettisoning surviving vestiges of amateurism. In his approach to policy-making, Heath displayed a predilection for expertise and it must be added, a ruthless disregard for opposition. Martin Burch observed that Heath had a preference for management techniques in his political management style.*(9) He held a special mastery of policy detail, and envisaged only manifestos whose contents had been thoroughly researched, argued and cost-cast. For example, between 1965 and 1966 he established 23 specialist policy groups, and after the 1966 general election the number of such groups was extended to 29. He also appointed a combined shadow team of 72 spokesmen, each with clearly defined responsibilities, from which they were not expected to stray. So did he initiate the practice of the Conservative Leader attending the entire Annual Conference, as well as specialist conferences of women, students, youth etc.*(10) Not for Heath was there the flexible dalliance of Churchill or introspective agonising of his successor, Margaret Thatcher. Above all else, he wanted to get the policy details right.

Second, was his passionate belief in the UK accession to the European Economic Community. In his memoirs, Heath enunciates his European beliefs – formed during student days when visiting 1930s Germany and France – which appear to have been strengthened by the course of post-1945 history, specifically the loss of empire, economic decline and excessive reliance on U.S. military and economic aid.*(11) He resented Britain's decline to becoming an American dependency, instead encouraging British participation in a new European regional economy based on free trade, economic, social and fiscal harmonisation.

Those conditions, if nourished, would, he believed, lead to a welcome degree of political integration.*(12) Hence he postulated the European cause with Jesuitical fervour, elevating it to centre stage in his economic and foreign policy. Europe was the hallmark of what Edward Heath believed to be a "... progressive Conservatism ..." attuned to the challenges of 1960s and '70s Britain. Accordingly, notwithstanding other disappointments of his Downing Street years, the United Kingdom's EEC entry in 1973 marked the crowning achievement of that premiership.

Third, Heath's Europe-centred agenda was coloured by disinterest in the Commonwealth. He cared little for the Conservative tradition of affinity with the Empire, regarding it as outdated and a symbol of past injustices, not to mention a digression from the reality of Britain's economic slide. Besides, Commonwealth economic benefits to the UK seemed negligible, and he made little secret of distaste for autocratic dictators from countries like Uganda, Nigeria and Pakistan. Hence regardless of a cool rapport with the Queen, Heath allowed the Commonwealth to decline.*(13) His priority was building Britain's future with Europe; he was not interested in an irrelevant, imperial 'old-boys' association.

Fourth, Heath's vision of dynamic Conservatism included a commitment to economic growth through the liberalisation of trade and tariffs, a policy most effectively realised through the mechanisms of the European Economic Community. It also involved tax cuts, investment in new technology, withdrawal of public subsidies for failing enterprises, and a review of social security with the overall aim of replacing universal benefits with aid targeted at the needy. Heath had no quarrel with the NHS, but sought greater efficiency there and in managing public utilities. Actually, he prioritised efficiency and productivity, for which parliamentary power could be utilised; hence New Right charges of corporatism. Heath was prepared to harness statutory powers where he felt circumstances required and, in later decades, was dismissive about New Right criticisms.

Fifth, as noted by Layton-Henry, Heath's modernisation agenda included a broadening of the Conservative social base, while assaulting surviving vestiges of racism, imperialism and class-based divisions.*(14)

120

He even countenanced a limited measure of Scottish devolution in response to the 1973 Kilbrandon report.*(15) Those measures were aimed at updating the party's credibility with voters and developing policies relevant to Britain of the 1960s and '70s. However, experiences with the Monday Club, Anti-Common Market League and Powellites, suggested crucial battles with traditionalists lying ahead.

Nigel Ashford has suggested that the authority of Conservative Leadership made factions an inevitable refuge for dissidents. In his study of Conservatives and Europeanism, Ashford argued that although the Leader's prerogative on policymaking enabled Macmillan and Heath to steer their party in a pro-European direction, in fact this course was dictated by pressure from other groups.*(16) In the late 1950s and '60s they included leading Conservative intellectuals, policy advisers at Central Office, a Euro-zealous faction in the parliamentary party, many youth activists, along with the Tory press and industrial lobbyists. Accordingly, when pursuing EEC accession, Edward Heath was soundly supported by an assorted coalition of Euro-converts and Europhile enthusiasts.*(17) At the same time, pro-European sentiments – encouraged by the Leader's office and Central Office – were resented by a vociferous nationalist/neo-imperial fellowship largely moored on the party's right. The latter had champions in Enoch Powell and Lord Salisbury and although unable to destroy Heath's accession goal, they encouraged a radical anti-European tendency whose support was demonstrated on platforms of the Monday Club and Anti-Common Market League throughout the 1960s and '70s.

Other issues arousing hostility on the Right included Northern Ireland, trade unions and the economy. Heath's economic U-turn after 1972, when the ailing Rolls Royce Aerospace was nationalised and miners pacified with a generous pay settlement, was in sharp contrast to the free market 1970 Selsdon Park manifesto which had promised to cut off 'lame-duck' industries, while bringing unions firmly within judicial authority. Such conditions enabled right wingers like Powell and his assorted disciples to carve a niche from which to stage rebellions within the party over that period.

The Right charged Heath with having betrayed basic Conservative faith by his economic policy U-turns, Euro-zeal and concessions to Irish and Scottish nationalists. This alleged apostasy made little allowance for unforeseen occurrences challenging Heath's vision, like the Arab oil embargo, international trade recession and the civic conflict engulfing Northern Ireland and domestic trade union militancy. There was also the ongoing Rhodesian UDI question and Ian Smith's rebel regime in Salisbury that had asserted independence in 1965. In fact, notwithstanding official abstention policy, actually the Conservatives in Parliament split three ways between opponents, supporters and abstainers when the annual Commons vote occurred over the renewal of sanctions on the Smith regime.

Heath's style was widely viewed as confrontational and unyielding. His personal manner was famously cool, something that made few friends and cost him dearly in the leadership contest of February 1975.*(18) Such was the stuff of which factionalism was made and, given the difficulties afflicting his government in its latter stages, it was inevitable that he would be challenged by an increasingly formidable and organised Conservative Right. Seyd's assessment of the Monday Club is useful, but only reaches up to 1972. The organisation evolved in a further right-wing direction throughout the mid 1970s assuming an elevated status over the last troubled two years of Edward Heath's leadership. This account aims to fill a gap and extend the inquiry to include those various campaigning organisations composing the New Right of that time.

5. Challenges from the New Right

Challenges emanating from the Right were many and varied. Some were British nationalists, others neo-imperialists, while others still were driven by a fear of excessive state power in the economy and social affairs and felt Conservatives ought to be reasserting the free market and individual autonomy. Additionally, there were anti-libertarian campaigners alarmed by the permissive society, along with social disciplinarians and Church (Anglican) and State convergence advocates ... all combining to give weight, personnel and causes to what by June 1970 was a rather heterogeneous Conservative Right. Indeed the Right by then fed off a range of anti-Heath tendencies, all working to undermine his leadership and anticipating defeat in the snap election called by Harold Wilson for that same month.*(19) That Heath, against all expectations, achieved victory served to buy time for the Progressives personified by the Leader and his soon-to-be short-lived Chancellor, Iain Macleod, while delaying the Right's rebellion.*(20) Yet that overview carries the benefit of hindsight, and was not obvious to either Conservatives, their political opponents, journalists or other observers of British politics.

Right wing challenges need be measured in character and origin. As earlier indicated, the Conservative Right was far from homogenous, and though nurtured on a common diet of anti-Heathism, its purpose varied among the different groups. At this stage, it may be instructive to examine those constituent elements making up the Right in June 1970, their characteristics, membership, leaders, campaigns and spheres of activity.

(i) *The Powellites* constituted an amorphous collection of anti-Heath dissidents gathered around the increasingly populist former minister, Enoch Powell. His 'Rivers of Blood' speech and the consequences marked a parting of ways for the two erstwhile One Nation bedfellows.*(21) Yet it had long been in the making. Powellism was driven by many causes including free market economics, resurgent British nationalism, sympathy with Ulster Unionists in Belfast, along with growing hostility towards the European Economic Community and United States. Yet Powellism was most widely characterised for its virulent opposition to immigration from the New Commonwealth and support for voluntary repatriation schemes. One Powell leftist biographer, the late Paul Foot, argued that he made racism respectable, while more sympathetic biographers like Shepherd and Cosgrave emphasised his challenge to the British liberal establishment to justify social effects of immigration on indigenous working class communities in the West and East Midlands, London, Sheffield, Manchester and the North.*(22)

It goes beyond the remit of this inquiry to evaluate the merits of Powell's policies and their impact on the Conservative Party and wider political arena. However, Powellites as a Conservative force may be likened to an evangelical crusade in that they possessed a recognised leader, multiple devotees, an evolving credo and major rallies for postulating their message. There was the added advantage of media interest, which in turn aroused popular enthusiasm in certain quarters – e.g. London dockers marched in his support – sufficient for sustaining momentum. Yet those assets were never utilised to maximum potential and, just as supporters of Rev. Dr Billy Graham's numerous British missions acknowledged, the need for follow-up by existing churches or creating new bodies, there the comparison ceases. Enoch Powell – as all biographers recall – refused to lead a movement bidding for control or influence within the Tories' higher councils.

Always a loner and primarily concerned with policy, Powell nursed no taste for factional politics; hence Powellites developed no group structures or campaigning organisation of any kind. Nor did any such body emerge at Westminster, even among Powell's most ardent admirers. Instead, he articulated a range of policies with a consistent nationalistic and free market ideological theme which aroused sympathy, even adulation, among many MPs, peers, constituency officers and activists on the Right. Moreover, Powell regularly accepted speaking invitations from the Monday Club and Anti-Common Market League, both of whose Conference fringe meetings boasted substantial attendances from which an enhanced profile and new supporters followed. So too was Powell's own reputation as a celebrity dissident enhanced, something that later facilitated his return to Westminster in October 1974 – as Ulster Unionist Member for South Down – following his final break with the Conservatives in the election of February 1974.*(23)

Comparisons of Powell with Margaret Thatcher and Tony Benn are of limited value.*(24) While Thatcher and Benn each patronised their respective political schools, Powell stayed aloof from factionalism. Dennis Kavanagh's observation of Powell as united with the other two in opposition to the post-war Consensus is valid, but therewith the likeness ceases. Whether or not Powell nursed any ambitions for high office after April 1968 or following his party's return to office in June 1970 looks unlikely. It is enough to note that while an articulate intellectual and a focal figure for right wing dissenters, Enoch Powell neither sought nor became embroiled in Conservative factionalism. Many of his devotees assumed leading positions in the growing network of rightist factions, especially after 1972, but Powell himself remained aloof from that arena. He is best viewed as an ideological rather than factional leader; specifically one who – like Labour's Anthony Crosland of the same generation – advocated an agenda rather than being involved with the power politics and group rivalries that it generated.

Powell's ideological critic, the cerebral Michael Foot, in a reflective essay viewed him as a natural loner for whom power held less attraction than articulating a vision, while defending the essential foundation bricks of the British constitution. Notwithstanding their differences, Foot acknowledged the sincerity of Powell's conscience, speaking as he did in support of a parliamentary system and national culture which he believed to be under threat from assorted Empire and European influences.*(25) In a most prescient evaluation of Powell from the outside, Foot also noted that Powell was a man who attracted disciples rather than troops sharing his faith and purpose. This assessment just about summarised Powell, his values, strategy and workings. Moreover, it drew the obvious conclusion that his voice had an arousing effect on others, but for all the latter Enoch Powell was no progenitor of disciplined legions of campaigners.

(ii) *The Monday Club* was a rare example of an organised Conservative faction. Founded in 1961, initially in response to Macmillan's 'Winds of Change' speech, it was a reactionary organisation with a credo reflecting dogged insistence on the continuation of Britain's great power role and revival of the free market in British politics.

Generally, the Club sought to counter the supposed 'leftist' influence of the Bow Group. It resented the decline of British imperial authority in Africa and looked askance at the domestic track record of 1950s Conservative governments in pursuing programmes of high taxation and public spending alongside management of state utilities and appeasement of trade unions. In particular, Monday Club members like John Biggs-Davison, Patrick Wall, Jill Knight and Julian Amery (all MPs then) were concerned at the diminution of British sovereignty visa-viz the USA and an apparent capitulation of successive UK governments to American interests. Plainly Suez and its aftermath had sounded alarm bells that continued to ring on the Tory Right!

The Club was unique for two reasons. First, by virtue of its organisational structure, the Monday Club swiftly developed an intensity of purpose that was uncharacteristic of the party. It set up a network of branches around the country, inclusive of the universities, and a membership serviced by a newsletter and journal, Monday World, that by 1971 had reached 10,000.*(26) Moreover, given its penchant for organisational activism – rather than fighting a battle of ideals – the Club aroused the concern of party leadership and attention from the wider body of political pundits. This was especially the case with its attempts in 1969 at forcing the de-selection of a Heath supporter, Nigel Fisher, by his Surbiton constituency party. There was also the Club's stated preference for having its people adopted as parliamentary candidates and constituency officers, and an evident willingness to pursue those goals*(27) Second, Monday Club energies were primarily directed at the party as a whole rather than the Westminster leadership, as tended to be true of other groups. In essence, the Club was an 'outside', indeed radical rightist force, that during the Macmillan, Home and Heath years (1961-75) provided a refuge for traditionalists disaffected by leadership centrist policies at Westminster.

Accordingly, although lacking the influence of the Bow Group and other 'insiders', the Monday Club exercised a measure of real independence that facilitated its purpose. It also provided a rallying platform for disaffected right wingers at a time when they were denied influence at Westminster and Central Office. Though always an organisation of the Conservative Right, actually its alignments did not manifest until the mid-1970s. In its first decade the Club attracted a broad stream membership, inclusive of parliamentary sponsors, peers and activists, and indeed was addressed by speakers from a wide spectrum of politics. Guest speakers included 1960s TUC General Secretary, George Woodcock, and Labour Deputy Leader, George Brown, while Macmillan's Foreign Secretary, Lord Home, received a Monday Club delegation to complain of British-made bombs used against Tshombe's forces in the Congo. The Club's Westminster sponsors, numbered 16 MPs in the 1966-70 Commons, a figure that increased to 30 in the 1970-74 Commons, including six members of Edward Heath's government.*(28)

126

Throughout its prominent years, the Monday Club maintained an active profile in three areas. First, was the publication of multiple policy pamphlets. These offered scope for the Club to define its policy stances while also raising issues for debate. Accordingly, the Club's range of pamphlets reflected both the causes and emergent direction of Conservative right wing thinking. The first Monday Club pamphlet deplored British withdrawal from Africa. It claimed a need for the educational and social advancement of the African population, such as had not been provided, nor any provision made for protecting the white population.*(29) Seyd noted the Club's poignant opposition to Kenyan independence, which offered no guarantees for the interests of ex-patriate Britons or Asians who would likely be threatened by post-colonial Africanisation.*(30) Indeed a Club founder member of imperial instincts wrote in 1970:

"The raison d'être of the Monday Club was the failure of successive British governments to grapple with the so-called Wind of Change in Africa. The Club was founded to fight a rearguard action to preserve the Central Africa Federation and to preserve a British presence in Southern Africa. On both counts we failed: the Federation was dissolved, and now a republican flag has replaced the Union Jack in Salisbury."(31)

Interestingly, early pamphlets were bereft of the racist overtones and strident nationalism characterising later platforms. Until the late 1960s the Club facilitated thoughtful Conservatives wanting a traditionalist alternative to the Bow Group; militant right causes being espoused then by other groups like the '92 Committee' which – as shown by the research of Lucy Grant at Hull University – had a large overlapping membership, not to mention similar policy goals to the Monday Club and League of Empire Loyalists.*(32) However, as was noted by Seyd, the critical year of change occurred in 1964 following the Conservatives' electoral defeat and removal from office. This event was to have a transforming effect on the Club both politically and in organisational terms.

"It [Monday Club] changed from its earlier position as a forum for intelligent, young Conservatives expressing opinions in pamphlet form to that of a mass organisation, explicitly anti-intellectual in its approach

to politics, and appealing to the right wing fundamentalist bitterly opposed to the Labour government's policies." {Seyd} *(33)

In a far-reaching organisational overhaul in 1965, the Club removed both the 35 years maximum age rule and requirement for recruits to be card-carrying Tories. The changes facilitated a wave of new blood into the organisation that was disaffected both with Harold Wilson's Labour government and the decolonisation policies of the previous Macmillan/Home Conservative governments. In essence, it marked the radicalisation of the Monday Club into a voice for the hard Right. While Seyd's previous description of the Club as "… a mass organisation …" – with 10,000 members – seems a little extravagant; there can be no doubting the acute impact that an enlarged and active membership, coupled with political radicalisation, had on the Club's raison d'être.*(34)

Seyd's 1972 membership survey showed a predominance of young middle-aged activists whose concerns on the shrinking empire, American hegemony, trade union power and public spending reflected the Right's perspective of the world at large.*(35) Moreover, the Club's various activist campaigns and radical policy pamphlets highlighted its emerging role as a vehicle for dissent on the outside right. For example, by 1970 the Club had published a host of pamphlets attacking sanctions against Ian Smith's UDI regime in Rhodesia, criticising trade union power, questioning public spending, defending the House of Lords in its then-current form and challenging the general direction of British post-war social and economic policy. So also did it prove a redoubtable ally – one of its few allies indeed – for the beleaguered Ulster Unionists whose credibility with the Conservative leadership had been drained after Edward Heath's proroguing of the Belfast administration in March 1972. The Monday Club facilitated a platform for Unionist speakers like ex-Stormont Home Affairs minister, William Craig, whose 'Shoot to Kill' speech to a Monday Club London audience in November 1972 made national headlines.

At the same time as its persistent attacks on Heath's leadership, the Monday Club divided over a key issue then wreaking divisions within the Tory party – Europe. The Club contained a number of prominent 'Europeans' like Julian Amery, Duncan Sandys, John Biggs-Davison and

Geoffrey Rippon, whose European credentials were directed towards achieving UK accession to the then Common Market. Their Europeanism sprang from optimism in enhanced trade prospects offered by continental markets, while rebuilding British foreign power status in Europe and thereby avoiding dependence on the USA or misplaced reliance on a Commonwealth unlikely to materialise as a global organisation. None of the Tory Right were federalists, con-federalists or even Euro integrationists, but instead shared General De Gaulle's concept of Europe des patries (i.e. sovereign nations). In his scholarly study of the Conservatives' European accession debate, Nigel Ashford calculated that anti-marketers probably numbered a majority among the Club's rank and file membership.*(36) Yet this advantage was offset by having only two senior figures on their side, namely Victor Montagu, formerly Viscount Hinchingbrooke (ex-Chairman of the war-time Tory Reform Committee), and Glaswegian Unionist, Teddy Taylor MP.

As Ashford noted, "There was anti-market activity within the Club, but it was handicapped by a lack of an alternative."*(37) The Club appointed the Atlantic-leaning Patrick Wall as Chairman of an External Affairs Committee that explored the NAFTA option, but could raise little enthusiasm. Ashford observed NAFTA being an unpopular cause within the Monday Club due to a residue of suspicion prevailing towards the United States, a legacy from the Suez debacle.*(38) Eventually, after a fulsome debate, the Club's Executive Committee determined that in view of poignant divisions no official position would be taken over European Community membership. It must be noted that whereas the Monday Club proved to be a regular and open critic of the Heath leadership, over Europe it provided no opposition or policy alternative.

Norman Tebbit – a parliamentary sponsor – recalled the Monday Club as rooted in the imperial era with attitudes barely in tune with conditions of the 1960s and '70s. The Club, Tebbit remembered, exuded an attitude of "… don't you just wish it was 1939 all over again …!"*(39) Tebbit's observation highlighted a serious flaw in the Club's psychology and perception of the world. This reactionary, indeed backward-looking tendency Tebbit viewed as an impediment to effectiveness. Given Tebbit's prominence on the Conservative Right and association with the Club, it is significant that he regarded the Club as too narrow and rather irrelevant to any useful purpose. Such scepticism was not confined to Tebbit either. It ensured that major rightist campaigns were fought on other platforms, something that eventually marginalized and killed off the Monday Club.

Overall, the Club was a vehicle for right wing dissenters lobbying Conservative voters and activists to put pressure on the party leadership to change policy direction. In the end, the Club was overtaken by events, not least the New Right's successful coup in ousting Heath from office in February 1975. That phenomenon and its relevance to the changing power structures in the party are examined in subsequent chapters.

(iii) *The Anti-Common Market League* (ACML) was the largest and principal pre-1975 organisation emerge against Europe from the Conservative Right.

Before examining rival campaign groups, it must be emphasised that Europe divided the Conservatives along lines transcending left/right divisions. While a substantial majority of the centre-left Tory Progressives supported European accession, there were exceptions such as Peter Walker.*(40) More poignant were divisions racking the Right over Europe. As shown in evaluations of the Monday Club, throughout the 1960s different views prevailed among Conservatives about British foreign policy alignments. There was a Commonwealth lobby, an Atlantic lobby (NAFTA) and European lobby, dividing between Common Marketeers and Euro-federalists, with all but the last category being represented on the Conservative Right. This debate and the various rival alignments it generated are comprehensively examined in Ashford's erudite study.*(41)

Notwithstanding diverse opinion on the Right about Europe, anti-EEC campaigners were driven mainly by assorted nationalist, Commonwealth and neo-imperialist sentiment. In the early-mid 1960s, a couple of other groups sought to seize the principal opposition mantle. One was 'True Blue Tories', a Home Counties based organisation headed by Major-General (Retired) Richard Hilton. This group did enjoy a limited profile at regional Conservative conferences and the Annual Conference of the National Union, but was kept afloat and funded mainly by the energies of middle ranking activists.*(42) In truth 'True Blue

Tories' suffered from the disadvantage of a narrow, right-wing membership, while lacking a national base and sufficient Westminster patrons to give it the 'punch' required for effectiveness.*(43) There was also the League of Empire Loyalists whose appeal went beyond Conservative quarters. Yet its credibility was limited by the militant campaigning tactics and absence of parliamentary supporters, such as rendered the organisation marginal. The League was largely represented at Annual Conference by shrill, middle aged and right-wing ladies who one former Conservative MP recalled less as threatening as more "quaint and eccentric than threatening".*(44)

The Anti-Common Market League was founded on June 26th 1961 at a meeting in London. Its two leading lights were a future Tory minister, Peter Walker, then a former Young Conservatives' National Chairman, and John Paul, former Chairman of South Kensington Conservatives, who emerged as first ACML Chair.*(45) The first Secretary was Michael Shay, then Research Director of Mobil Oil (UK), while the youthful David Clarke became Treasurer, before being replaced by Sir Jeffrey Reynolds.*(46) It is significant that among the early backers – including platform speakers – were Derek Walker-Smith, Robin Turton, John Biggs-Davison, Lord Hinchingbrooke (ex-TRC Chair) and right-wing historian, Sir Arthur Bryant. The latter figure later contributed to the flow of anti-EEC literature with a polemical text on the subject.

By 1962, the League was claiming to have organised some 240 meetings – with 35 public gatherings, 35 educational events, 34 Rotary and business clubs meetings and a further 20 meetings held in conjunction with the National Farmers Union. One super rally took place at Methodist Central Hall, Westminster and attracted an audience of some 2,000 people.*(47) The League's revenue was raised partly from passing the hat around supporters at meetings and partly large, if also occasional donations from sympathetic business sources. Reynolds's company, Garfield and Weston, donated £2,000, while the Commonwealth Industries Association gave the not-inconsiderable sum in 1962 of £250. There was also a special donation of £35,000 forthcoming from quasi-public sources for offsetting the costs of a Rally to the Commonwealth in September 1962.*(48) Yet, as Ashford noted, notwithstanding the League's high profile, in fact its finances were always precarious, which in the longer term weakened both the organisation and its appeal.*(49) It was in no position to match the pro-EEC lobby inside or outside the party, and its confrontational style throughout the 1960s belied the reality of impotence.

A measure of the League's limited impact can be found in the crucial debate at the 1969 Conservative Annual Conference. At that event, six motions were submitted by constituency associations backing Edward Heath's pro-accession policy, with a further three critical motions variously expressing concerns about where the EEC would leave Sterling, British agriculture and the Monarchy.*(50) In the debate that followed, with Powell opting not to speak, the anti-EEC Right's case was put by Neil Marten and Derek Walker Smith – both of ACML – against the leadership's line put by Eldon Griffiths, Duncan Sandys and two enthusiastic Young Conservatives, David Atkinson, and one who emerged prominent in the Tory Charter Movement, Eric Chalker. Approval for Heath's policy ran to a decisive 1,452 votes as against 475 dissenters.*(51) Also, a *Spectator* poll of 1969 Conservative Conference representatives found 73% admitting to being pro-European, 19% anti-EEC and a further 6% of 'Don't Knows'.*(52)

Ashford concluded that Heath had emerged from the Conference's European debate with his leadership more firmly established than before. Yet he was concerned not to allow internal-divisions to accentuate or even manifest before the coming election.*(53) This need for unity had assumed special priority in light of the damaging impact of Enoch Powell's rebellion the previous year over immigration and European accession.

Accordingly, it is indicative of how ineffectual the League had become that by the early 1970s, when key battles over British EEC membership raged, ACML was little more than a fringe platform for anti-Heath forces. Significantly, there occurred some overlapping membership with other Rightist groups, e.g. Monday Club and the '92 Committee, where there existed much sympathy for their views. Overall, ACML was a poor lobbyist in the constituencies and even poorer publicist at Annual Conference.*(54) ACML failed to attract the full range of Tory anti-EEC opinion, made scarce impact on outside groups in industry, commerce and agriculture, had a poor media profile, and was bereft of influence resulting from having limited numbers of peers and MPs as sponsors.

Two other factors hindered the League's development. First was that opposition to the EEC was limited to an irreconcilable school on the Conservative Right. The 1970s Right – unlike the 2016 Right – was not entirely of one mind on Europe, and those divisions affected other rightist groups like the Monday Club and '92 Committee'. Of particular significance was the presence of right wingers like Duncan Sandys and Julian Amery in the vanguard of pro-EEC lobbies, while on the other side Peter Walker and Viscount Hinchingbrooke occupied Euro-sceptical positions. This lack of ideological consistency created ambiguity, thereby minimising MPs and activists of the Right constituency. Second, with the EEC debate having transcended the political parties, this elevated cross party organisations like the rival European Movement and 'Get Britain Out' campaigns, who each came to dominate debates. Such was enhanced by a coalition of pro – and anti – EEC advocates emerging across the party spectrum. The effect of this development was to transfer the initiative to external campaigning groups at the expense of party factions. Actually, this phenomenon was consolidated, indeed accentuated and highlighted by the ensuing referendum called by Prime Minister, Harold Wilson, for June 1975.

Given the circumstances of the British European debate, the decline of the Anti-Common Market League in the early 1970s was as predictable as it was definite.

(iv) *Other Rightist groups*: There were a number of other organisations whose activities registered some significance in the ongoing Tory debates of the period. Some emerged in reaction to events then, while others had been established over previous years and enjoyed a defined ideological and/or policy purpose.

The '92 Committee' was among the better-known right-wing groups of the time. Formed in 1965 by a group of Conservative backbenchers, headed by Patrick Wall – drawing its name from Wall's London abode at 92 Cheyne Walk – this organisation defined its mission as to "… keep the Conservative Party Conservative". As noted in Lucy Grant's study of the group, it remained a Westminster-based organisation with membership restricted to MPs alone, although Conservative peers were later admitted, along with women.*(55) The '92 Committee' acted as a pressure group primarily within the Conservative Parliamentary Party, broadly holding the line for the Right. Interestingly, though abounding with right wingers like George Gardiner, Ronald Bell, Jill Knight, William Clark (from John Major's 1992 campaign team), Peter Hornden, Frederick Bennett, Peter Emery (Bow Group co-founder) and John Townsend, actually the group maintained a broad ideological perspective but avoided divisive alignments. So also did it refrain from publishing pamphlets, instead allowing other rightist groups, e.g. the Monday Club and Anti-Common Market League, later Bruges Group, to take the direct initiative.

Grant noted the '92 Committee' as an informal body with a membership that grew to 40 MPs in the 1970-74 Parliament, and with a principal purpose to manage elections to the 1922 Executive and various backbench committees.*(56) However, its remit went further than a dining club. In seeking to have its people on the 1922 Executive and policy committees, not to mention influencing leadership elections throughout the 1970s and beyond, Patrick Wall's group acted as a vital Trojan horse for encouraging the New Right.*(57) There was an element of secret, almost Masonic politicking about their style, which was well illustrated in the Grant study. For example, new members were enlisted by invitation, a practice that ensured a perpetuating ideological line that Grant noted to have changed little over three decades.*(58) Also, the group was guarded about meetings, along with the business discussed and the various strategies planned.

It is difficult to determine how influential was this group throughout its lifetime, but for the period 1965-73 acted as a rightist backbenchers' watchdog. In Grant's account, there is mention of the '92 Committee' having had a "... generally good ..." relationship with Heath throughout the Opposition period and even for the first two years of his premiership. However, following the collapse of the Selsdon programme by 1972, predictably the relationship became increasingly antagonistic. Heath's icy manner and unwillingness to make concessions to backbenchers exacerbated tensions. Therefore it can hardly have been surprising that from the '92 Committee' ranks many New Right advocates and Thatcher campaigners emerged over the ensuing three years.*(59)

There were also a few 'think tanks' whose combined impact provided impetus for the New Right. Most functioned outside the formal parameters of the Conservative Party, but as Kavanagh's 1987 study showed, those groups aided the rise of Thatcherism.*(60) Most acted as 'brains trusts' servicing the growing body of ideological dissenters who challenged the policies and general direction of the Conservative Party under Edward Heath's leadership. A mixture of nationalists and free market zealots, theirs was a potent cocktail that appealed to a growing section of the Party especially as Heath's travails in government grew ever more critical and success prospects increasingly remote.

The Institute of Economic Affairs (IEA) was founded in 1957 as a "… research and educational trust ..." to study the role of markets and pricing. Its chief architect was Anthony Fisher, himself also founder of the commercial operation, 'Buxted Chickens', and a devotee of free market guru, Frederick Hayek. In fact Fisher was persuaded by Hayek of the need for this organisation to champion free market ideals. In particular, according to Kavanagh, the IEA set itself the task of re-fashioning the climate within which politicians worked to promote the virtues of a deregulated market and enterprise culture. It was funded by donations from sympathisers in industry and the city, and employed a small team of researchers and pamphleteers to promote its message.*(61) Though never formally linked to the Conservative Party, its strategy was to promote ideals of private enterprise among the party faithful. Kavanagh says:

"The Institute makes much of not being formally attached to a political party nor being financed by one. It is firmly in the libertarian tradition, ... and perceived .... as the latter day equivalent of the Anti-Socialist Union and the Liberty and Property Defence League of the early decades of the {twentieth} century.." *(62)

The IEA published many seminal papers throughout the 1960s and '70s which sustained the free enterprise flag, while counterpoising Keynesianism of the post-war Settlement.

It is significant that leading IEA figures featured among Margaret Thatcher's entourage. For example, the Editorial Director was Arthur Seldon (later knighted by Mrs Thatcher), while the General Director, Lord Harris, was ennobled by Mrs Thatcher in 1979. So also was the IEA's 1970s/early '80s Deputy Director, John Wood, an ardent Thatcherite. Although not a faction under the political scientist's definition, ILEA was actively propagating an ideological alternative to that of the leadership. Its greatest impact lay with the weight underlying its alternative economic agenda such as undermined official policy and, ultimately, the Leader. So too did ILEA's 'high priests' like Seldon, Harris and Wood counterpoise the official leadership, operating from the sidelines, attracting intellectual recruits and thriving on the failings of Heath's frontbench team in opposition and government.*(63) Perhaps its greatest significance lay in the timing and pitch of its outpourings; these augmented the culture of grassroots and middle ranking dissatisfaction with Heath's leadership, as well as strengthening the climate that favoured the New Right. Such proved a vital aid to the rise of Thatcherism in the mid-1970s.

Other right wing campaigns had a historic lineage and might be more accurately termed pressure groups rather than factions. Yet it is in the nature of Conservative factionalism for outside campaigning organisations of a pro-Conservative persuasion to exercise an influence on party direction. Pressure groups like the right-leaning Institute of Directors (founded 1906) with its 30,000 members and pro-free enterprise Aims of Industry (founded 1942 to counter nationalisation) were always assured of a warm reception by the Conservative Right. Their policies squared with the Right's credo. Inevitably their protests against leadership were seized upon as evidence of party voters' distress with leadership. Such was the Right's strategy for undermining Heath's leadership after 1968.

As will be shown in Chapter 6, the number of right wing pressure groups mushroomed over the ensuing 16 years of Mrs Thatcher's leadership, February 1975 - November 1990. Additions included the National Association for Freedom (re-named Freedom Association), Centre for Policy Studies, Adam Smith Institute and Social Affairs Unit. All represented a burgeoning shift away from the mixed economy towards free market economics and the revival of state authority, both twin goals of the New Right.

6. Tory Progressives:- Heath's Loyal Publicists

It is tempting to view the decade of Edward Heath's leadership as one of constant struggle between a centre-minded leader in conflict with a rightwards-moving party. Such a view begs from an exaggerated profile of the numerous right wing dissenters of the Powell ultra-nationalist and free market schools previously listed. Yet this view presents neither an instructive nor accurate picture. That the Right were on the ascendant from 1968 onwards is evident, but there was nothing inevitable about their eventual triumph. Indeed the crucial determinants of that struggle appear to have rested on the failings of Heath's government along with defeat in both 1974 elections. Notwithstanding the Right's rising profile, the party mainstream remained largely loyal to Heath up until his fall in February 1975. Very importantly, a campaign was sustained by Heath's loyal followers on the centre to promote the merits of his policies throughout the party.

There were three areas in which supporters of Edward Heath's leadership operated within the Conservative Party of his time. First was domination of official party organisations by Tory Progressives promoting leadership policies on the economy, Europe, foreign affairs and domestic social issues. "Official" bodies included Central Office, a majority of constituency executives, Annual Conference, the National Union Executive and Central Council, plus various ancillary groups like Conservative women, students and youth, most of whom backed the Leader during his term.*(64) Such was also true of Tory MPs and peers, they being prime sources of Heath's authority. There were dissenting rightist voices after 1968, but they were kept in check and did not threaten the Leader's authority until after defeat in February 1974 and more so following the defeat of October.*(65)

Second, were the great policy debates of the Heath years, principally on Europe, the economy and immigration. It was a defining characteristic of Tory Progressives that they echoed Edward Heath's vision of a Britain whose economy was united with Western Europe, and where the rule of law governed trade unions, protest groups and other would-be challengers to parliament. Also, in the Progressive mind, immigration rules would be devoid of the colour dimension and avoided the harsh rhetoric of Enoch Powell and the Right. Active Tory Progressives in 1973 included Jim Prior, Christopher Soames, Peter Walker, Douglas Hurd, Norman St John-Stevas and Quintan Hogg (Lord Hailsham).

Third was the fringe of campaigning groups, which were few on account of prevailing Tory Progressive control of the party. Factional politics are often a recourse for disaffected bodies of activists who having dissented from leadership or lost control of a party realign in an unofficial group dedicated to their vision. Heathites were not then experiencing such travails, hence their preference for working through official structures. Yet with the growth of rightist challenges after 1968 the Tory Progressives had to demonstrate their heart and soul by the cogency of campaigning vision. Such was necessary for the sake of keeping the loyalty of Conservative grass roots, as well as presenting a positive defence of leadership policies.

The war-time Tory Reform Committee had long been dissolved by the Heath era, but other successor groups had emerged. None were greatly significant in terms of corporate organisation or campaigning tactics, and none made a strong impact on the party's power balance even at the height of Heath's leadership authority. Instead they acted as publicists for Heath's leadership while underlining the ideological vigour of Progressive Toryism in a party that was slowly shaping up for a battle of ideals. Throughout the early 1970s there were three organised ideological tendencies on the Tory Progressive wing. Pressure for Economic and Social Toryism (PEST) was a small, rather exclusive fellowship largely composed of students and policy researchers dedicated to continuing Butler's One Nation agenda during the Heath years. Founded in 1963, it remained small and London-centred, with a penchant for lobbying and publishing pamphlets to counter the contentious profile of the Monday Club, ILEA and Powellites. The group also ran occasional seminars and Conference fringe meetings, enabling it to put forward an agenda, aided by a handful of parliamentary sponsors. However, it did not engage in power politics and avoided activists' slates, policy resolutions, AGM campaigns and candidate selection efforts, all so typical of the Monday Club and other factional groups of the party.*(66)

Two other small organisations functioned along comparable lines. One was the Macleod Group based in the North West of England. This One-Nation fellowship was fashioned in the image of its personifying guru, which assumed a folksy dimension after the short-lived Chancellor's untimely death in July 1970. Another was the Home Counties based, Social Tory Action Group (STAG) which represented the same values and ideals as its Northern sister group. It too had operated throughout the 1960s and early '70s with a small cadre of stalwarts drawn mainly from the middle ranks of researchers and graduate enthusiasts.*(67) There was also the Conservative European lobby, initiated some years earlier, with a dominant centre-left/Progressive tendency. However, while favoured largely by Progressives, Conservative Europeans also included assorted elements drawn from the Conservative Right. Generally, European sentiment in those times was an inexact barometer for measuring pro-Heath opinion within the Tory Party.

Those groups generally kept the Keynesian flag flying, acted as ideological publicists for the party leadership and countered hostile campaigns by the Right on the free market, race and immigration. While impact is difficult to measure, throughout the early 1970s clearly the tide moved against Progressives as the difficulties faced by Edward Heath's government multiplied. Yet it was precisely those troubles on the government's front – ranging from Rolls Royce's bankruptcy, failing industrial relations, inflation, economic stagnation, the oil crisis, etc. – which sealed both Heath's fate and that of his beleaguered Tory Progressives. That sequence of events is relayed more fully in Chapter 6.

7. Conclusions

The cut-off point for this chapter has been – curiously to the minds of some – placed at 1973 on account of the domino events resulting from Heath's loss of office the following year. That phase carries connotations for the Conservatives best relayed through a separate chapter, largely because it spelt the end of an era for the post-war 'Consensus' and triumph of Margaret Thatcher's New Right. Such events and their ramifications merit a comprehensive assessment which comes later in this book. Yet the Heath years fashioned conditions that precipitated his downfall, while refashioning the Conservatives in a new ideological direction for the next two decades ahead.

Previous evidence suggests developments to be paving the way for the Right's successful challenge over the twelve months following the party's election defeat in February 1974. First, the economy was visibly faltering. A combination of inflation, economic stagnation, industrial instability, recurrent trade deficits, manufacturing decline and unease over high taxation, government subsidies and welfare spending all served to feed public dissatisfaction. This situation enabled the Right to attack the policy framework of the 'Consensus' and demand a change of direction. Indeed the Conservatives' adoption of the Selsdon Park manifesto (1970) showed the extent of changing opinion and how prevailing conditions and longer term trends favoured a slow revival of the Right.

Second, the Consensus was under further assault from high profile dissenters within the party. Chief among these was Enoch Powell, who attracted a small following at Westminster but a larger devotion among Conservative middle management and party grass roots. Other occasional dissenters paled to insignificance when weighed against Powell. Though devoid of an organisation, Powell counterpoised official Conservative policy most effectively through his intellectual stature, combined with a populist style. More significantly, as noted by Kavanagh, Powell's post-1968 rebellion marked the most serious challenge to the post-war Consensus.*(68) From that point onwards the Consensus faltered under the sustained weight of attacks from left and right, leading to its eventual collapse and replacement by Thatcherism after 1979. Powell proved to be an icon for those on the Right wanting change. Hence, though not himself a factionalist, still Powell's legacy was utilised by convivial groups on the Conservative Right – nationalists and economic Whigs alike – demanding a break with 'Consensus' politics.

140

Third, by the late 1960s the Conservative Right had regained momentum, but not enough for seizing control of the party. The political climate was favourable to their cause, and clearly a continuation of economic and social pressures would eventually bring them to the fore. Yet it was the Tory Progressives under Edward Heath who controlled the party and its policy agenda at that time. Their causes like European Community accession, quasi-Keynesian economics, maintenance of public welfare and progressive taxation characterised the Heath government's programme. Conversely, the Right's protests about a "U-turn" failed to force any significant change of direction. Accordingly, throughout the 1960s, and especially after 1968, the Right sought to rebuild appeal through campaigning groups like the Monday Club and Anti-Common Market League. This strategy encompassed the reinvigoration of existing right-wing think-tanks like the Institute of Economic Affairs, Aims of Industry etc. along with the Monday Club, the most pertinacious Tory campaigning force. Such organisations mushroomed after 1973.

Fourth, Heath's authoritarian and dogmatic political style encouraged his opponents to re-group on the fringe. So did his scarcity of warmth and poor rapport with backbenchers cause unnecessary alienation of political allies at Westminster and throughout the party, which cost him dearly in the leadership ballot of 1975.

Fifth, Tory Progressives operating during the Heath years acted more as publicists than campaigners. Their ideology was in broad sympathy with the Heath government, but they organised into their own groups. Frankly, they lacked independence, and despite making inroads into ancillary groups as Conservative students, youth and women etc, theirs was always a marginal campaign devoid of real grass roots or other popular links.

This was the troubled state of the Conservative Party after bowing out of office in 1974. Such conditions paved the way for a final break with the Consensus and the subsequent emergence of Thatcherism and the New Right later in that decade.

FOOTNOTES and REFERENCES

1. Richard Rose - Political Studies (1964).

2. Heath won 150 votes to Maudling's 133 and Powell's 15. Although under the rules, a second ballot was required, Maudling withdrew, leaving Heath outright winner, the first ever Conservative leader to be elected by MPs.

3. Heath (1998) - Chap. 10, pp. 274-282.

4. Heath (1998) - Chap. 8, pp. 201-204.

5. Gamble (1988) - Chap. 3, pp. 67-73.

6. Nigel Ashford - Chap. 5, Layton-Henry Eds. (1980).

7. Ibid.

8. A recurrent message from interviewing former Westminster colleagues was that Heath's style provoked antagonism; e.g. Norman Tebbit and Peter Temple-Morris.

   Another One Nationite, Michael Heseltine, acknowledged that Heath's manner was why he abstained in the leadership election of February 1975. Ref. Michael Heseltine interviewed by Peter Hennessy, BBC Radio 4, 2nd August, 2016.

9. Burch - Layton-Henry (1980), pp. 166-172.

10. Ibid.

11. Early Euro-zealous ideals coloured Heath's memoirs (1998), Chaps. 3, 4 & 8.

12. Heath (1998), Chap. 25.

13. Journalists maintain that Heath's relations with the Queen were cool on account of his preference for Europe over the Commonwealth. Such has never been confirmed by state papers and was avoided by Heath in his own memoirs.

14. Heath (1998), Chap. 16, pp. 451-454.

15. Layton-Henry (1980), Chap. 3, pp. 60-66;Vernon Bogdanor, Chap. 4, pp. 80-91, Layton-Henry Eds. (1980).

16. Nigel Ashford - 'The Conservative Party and European Integration, 1945-1975.' Introduction. - Unpublished Ph.D. thesis, University of Warwick, 1983.

17. Ashford thesis (1983) - Chap. 5, pp. 227- 229.

18. Peter Temple-Morris admitted to the author that Heath's coolness and poor style had cost him his vote in the leadership election of February 1975.

    Interview - Peter Temple-Morris, MP/V. McKee, 24th October, 2000.

19. See Robert Behrens (1980), Chap. 2.

20. Norton (1996), Chap.3, pp. 53, 54.

21. Times, Guardian, Daily Telegraph and Birmingham Post reports; 23rd April, 1968.

22. Robert Shepherd - Enoch Powell: A Biography, Chap. 15, pp. 349-359, (Hutchinson, 1996).
    Cosgrave (1989) - Concluding chapter.

23. Powell was elected - albeit after a close contest with the SDLP candidate, Sean Holywood - as United Ulster Unionist Coalition MP for South Down in October 1974. He held this seat through two general elections (1979 and 1983) and a by-election (1986) before losing marginally to the SDLP's Eddie McGrady in 1987.

24. Kavanagh (1987), Chap. 3, pp. 69-71.

25. Michael Foot - Essay on Powell, 'A Miscellany of Crossbreeds', pp 185-193, Loyalists and Loners (Collins, 1986).

26. Monday Club Newsletter, 69, May-June 1971, p. 3.

27. Patrick Seyd 'Factionalism within the Conservative Party: The Monday Club'; pp. 482-486, Government and Opposition, Vol. 7, 4, Autumn 1972.

28. Geoffrey Rippon, Julian Amery, John Peyton, Teddy Taylor, Jasper More and Victor Goodhew were the six ministers from Heath's 1970 government team who also held membership of the Monday Club. - More later resigned.

29. Cited in Seyd - <u>Government and Opposition</u> (1972), p. 468.

30. Ibid.

31. Editorial, Monday World, Spring 1970.

32. Lucy Grant - 'Clear Blue Water: Secrets from the Deep: - A study of the 92 Group within the Conservative Party'. - Unpublished M.A. Dissertation, University of Hull, 1999.

33. Seyd - Government and Opposition, p. 470.

34. Seyd, - Government and Opposition, p. 471.

35. Seyd (1972), Tables 1-4, pp. 474, 475.

36. Ashford thesis (1983), Chap. 5, p. 241.

37. Ashford (1983), Chap. 5, p. 242.

38. Ashford, Chap. 5, pp. 241-242.

39. Interview - Lord Tebbit/V. McKee.

40. Ashford, Chap. 4, p.149.

41. Ashford, Chaps. 1-5.

42. 'True Blues Newsletter'- Annual Conference edition, October 1957.

43. Impressions of former activist (interviewed by author) who asked for anonymity.

44. Impressions of Peter Temple-Morris, MP in interview with author.

45. Ashford, Chap. 4, pp. 175-180.

46. Ashford, Chap. 4, p. 178.

47. Ibid.

48. Ibid.

49. Ibid.

50. Ashford, Chap. 5, pp. 243-245.

51. Ashford, Chap. 5, p. 227.

52. Ibid.

52. Ashford, Chap. 5, 228.

53. Ashford, Chap. 5, p.p.-228-230.

54. Grant Dissertation (1999), p.p. 6-8.

55. Grant, p.p. 9-11.

56. Grant, p.p. 12-16.

57. Grant, p 7.

58. Grant, p 8.

59. Kavanagh (1987), Chap. 4, pp. 111-118.

60. Kavanagh - Chap. 3 general.

61. Kavanagh (1987), Chap. 3, pp. 80-84.

62. Kavanagh, Chap. 3, p. 81.

63. Ibid

64. Gamble (1975), Chap. 1 - a recurrent theme for the book.

65. The steadfast allegiance to Heath of the various official organisations is confirmed by most contemporary historical accounts of the Thatcher-Heath contest. See Blake (1985) Chap. 10; Seyd in Layton-Henry, Chap. 10; Charmley, Chap. 10; Ramsden, Chap. 15.

66. Interviews - Author/Editor, Giles Marshall - Tory Reformer, 23rd March, 2000; Author - Justin Powell-Tuck, 22nd February, 2000.

67. Ibid.

68. Kavanagh (1987), Chap. 3, p. 73.

Forty Shades of Blue

CHAPTER 6

ENTER MRS THATCHER

THE CONSERVATIVES' QUIET REVOLUTION 1973-79

This chapter will examine the political and ideological transformation of the Conservative Party from the fall of Edward Heath from office in February 1974, his loss of party leadership in February 1975, the emergence of a New Right ideology, and the party's return to office under Margaret Thatcher in May 1979. Essentially, the chapter is concerned with evaluating the growth of Thatcherism, its effects on policy and power balances, and the extent to which group activities played a part in fashioning this process. Significantly, among questions to be addressed, is that of how far rightist and centrist groups acted as agents of the rival New Right and One Nation camps. So also will there be a highlighting of the extent to which factional politics assumed centre-stage in the Conservative Party during the crisis period when Heath's authority was under challenge and a rival school were planning their 'putsch'.

Initially it is necessary to examine the roots of that challenge. This may be found in the last months of the Heath government, when a combination of troubles like the Arab oil embargo, three-day week, inflation, trade deficits and miners' industrial action imposed endless afflictions. Heath's problems with his own rebels and ideological dissidents were exacerbated by the loss of public confidence that partly accounted for the government's defeat at the polls in February 1974. Such an experience facilitated the right wing challenge that followed over late 1974 and early 1975 having been further aided by the second election defeat of October 1974. For this failing, Heath paid the ultimate price.

What is also important is the degree to which his successor set about redefining the programme of Conservatives in office. Some 30 years of post-1945 orthodoxy were set aside as the New Right under Margaret Thatcher revived the libertarian economics and nationalism in a desperate bid to halt what appeared then as a serious and prolonged electoral slide. Factional activity was utilised to advance the Thatcher cause at all levels of the party. However, factionalism also became a mechanism by which the record and credibility of displaced Tory Progressives was defended after 1975, and just as the New Right forces had operated from 'Think Tanks' like IEA, Selsdon Group and Centre for Policy Studies over 1973/74, so did the Tory Reform Group provided a refuge for Heath's people after Thatcher's accession. This turbulent period will now be examined.

1. Introduction

Churchill considered the Conservative leader's position to be comparable to that of a renewable lease. It carries full authority over policy-making and cabinet/shadow cabinet appointments, as well as senior appointments to Conservative Central Office and the party organisation at large. Perhaps most significant is the authority to determine the party's election manifesto. Indeed, as Norton suggested, the Conservative leader's power is as near absolute as may be found anywhere in the democratic world.*(1) Nor has the position altered much, even since the inception in 1998 of William Hague's democratised party constitution with its emphasis on rank and file ballots and final choice of leader etc.

Meanwhile, by November 1974 Edward Heath's position had become impossible. Plainly, he had failed the supreme test of all Tory leaders, notably winning power. Under him, the party had lost three out of four elections, the vote share of October 1974 was the Conservatives' lowest since 1945, and everywhere questions were being asked about whether the party would govern again. Given the manner in which Conservative leaders have been raised and ousted over the past 150 years, it is surprising that Heath or his lieutenants ever thought his leadership could have survived this crisis. Yet reliable accounts of the 'goings on' between October 1974 and February 1975 suggest that Heath was stunned, even hurt by the challenge that emerged.*(2) Nor did he expect to lose either, thereby causing grave shock when he was so comprehensively beaten by Margaret Thatcher in the first round held on 5th February.

In order to understand the significance of the Conservatives' loss of power in 1974 and Heath's subsequent rejection by Tory MPs, it is necessary to evaluate cumulative events from the last months of his premiership. Therein lay the roots of troubles, both with the party at large and the ascendant Right in particular. It was his manner of handling dissenters, plus a general imperviosity to back-benchers, that raised issues after his government's failure to deal effectively with striking miners, shield Britain from the ravages of the 1973 Arab oil embargo (including the three day working week), conquer inflation or even halt the growing trade deficits. There was also a growing debate over Scottish and Welsh devolution following the Kilbrandon Commission report's publication (something he did not reject), plus alienation of Ulster Unionists after his suspension of the Stormont regime (March 1972) and introduction of power sharing between Unionists and Nationalists in N. Ireland as determined by the 1973 White Paper.

Heath had unavoidably made enemies on his own right wing, e.g. Ulster Unionists and anti-EEC zealots, but his personal manner strained some MPs who actually shared his aims.*(3) As Margaret Thatcher herself was to discover some fifteen years later, alienating colleagues amounted to poor politics when leadership votes were needed, but that same lesson Heath learned bitterly in 1975. Of course it is debatable whether he would have survived anyway in the unpropitious conditions following the two defeats of 1974. However, he made his own demise more likely by an imperious and self righteous manner that played into the hands of opponents just at a time when support was crucial.

It is important to analyse how the Heath government's travails rejuvenated the New Right while spelling concomitant decline for Tory Progressives. Even before Heath sought a fresh mandate, evidence manifested of voter dissatisfaction. Aside from unpromising opinion polls showing the Conservatives throughout 1973 lagging an average of 7 points behind Labour, local elections in May 1973 had resulted in substantial Labour gains. There were also signs of a mini-Liberal revival, with by-election wins in Rochdale, Isle of Ely and Richmond, while the nationalist tide was gathering in Scotland and Wales. Actually both 1974 elections demonstrated a process of voter de-alignment to be underway at the expense of both major parties.*(4) However, it was the Conservatives who bore the brunt, something later blamed by rightist advocates on the legacy of Heath's government. Therewith Mrs Thatcher and the Conservative Right developed their questionable thesis of Conservatives losing ground on account of successive Tory governments' collusion in a left-led and state-orientated post-war settlement.

As for the 'Consensus', it was visibly disintegrating along with key defenders. The different radical schools of left and right were questioning the orthodoxy of policymaking in the wake of long-term economic stagnation and social disorientation in mid-1970s Britain. Edward Heath's troubles seemed all too redolent of the declining post-war socio-economic system, which was being overtaken by a mixture of inflation, poor growth, union militancy and overbearing taxes, none of which bode well for government plans. All those factors effected substantial shifts in the political ground. Indeed the fault-lines were becoming ever more marked and there was every chance of a different orthodoxy emerging to that which had been around since the late 1940s. Kavanagh considered the rise of radical right wingers in the Conservative Party to be symptomatic of a failing 'Consensus', and is generally supported in this view by Charmley and Blake.*(5) This seems much like wisdom with the benefit of hindsight! Yet it was underway. So also was a comparable phenomenon underway in Labour ranks through the rise of the Bennite left.

A poignant indicator of the declining 'Consensus' was the continuing rise throughout the early 1970s of right wing lobby organisations. Additional to familiar names like the Monday Club and Anti-Common Market League, several new right-wing 'brains trusts' emerged, such as Keith Joseph's Centre for Policy Studies, established to promote free market -orientated policies on socio-economic issues. Others included the Selsdon Group, IEA and National Association for Freedom (already covered).

Even the Bow Group was inclining towards deregulation as a main framework for future policy making.*(6) Kavanagh viewed this trend as significant because it lent weight to the growing strength of the Conservative Right both inside and outside Parliament.*(7) At the very least, such groups provided an alternative focus for disaffected right-wingers, and came to rival the Conservative Research Department and Central Office for generating policy pamphlets and spokesmen. Edward Heath showed disdain for the Right on the grounds that they undermined his authority at Westminster and in the country.*(8) Yet internal realignment was taking place and re-ascendant rightist groups were important functionaries in that process. The fact that it did not wholly manifest until after October 1974 meant that the rebellion against Heath availed of widespread rank and file discontent emanating from a serious loss of confidence in his leadership.

2. Evaluation of the Conservative Right

A serious appraisal of the Conservative Right must address certain key questions. Firstly, in what sections of the party did the Right organise? What were its principal platforms? Did the Right have a campaigning strategy, and how did it propagate ideological and philosophical arguments? Who were the major right wing figures? What ideological schools operated on the Conservative Right and to what degree did they collaborate?

All those issues are relevant for assessing the Right's character as it tried forcing an historic shift of power in the party and held fundamental consequences for both party and country over the ensuing two decades. Comparisons may be made between the Thatcherite New Right and earlier generations of right-wingers functioning at other stages of post-war history. Such says much about the Conservative Party, various rightist groups, their agendas and the conditions in which they operated. Factions being agents of political change and internal rivalry, it followed that Conservative factional politics throughout the mid-late 1970s offered a mirror on the party's direction then.

The causes feeding the Conservative Right were outlined in Chapter 4. They were further galvanised by Heath's accumulating policy failures, U-turns and electoral setbacks. Overall, the New Right protested against the corporatist-leaning post-war system with its emphasis on state-run utilities, powerful trade unions, universal welfare benefits and high taxation. Instead, as was argued in a collection of essays edited by Rhodes

Boyson, the Right's priorities included a return to the free market, major tax cuts, deregulation, restoration of parliamentary authority and a revival of British stature in international affairs.*(9) Significantly, two schools emerged on the New Right: New Whigs and Nationalists/Neo-Imperialists. Despite having separate priorities, those two possessed enough common ground for constructing a grand political crusade headed and personified by Margaret Thatcher.*(10) Both merit closer examination.

3. New Whigs

The New Whig school was composed of free market ideologues seeking a revival of earlier faith in the merits of free enterprise and minimalist government. Their cause owed as much to nineteenth century classical Liberalism as anything related to Conservatism. Indeed some One Nationites, most notably Ian Gilmour, suggested this updated version of Victorian Whig thinking to be alien to Tory traditions.*(11)

(i) *New Whig Agenda*

Generally, this school viewed state utilities as inefficient, non-profitable, a bastion of entrenched trade union interests and a burden on the public purse. Comprehensive welfare provision, they felt, had become excessive and monopolised by the least deserving. It served to undermine the work ethic while swelling the tax bill, thereby hastening a decline in the culture of self-help and enterprise in contrast to Victorian glories. Also, education, broadcasting, state quangos and the trade unions had lost their way under leftist influence from Whitehall, resulting in the British national character experiencing irreversible mutation. So also were property ownership and individual initiative compromised by an assortment of crippling taxes, restrictive union practices (especially the closed shop) and a nanny welfare system that was unduly comprehensive and undermined the family. An example of 'nannying' was the reluctance of Labour-led local councils to allow tenants to buy their homes, generating town hall 'clientelism' so beloved of socialists.

Robert Behrens offers the broad-sweeping 'die-hard' label for describing the New Right.*(12) He did not distinguish wholly between those right wingers whose major priority was economic liberalisation and those with a nationalist agenda. Nevertheless, Behrens's appraisal of the New Right's dispute with Heath and his corporatist-minded Progressives is entirely apposite. The principal goal of New Whigs was – as Margaret Thatcher proclaimed – "… to roll back the frontiers of the state." Privatisation, deregulation, tax cuts, union power curbs, welfare spending cuts, dismantling sections of the state apparatus in favour of voluntary groups, while regenerating private enterprise all dominated the Whig agenda. There was also a view that Parliament had become subservient to "improper challenges" from outside groups. Thus Whigs opposed constitutional changes that weakened central government while reasserting parliamentary sovereignty and authority for curbing internal and external threats.*(13) New Whigs were mainly concerned with economic liberalisation so as to boost free enterprise and curb the 'dead hand' – as it was perceived – of the state and corporate interests. Adopting nationalist causes served to underline the broad-based nature of the New Right coalition.

Significantly, Mrs Thatcher's greatest appeal was to this school, and her patronage meant an enhanced profile for its protagonists. So did Thatcher lieutenants like Keith Joseph, Rhodes Boyson, Nicholas Ridley, Arthur Seldon and Professor Alan Walter all raise their heads over the fifteen months after November 1973. Other recruits emerged, but not until the Thatcher campaign took off in earnest in January 1975 did the New Whigs assume a specific raison d'être. As will later be shown, throughout the mid-1970s New Whigs embraced various free market lobby groups operating around the Conservative Party. They included existing bodies like the Institute for Economic Affairs along with the newly-founded Selsdon Group, Keith Joseph's Centre for Policy Studies (founded 1974), later the ultra-radical Libertarian Alliance, the Adam Smith Institute and sections of the National Association for Freedom. The Bow Group moved in that direction after 1973 and its journal, *Crossbow*, offered a platform for New Whigs advocates. Another ally was *The Daily Telegraph*, whose opinion pages and editorials from 1974 onwards proved increasingly partial towards the free market cause.*(14) Throughout the 1980s, the paper – under Max Hastings's editorship – proved a key Thatcher supporter, while facilitating policy debates among diverse strands of the Conservative Right.

(ii) *Nationalists and Neo-Imperialists:*

This school comprised a collection of nationalists, old style imperialists and political malcontents whose primary worry was declining British authority at home on the world stage. Their concerns were with remnants of the Empire, UK-US relations and the legacy of Suez, the Smith regime in Salisbury, Anglo-South African relations, EEC influence, Soviet threats and growing appeal of Celtic nationalists. Also, they were concerned about 1970s military and naval reductions, as well as socialist plans to curb public schools and abolish the House of Lords.*(15) Essentially, nationalists defended traditional British institutions, propagated sovereignty, asserted the Anglo-Irish and Scottish Union and promoted British influence in global affairs. Previously they were in favour of imperial union, opposed decolonisation, disliked GATT, were disinclined towards Europe, favoured Eden's hawkish line on Egypt and sought a British presence East of Suez. By 1974/75, they opposed further immigration, defended the white regimes in Pretoria and Salisbury, asserted UK sovereignty in NATO, while backing Unionists in Scotland and Northern Ireland. They also preferred a free market economic strategy.

Prominent advocates of this school were drawn partly from the ranks of old imperialists – more numerous in the 1970s than three decades later – plus contemporary nationalists. They included Lord Salisbury (co-founder of the Anti-Common Market League), Enoch Powell, Julian Amery, Scottish Unionist and monarchist Teddy Taylor, John Biggs-Davison and political philosopher, Roger Scruton. Previous gurus numbered the former Ulster Unionist premier 1943-63, Basil (Lord) Brooke, Churchill's ally, Leo Amery, and Viscount Hinchingbrooke, the ex-Tory Reform Committee chairman whose nationalist sympathies and anti-EEC sentiments caused him to realign with the Right.*(16)

Nationalist/neo-Imperialist groups functioned variously according to the political climate. Throughout the 1960s an East of Suez Group operated at Westminster, along with the Anglo-South African and Rhodesian Friendship Societies. Also, there were the Anti-Common Market League (1960s and early '70s), Monday Club, Tory Action (ultra-rightist) and sections of the National Association for Freedom.*(17) Additionally, Ulster Unionist links to some Conservative parliamentarians and rank and file alike were maintained through organisations like the Monday Club; it having hosted speakers from Belfast like hard-line former Stormont Home Affairs minister, William Craig, and several bedfellows. Essentially, the Monday Club facilitated those disaffected Ulster Unionists – the Conservatives' former allies – whose fury at the dramatic loss of Protestant political power in Northern Ireland in March 1972 was vented at Ted Heath.

As for Fleet Street platforms, they were provided by the *Daily Telegraph* and *Daily Mail*. There was also Monday World (Monday Club journal), whose regular outpourings on policy received prime media attention, especially after the Right were perceived as serious challengers to Heath following the election defeat of February 1974. The Monday Club became a platform for arguing policy alternatives and facilitating rebellious scribes like Powell, Biggs-Davison and Rhodes Boyson. Its successor journal, *Salisbury Review*, offered a similar role and throughout the late 1980s and '90s served as a leading right wing magazine – nominally independent of both Club and Party – for examining ideals and policies. Ironically, its declining influence may be linked to a sense on the Right – earlier articulated by Tebbit – that its ethos belonged to a past era.

Another ultra-right fringe group, Tory Challenge, operated mainly in London and the Home Counties. This organisation lacked MPs and funds, and had little access to Central Office; its conference meetings were shrill but otherwise unspectacular. Tory Challenge articulated a message from the party fringe that more than anything else highlighted the extent of imperialist estrangement from the party mainstream by 1974. By the late 1970s, with Mrs Thatcher at the party helm, the organisation faded.*(18)

(iii) *Right-wing Coalition*

The Conservative Right was in every sense a coalition of Nationalists/neo-Imperialists and New Whigs who combined faith in the free market with renewal of traditional Conservative causes like the Union, parliamentary sovereignty, the family, law and order and a powerful British state with revived influence in international affairs. Although this framework distinguishes between Nationalists and New Whigs, there were many figures on the Right who articulated both persuasions in semi-equal measure. Examples included Norman Tebbit, Alan Clark, Airey Neave, Ronald Bell, Julian Amery and Enoch Powell, along with Margaret Thatcher. So also did some organisations straddle the same divide, most notably the National Association for Freedom and the Monday Club.

The Right's ascendant profile was evident by the Summer of 1974 and underpinned by an evolving agenda of liberal economics, nationalism and social conservatism. This phenomenon appealed to a party many of whose grass roots and parliamentarians were losing faith in the Keynesian orthodoxy and Consensus politics of post-war years. Given the party's slide from previous hegemony to something approaching a voter crisis under Heath, there was a perceived need for finding a new agenda that chimed with traditional beliefs and looked likely to restore electoral prospects. Hence for the emergent New Right, this diet provided the basis for what was to become known as Thatcherism.

Starting out in opposition to Ted Heath's regime in the early/mid-1970s, the New Right's gestation was facilitated by the accumulated failings of that government and its hapless leader. It gained momentum from Heath's fall and the election of Margaret Thatcher to the Conservative helm with her declared commitment to a departure from "... the failed policies ..." of the post-war Settlement. Mrs Thatcher's emergence as Conservative leader signalled a shift to the Right, and her New Right coalition proved redoubtable champions in promoting that new direction to the party at Westminster and to rank and file Conservatives throughout the country. The manner in which her cause was postulated and the groups involved will be a primary focus for this study.

4. Effects of the Conservative Defeats, 1974

Kavanagh has emphasised the Conservative Party to be a poor loser in elections. As a party fashioned on state-craft, opposition after February 1974 did not sit well; even less promising was the party's longer term electoral crisis. The latter only became apparent following the second defeat of October that year. With the vote at 35.8, the party's lowest share since World War 2, fears of terminal decline surfaced. Given demographic trends, questions were asked about whether the party could win office again, or might be reduced to a middle class rump bereft of the nationwide support Conservatives have long claimed as their heritage. There was also a feeling among others that the party could only return to government through a national coalition. Such a view had been given credence by Heath in the October (1974) election campaign when openly talking about the desirability of a national government for meeting the economic crisis. This confidence crisis had the effect of galvanising Conservative MPs and activists into various forms of defensive action.

The state of the Conservative Party over the last months of Edward Heath's leadership has been thoroughly chronicled by various academics, journalists and contemporary observers, not to mention the innumerable memoirs and biographies dealing with the period, including those of the prime actors, Mr Heath and Mrs Thatcher respectively. The same atmosphere produced an upsurge of debate, along with divisions, rebellions and challenges, in turn leading to a proliferation of factionalism. Patrick Seyd viewed the Conservatives as especially susceptible to factional politicking when leadership is under challenge.*(19) This view appears to be borne out by the level of internecine conflict characterising the Conservatives over the critical months preceding and immediately following the leadership election of February 1975. John Barnes' view of Conservative factions being a manifestation of competing ideological tendencies has been lent weight by events from that period.*(20) While each group articulated its causes, the overriding feature was ideological crusaders campaigning in the colours of the Conservative centre or right. The 1974/76 battles between Heathite Progressives and New Right Thatcherites highlighted the divisions and consequences for the whole party.

Behrens' account of the effects and aftermath of the 1975 leadership change on the party highlights the unsettling impact that it exerted on Central Office and the constituency associations.*(21) It was mainly the Right who made the most running. An array of right wing groups sprang up over the two-year period from Autumn 1973 to Autumn 1975, all postulating radical free market and/or nationalist agendas. They included the Centre for Policy Studies, Selsdon Group, Adam Smith Institute and National Association for Freedom (NAFF). Other groups were already there, including a revamped Monday Club, Institute for Economic

Affairs, Institute of Directors and an increasingly pro-Thatcher Bow Group which after Heath's fall moved towards a free-market orthodoxy.*(22) Some groups functioned within the party while others operated on the outside. In any case, the common theme uniting all was a desire for fundamental policy change. The latter process began with Edward Heath's removal from the leadership, as happened in February 1975.

This goal continued to dominate the Right's agenda from the first election defeat of February 1974 through until Margaret Thatcher's election in February 1975. It was to have a divisive impact on the internal party atmosphere and was deployed with unremitting verve until Heath and his people were finally driven from the party helm.

The Right's assertive profile attracted numerous patrons and advocates from Westminster as the battle for the Conservative leadership got underway. Though the formal challenge from Margaret Thatcher did not emerge until late January 1975, in fact from October 1974 onwards a phoney war was underway. Following the loss of office, Conservatives lacked direction, and it was 'open season' for revolts. The latter played into the Right's hands, whose assorted legions attacked the record and direction of Heath's government, demanding simultaneously a return to older Conservative preferences for the free market, self-help and a strong, unified state. By contrast, Heath's defenders appeared staid and lacking in ideals, not to mention de-facto apologists for a government that had reneged on its manifesto, failed in key policy objectives – except Europe – and had been rejected by voters at the polls. Also, Heath in 1975 lacked an effective campaign fired up to take his message to Conservatives at Westminster and in the country. Instead he relied on the authority of his captaincy and lobbying by lieutenants for winning the day. Given that a cocktail of discontent had long been brewing, such was plainly not going to happen.*(23)

5.   State of the Conservative Right in January 1975

Most reputable party histories point to the Right's rebellious state at the beginning of 1975. There was a strong sense among discerning observers that Heath's days were numbered, and though the forthcoming contest was by no means a formality, still his campaign lacked the passion of the challenger, Margaret Thatcher. It was not well coordinated, nor were backbenchers effectively mobilised in the Leader's support. Conversely, the Thatcher campaign – directed by Airey Neave – assumed an increasingly poignant momentum that gathered more confidence by the day. While outside groups were not directly involved in either candidate's campaign, still rightist groups actively promoted the persona and agenda of Mrs Thatcher.

It was noticeable that in the period 1974-76 certain groups provided an alternative focus for the allegiances of right wing activists. Those bodies were of a disciplined and structured kind, with the Monday Club and newly launched National Association for Freedom being the most prominent examples. So also did the growing array of right wing 'brains trusts' like the Centre for Policy Studies and Adam Smith Institute rival official party organisations. While Conservative Central Office and the Research Department defended existing orthodoxy up until Thatcher's succession, it was those cerebral rightist groups that offered an alternative political home for followers alienated by the leadership of Edward Heath. Yet the New Right agenda had to wait until the party leadership passed to Margaret Thatcher before entering the official frame, and even then only by degrees.

Theoretically, the conduct of the Monday Club and other hard right groups over this period amounted to a classical exhibition of factionalism in action. Richard Rose wrote of factions as highly disciplined internal groups possessing their own structures and acting as 'parties within parties', offering a home to disaffected activists throughout periods of hostility in the parent party.*(24) This view holds considerable relevance to the Monday Club during its 'Babylonian exile', when throughout the final two Heath years it virtually counterpoised the official Conservative organisation in policy output and bidding for activists' loyalties. The same point applied to the right wing 'think-tanks' whose preference for independent policy analysis undermined the Conservative Research Department. It also encouraged the Right to tacitly develop preparations for a challenge, which following election defeat in February 1974 looked inevitable in the short term.

How and what strategy might have been adopted had the Right lost their bid for the party leadership is unclear. Moreover, as far as can be established from literature, group pamphlets and this author's interviews with key figures of the period, there were no plans anywhere on the Right to set up a rival party.*(25) Instead the consensus of rightist opinion was that their day was dawning, and even if Heath had hung on in the leadership contest, his authority would have been weakened by two electoral defeats and subsequent defections of key former colleagues as Joseph, Howe and Thatcher to a rival camp.*(26) Either way, his captaincy was clearly on the wane, and to observers of the time events – if not formal procedures – would shortly require his exit from the bridge.

Hence, though the Right was characterised by nationalist and free market campaigns, the key unifying strategy was to oust Edward Heath and his lieutenants from leadership. This strategy galvanised the Right both at Westminster and in the country over those critical months: October 1974 to February 1975 and – from their viewpoint – yielded a positive result. Before that, came the all-important Conservative leadership contest which set the pace for the party's ideological re-direction over the ensuing two decades.

6.   The Conservative Leadership Contest of February 1975

This seminal event was settled at Westminster without much involvement from outside groups. Although there was some input to debates from the Monday Club and its allies on the Right, in fact they had only marginal importance. Rather more significant was the outcome on the Conservative Party generally and the ascendant Right particularly.

First Ballot 4th February 1975		Second Ballot 11th Feb 1975	
Edward Heath	*119*	*Margaret Thatcher*	*146*
Margaret Thatcher	*130*	*William Whitelaw*	*79*
Hugh Fraser	*16*	*Geoffrey Howe*	*19*
		James Prior	*19*
		John Peyton	*16*

160

The Conservatives now had a new leader from the Right. It was the beginning of the Thatcher era, which was to last another sixteen years through three consecutive election victories and eleven and a half years in government. So also was the party transformed in policy terms; it would renounce the beleaguered post-war Settlement in favour of a new agenda of economic liberalism and nationalism that was later to sweep the country.

The Right's victory raised several questions about future direction under Thatcher. First was the prospect of an internal Thatcherite revolution. Given the political composition of her election team, most especially her campaign manager, Airey Neave, and ideological mentor, Sir Keith Joseph, there was every possibility of the Conservatives changing direction under her leadership. Such might mean repudiating the Heath legacy and indeed the general drift of successive post-war Conservative governments. It was not an appealing prospect to supporters of the fallen Tory leader or many others. Only die-hard opponents of Consensus politics like Neave, Joseph, Nicholas Ridley and the upward moving Norman Tebbit welcomed such changes. Second, there was a need to carry the party faithful in a new direction. Although Heath never struck a warm chord with grass roots, he still enjoyed a residual loyalty manifested in the majority preference for him over Thatcher in unofficial soundings taken amongst constituency party chairmen. It was unclear then whether Thatcher could win over grass roots loyalties in the course of the next four years. Third, with the Right now in charge of the party, clearly the power balance had shifted away from the Tory Progressives to economic libertarians and nationalists of the New Right. Where this left the old Heath rump was very unclear.

At the very least, a new leader meant fresh direction for the party, along with new faces on the front bench and a new team of Central Office managers. Though the innovations have been adequately covered in other party histories, for this purpose only events pertaining to divisions and factional developments are of interest. Accordingly, the new leader's cautious strategy of attending to key front bench positions and Central Office was accompanied by the retention of certain Heath figures. In came allies like Joseph, Neave, Sir Geoffrey Howe and Norman Tebbit, but certain Heath men were either retained or recalled including Peter Walker, Reginald Maudling and Jim Prior ... to name a few. So also did other Progressives find places in Mrs Thatcher's Shadow Cabinet, most notably William Whitelaw and Norman St John-Stevas. Nevertheless, there was an overhaul of party organisation; the latter included the enforced resignation of Sara Morrison from the Vice Chairmanship, the dismissal of Michael Wolff as party Director-General, and the return – as Central Office Chairman – of Lord (Peter) Thorneycroft.

Behrens observed that Thatcher was not willing to risk divisions stemming from the exclusion of ideological opponents from the party's front bench.*(27) Moreover, it was noted by several colleagues that she skilfully cultivated relations among backbenchers sufficient for avoiding the angst of disaffected parliamentarians that had cost Heath so dearly when facing Conservative MPs.*(28) Whether it was the counsel of mentors or her own survival instincts, she trod a careful course in imposing her leadership and defining a policy programme throughout the 1974-79 Parliament in preparation for the forthcoming general election that was to bring her to government. Only in formulating and articulating policy did Thatcher effect major changes, and that process she undertook by degrees.

7.   Who were the Principal Rightist Groups?

The Conservative Right was boosted by the defeat of Edward Heath and emergence of Margaret Thatcher at the party helm in February 1975. Given Heath's antipathy towards the Right throughout his tenure, there was relief at his departure and replacement by a leader pledged to reinstate traditional Conservative beliefs. So too was there hope that under the new leader Conservatives might experience electoral recovery. Yet Thatcher's accession meant a changed role for the Right. No longer were they the 'outsider' forces of previous decades, accommodating dissenters and arch-traditionalists, but instead were recast as supportive publicists for the new leadership. Plainly the Right had become adjuncts to the Thatcher regime. This role rather compromised their independence, but the overriding priority was to support the new leader. For Monday 'Clubbers' and other free marketers of the IEA, Bow Group and CPS, Thatcher represented the best chance for policy advancement since 1945.*(29) Hence the need to assist her opening batting!

In Chapter 2, it was noted that factions and tendencies are often ideological and leader-driven. The prototype party model offered by William N. Chambers bears a partial resemblance to highly organised sections of the broad Right school like the Monday Club and, later, National Association for Freedom. Yet Ralph Nicolas' emphasis on group leadership was the one vital missing factor from the Right's organisation, since no single leader had existed until then. As was shown in the previous chapter, notwithstanding his dissenting platform, Enoch Powell was unwilling to accept any formal position on the Conservative Right, even after dismissal to the back benches in April 1968, nor during his self-imposed exile of 1970-74. Other right wing 'pretenders' had emerged over the period 1974-75 e.g. the cerebral but tactless Keith Joseph, Hugh Fraser who – as shown by his 16 votes in the leadership ballot – had scarce backbench support, and Airey Neave whose ambitions were sacrificed to Margaret Thatcher's as her campaign manager in 1975. Now, with Mrs Thatcher at the party helm, her writ ran large across the full range of Whig and nationalist organisations composing the Conservative Right.

The Rose model of ultra-disciplined factions and looser tendencies, supplemented by single cause groups, bears some resemblance to the Conservative Right in 1975. That disciplined organisations like the Monday Club and – on the outside – NAFF existed, testified to advanced organisation on the Right. Yet more common were tendencies like the Bow and Seldon Groups' and single-issue groups like the Conservative Family Campaign, Charter Movement, Tory Environmentalists, pro and anti Common Marketers and the Conservative Life Group. It was those campaigning organisations with ideology or specific cause – often both – who accounted for most right wing activists. This trait applied to various groups of the Conservative Right, whose goals, activities, members, Westminster patrons, status and ultimate impact are explored herewith.

8.   The Monday Club

The Monday Club remained a major organisation of the Conservative Right, but, as described in Chapter 4, it had become narrow and nationalistic, posturing hostility towards the Heath establishment over its final three years. With Thatcher now in charge, ironically, Monday Club influence began to wane. Its revenue which had been entirely self-generated – from a mixture of internal fund raising and large donations from sympathetic wealthy benefactors on whom the Club maintained absolute silence – began to dwindle after the party passed under rightist control. While retaining an 8,000-strong membership, complete with its compliment of parliamentary patrons and officers, the Club continued to exert public pressure on the new leadership through a series of pamphlets, conference fringe meetings and its journal, *Monday World*. Yet by October 1976 the Club had clearly passed its peak, something borne out by the following facts.

The need to support Thatcher after February 1975 restricted the Club's independence. This restriction proved critical in respect of Thatcher's conciliatory attitude towards the Heathites and caution over policy change. Monday 'Clubbers' wanted an immediate renunciation of the post-war political legacy and purges of Heath functionaries at Westminster and Central Office. No change was ever sufficient or effective for meeting their demands.*(30) Whereas Mrs Thatcher's first major policy statement of 1976 initiated a new commitment to the free market and deregulation, the Monday Club were demanding whole scale privatisation, major tax cuts, fulsome backing for Ulster Unionists and swift curbs to immigration. Put simply, however rightwards the party's direction, the Monday Club wanted to go further, much further.

Moreover, Monday Club tactics became increasingly outlandish beyond the norms of conventional campaigning. For example, aside from the concerted – and failed – attempt at forcing the de-selection of Tory Progressive, Nigel Fisher, in his Surbiton constituency, Monday Club activists fought bitter battles in the mid-late 1970s with Tory Progressives for control of the centrist-leaning Federation of Conservative Students.*(31) Their literature took an uncompromising stance against black nationalist forces in Rhodesia-Zimbabwe and in defence of the respective Smith and Afrikaner regimes of Salisbury and Pretoria, while inveighing against devolution in Scotland and Wales and Irish nationalism in Northern Ireland. It defended vigorously the House of Lords, while asserting independent British nuclear deterrents and a sovereign defence policy.*(32)

Overall, the Monday Club throughout the 1970s was a repository for right wing causes and activists. Its tactics became increasingly shrill, its reputation reactionary and its key figures gradually estranged from mainstream Conservative politics. Even in the Thatcher-led Conservative Party, the Monday Club diminished to the fringe becoming an embarrassment to the leadership, not to mention anathema to centrists and survivors of the Progressive/One Nation school.*(33) Norman Tebbit acknowledged that by 1979 the Monday Club had not so much fallen out of favour as more been rendered an irrelevance by the course of events. Yes, the party had shifted towards the Right and was back in power by May 1979, but not on the assorted nationalist and neo-imperialist causes which defined the Monday Club.*(34) Its real influence by that time was minimal, and the Club's loose associations with external rightist groups e.g. Tory Action, NAFF and fringe Ulster Unionists – showed its distance from the party mainstream.

Yet the Club retained a litany of Westminster patrons like John Biggs-Davison, Jill Knight and John Stokes; it had resources for employing three full time staff, maintaining a London office and publishing glossy pamphlets on various causes e.g. Ulster Unionism, immigration, trade union reform and Rhodesia. By 1985, the Monday Club had 18 MPs and 15 peers, though it must be added that all were backbenchers. While Tebbit's assessment of the Club as "marginal" was true, it remained an active and formidable force in Conservative politics over three decades until splitting in the early 1990s.*(35)

Aside from the shrillness of the Monday Club's political agenda and its confrontational strategy, following Heath's fall in 1975, many right wingers previously active in the Club transferred first allegiance back to the Party. The Club had served its purpose as a focus for dissenters during the Heath years, but now with Thatcher at the helm they felt more willing to serve the Conservative drive for a return to power.

9.   Anti-Common Market League

The Anti-Common Market League – surprisingly in view of later developments in Britain's relations with Europe – was not revived by Mrs Thatcher's emergence as leader. Although there remained an enduring Conservative school hostile to the European Economic Community, it was adapted to the course of events affecting Britain. For one thing, the 1975 EEC referendum settled the issue on terms preferable to both the former and new leader respectively, thereby leaving anti-EEC campaigners marooned to what then seemed like a lost cause. Second, the positive verdict of voters reflected a consensus of resignation – albeit unenthusiastic – prevalent among business people, financiers, educationalists, some trade unionists and many social institutions of that time towards the Community. Thereafter, following the 1975 referendum victory of Europhiles, former League supporters shifted over the next 15 years towards Euro-scepticism, a cause shared with British sovereignty advocates, not least Norman Tebbit, Nicholas Ridley, William Cash and Margaret Thatcher herself at Downing Street and beyond.

Generally, the League – as shown by Nigel Ashford – was a spent force by early 1975, continuing its existence but bereft of influence and increasingly reactionary.*(36) Its fringe meetings at Conservative Conferences continued until 1978, its literature was being distributed until around the same time, and its activists maintained a profile and discipline right up until the 1979 general election. In the immediate years following the referendum, anti-Brussels proponents kept their flickering cause alight under the guise of "safeguards campaigners". The League did not disappear so much as being 'mothballed', from which it never emerged. It was a monument to the raging debate within a party whose right wing had never really accepted the British Empire's wind-up nor declining British international authority that followed. Moreover, while the League exited from the political scene, its protracted conflict with Brussels remained to fashion debates and alignments within the Conservative Party over the next four decades.*(37)

When European scepticism and eventual Brexit campaigns resurfaced in the 1990s, the cause was driven initially by the Bruges group. Later that organisation was superseded by numerous campaigning organisations seeking UK withdrawal in the referendum that took place in June 2016. Those groups we shall return to examine later in the book.

10. National Association for Freedom

The National Association for Freedom was formed in December 1975. Its launch was initiated by a group centred around Norris McWhirter, whose brother Ross had earlier been murdered by the IRA. McWhirter was also involved with publishing the Guinness Book of Records. Like many such groups, NAFF had no formal affiliation to the Conservative Party, but numbered a dozen Conservative MPs as patrons and members of its National Council, plus sponsoring peers. It recruited a membership across the country, largely based on Conservative activists and supporters, and was especially strong in the Home Counties and south London.*(38) The Association shared the neo-Whig dislike of state economic authority and public sector industries, and sought curbs on taxation, trade union powers and centralised regulation. It further argued for a revival of free enterprise, and promoted the culture of entrepreneurialism. The Association asserted generally that citizens' liberties were undermined by current practices. Hence NAFF committed to abolishing workplace closed shops, limiting LEA intrusions to parents' choice of schools, council tenants right to buy their homes, abolition of compulsory students unions at universities/colleges, tax cuts, a Bill of Rights and Supreme Court in Britain.*(39)

Generally, NAFF was a vigorous anti-Communist organisation, viewing the USSR as a major threat to be met by a strong British defence policy that included the nuclear deterrent. Through its journal, *Free Nation*, NAFF's case was cogently expounded, and a series of Conference fringe meetings extended its profile. NAFF's formal independence of Conservative Central Office ensured the propagation of causes appealing to right wing Tory populists of the nationalist and free market schools who were numerous among rank and file. It strengths may be evaluated on a three-fold basis,

First was NAFF's political acceptability to Margaret Thatcher, who gave the organisation her tacit backing, even addressing a NAFF dinner in 1977. Generally, their causes were hers, and even if their tactics were confrontational, NAFF constituted a battalion in her broad army of the Right. Their combined goals were to re-instil in the Conservative Party those prime values of thrift, enterprise and defence of the nation state that had delivered it to government in times past. Second, NAFF had access to considerable resources from affluent sympathisers, enough to initiate polemical litigation throughout the 1970s and early 1980s. They assisted George Ward, proprietor of Grunwicks Reprographics, in his bitter 1977 dispute and lock-out with the clerical union, APEX. Ward further acknowledged NAFF's support throughout his dispute.*(40) It also provided legal backing to the Conservative-controlled Tameside local education authority in its dispute with the Wilson government over eleven-plus selection in 1976.

Other causes included obtaining High Court injunctions against the Post Office in 1977 over sorting officers' unwillingness to handle South African-bound mail, petitioning the European Court of Human Rights in 1979 in defence of three rail workers dismissed for refusing union membership in defiance of a closed shop agreement, sponsoring the appeal of non-union worker, Joanne Harris, in 1981 against dismissal from her municipal inspectorate also in protest against the closed shop.*(41) Indeed the Association developed a 'writ-happy' reputation that stemmed from numerous litigation threats against newspaper and journal critics across the British Isles.*(42)

Third, at a time when the Conservatives were experiencing transition, NAFF – renamed the Freedom Association in 1979 – offered an alternative vehicle for the propagation of New Right values throughout the party. Actually, NAFF of the 1970s represented a microcosm of the Thatcher-led Conservative Party of the 1980s. Thus its many battles in the courts, universities, industrial and political arenas were conducted on issues dear to the hearts of New Right idealists. Interestingly, after the second Thatcher election victory of 1983, the Freedom Association became semi-redundant, largely as a result of its role being overtaken by government. Like many right wing bodies, it was maintained by activists, funded by business donations, subscriptions and much McWhirter money.*(43) Yet without the profile, causes or prominent sponsors of earlier years, when it challenged a Labour government managing a leftist political system, it gradually lost purpose.

11.   Right wing 'Brains Trusts'

Additional to groups mentioned, there existed a growing raft of 'think tanks' dedicated to propagating the New Right cause throughout the Conservative Party. Most tended towards the Whig school, were nominally independent of the party, self-financed and relied heavily on the patronage of leading Conservative patrons. Input to the groups' various publications came mainly from sympathetic academics and policymakers, while parliamentarians also contributed to select journals and pamphlets. Some well-endowed groups like the Centre for Policy Studies had offices and a professional administrator, while others like the 1980s Libertarian Alliance ran on a small budget from members' homes in London, St Andrew's and Coventry sustained by enthusiastic volunteers.*(44)

(i) *The Centre for Policy Studies* was among the most formidable of the 'brains trusts', and certainly among the more durable. Founded in August 1974, with Sir Keith Joseph as its first Chairman, Alfred (later Sir Alfred) Sherman its Director and Margaret Thatcher its President, the primary goal was to review policy at home and abroad – observing practices in West Germany and Japan especially – with a view to preparing the party for a return to government. Yet as events gathered momentum over Autumn 1974, predictably the organisation fell under the guiding hand of the Conservative New Right.

CPS provided a residue of pamphlets that criticised trade union powers, publicly-owned industries, state welfare and high taxation, arguing instead for a culture of enterprise, low taxes, privatisation and curbs on union powers. Moreover, its position on the Right as a proponent of Thatcherism conferred an elevated status counterpoising the party Research Department (CRD) which the Right viewed with suspicion. Kavanagh said: *(45)

"The Conservative Research Department of course reflected the policy outlook of the leadership, and it was this that Sir Keith [Joseph] wished to question. Challenging established views and widening the range of free market options for a future Conservative government was, it was argued by Sir Keith's backers, best done by an organisation which had some distance from the party machine."

After Thatcher declared her hand for the leadership, she turned to CPS for support. According to Kavanagh, right wingers believed CRD to be staffed by Heath's 'One Nationites'; hence CPS as an alternative. After her accession, CPS operated as a right-wing research body, propagating free market ideals, publishing papers, staging seminars and conferences while attracting the loyalty of supporters and ire of critics within and beyond the Conservative Party. CPS adopted strident policies on education, seeking the revival of an examinations culture, while also demanding increases in technological and scientific courses in place of Arts and social sciences, such as would address the needs of the economy. Its principal role was as an ideological pressure group promoting the New Right crusade so beloved of Mrs Thatcher, Keith Joseph and fellow Whigs. Other figures associated with CPS included Sir John Hoskyns, Sir Alan Thomas, Lord Young, Lord Thomas of Swynnerton and its 1980s Director, David Willets, now a Conservative MP.

CPS finances were never transparent, nor were donors. Yet the organisation was wealthy enough to afford a full-time London office, director and supportive researchers, along with an extensive budget for publishing and promotions. So also has it stayed the course over the ensuing 43 years up to the time of writing. A likely revenue source was business, specifically anti-Socialist industry captains whose donations to Conservative funds were matched by sponsorship of an organisation campaigning to replace what they viewed as an over-taxed and over regulated British state with a private enterprise defender.*(46)

It is a moot point whether this organisation was primarily a faction or pressure group. In output, CPS aimed at fashioning a climate within the party favourable to its free market and enterprise programme. Its literature and lobbyist efforts were directed at the party leadership, it advocated the Conservative political cause, many officers were leading Conservatives – as were principal patrons, its donors were Conservative supporters and the CPS writers and researchers were of the Conservative persuasion. This made CPS an organisation of the Conservative Party, whether autonomous or independent. Yet CPS was not formally connected to the party or subject to party discipline. Moreover, it acted entirely independently throughout the late 1970s and 80s, and far beyond the scope of a ginger group. The profile included presenting evidence to select and parliamentary committees, achieving multiple publications (over 230 by 2016) in the areas of public services, industry and education, and lobbying on the Thatcher front bench from 1975 onwards. Plainly CPS thrived on Thatcher's elevation to the party helm, and acted to promote the Whig ideals with which she was so openly associated.

(ii) *The Adam Smith Institute* (ASI) was another right wing brains trust operating on the Conservative fringe after 1977. Founded in that year by two St Andrew's University academics, Dr Madsen Pirie and Dr Eamonn Butler, this organisation aimed to promote the free-market cause through research, publications and quality debate.*(47) Pirie in particular became prominent over the ensuing two decades as his organisation's profile grew among the lexicon of Conservative and non-aligned free market lobbyists.

The Institute attracted ambitious talents, including future Tory MPs like Christopher Chope, Michael Forsyth, Michael Fallon and Robert Jones. Most prominently, it proved a staunch advocate of privatisation and tax reform, with an array of pamphlets arguing for tax cuts, deregulation and privatisation of state industries and public services. Indeed the Community Charge – central to Thatcher's 1987 programme – along with school vouchers were first mooted by the Adam Smith Institute, causing it to act as an 'auditor'.

As with CPS, the Institute attracted considerable funding, covering a central London office, full-time staff, promotional events and a range of publications. The precise sources of that funding remain unclear, but one must assume its multiple contacts among Westminster Conservatives brought rewards. It enjoyed the ear of leadership, prepared briefings for frontbench spokesmen, ran meetings at Annual Conference and had privileged access to ministers.*(48) An outsider faction would never have enjoyed such influence or resources, thus putting it in the category of a free market pressure group and thus a Tory ally. Significantly, the Institute's ideological alignments with Thatcher placed it squarely in the New Right camp for which it provided ideas, policies and shock troops.

Additionally ….. there were other, smaller groups on the Conservative Right. They included the resurgent Institute of Economic Affairs (IEA) and Selsdon Group, both described in Chapter 5 and receiving fresh impetus from the Thatcher ascendancy. Such groups were important protagonists of the New Right, and lobbied party elites, parliamentarians, policy makers and external benefactors. So also did many adherents by virtue of their positions as researchers, writers, MPs, peers, commentators, etc. secure prominent press outlets which in turn led to an enhanced profile.

Throughout ensuing years, a wave of campaigning groups emerged to propagate such causes as multilateral nuclear defence, the Union, family renewal and moral revival, as well as local and national tax reform and curbing trade union powers. Whether those renewed causes fed off the ascendant New Right – as argued by Kavanagh – is a question beyond the scope of this study.*(49) Significantly, many like the anti-Marxist Western Goals Institute, Women and Families for Defence (a 1980s group headed by future Tory MP, Lady Olga Maitland) and the Coalition for Peace and Security, though nominally independent, were composed largely of Conservative supporters and activists. So also were their principal lobby efforts directed at the Conservative Party. Their spokesmen served a publicist function for the New Right; many were patronised by Conservative MPs, while others like the 1980s Conservative Family Campaign provided a quota of candidates as prospective parliamentarians.*(50)

There was also the Westminster-based Union Flag Group, established in 1975 to counter support for Scottish and Welsh devolution. While small in numbers (250), its overt unionist cause found much favour with sections of the British establishment, as well as Mrs Thatcher, who held little sympathy for Celtic nationalism, devolution or the 1973 Kilbrandon Report, which had been accepted in principle by her predecessor.

Overall, the combined New Right forces worked to cultivate a climate conducive to Mrs Thatcher's electoral victory of 1979.

12. Displaced One Nation Tories and revival of Tory Reform Group

Mrs Thatcher's accession meant changed power balances that left 'One Nationites' marooned and marginalized. Heath's defeat had put the Right on the ascendant and Tory Progressives on the decline, a factor accentuated by the demise of Heath people on the front bench and at Central Office. Alistair MacAlpine's appointment as National Treasurer, Lord Thorneycroft's return to head Central Office and the Heath supporter, Sarah Parkin's dismissal as Director of Organisation meant a thorough clear-out! As for the former leader, his sulking in Opposition and coldness towards his successor compounded the low morale of fellow Progressives. Indeed after his fall, Heath declined to play any constructive party role. Only the European cause attracted him, campaigning for a "Yes" vote in the June 1975 EEC referendum. As a result, within less than twelve months the tide of party opinion ran heavily against Heath and the Progressive legacy which over previous years he had done so much to advance.

Heath's fellow travellers dispersed in various directions. In 1975, Norman St John-Stevas shifted allegiance to the Right and served in Thatcher's Shadow Cabinet, while the un-reconstructed Reginald Maudling, Jim Prior and Ian Gilmour also accepted portfolios under the new leader. Peter Walker went to the back benches, only to be recalled later to government. Mrs Thatcher's position over 1975-79 was so precarious as to rule out a predominantly right-wing front bench – hence the proliferation of lingering Heathites.

This situation continued until she became more secure after the victory of 1983. Yet the Conservative tradition of serving the party leader enabled operatives of the former regime to remain in post even while their major policy handiwork was being dismantled by Mrs Thatcher. For the time being, this convention worked to the new leader's benefit as it gave the appearance of unity and renewed purpose. However, ultimately it showed up ex-Heath ministers as shallow compromisers and, in some cases, outright careerists whose presence in Mrs Thatcher's front bench teams only served to strengthen the Right's hand.

It was against this unpromising background that initiatives were taken to galvanise surviving elements of the Progressive Tory coalition. In July 1975, a few weeks after the European referendum, a new organisation was set up to promote the Progressive cause, Tory Reform Group (TRG). TRG was formed on the joint initiative of Peter Walker, MP and Michael Spicer, MP from a merger of three regional groups: notably the London-based Pressure for Economic and Social Toryism (PEST), the Northern Macleod Group and Home Counties-based Social Tory Action Group.*(51)

The logic of this move was brought home by the beleaguered state of the Progressive Tories in Mrs Thatcher's party – hence the need for pooling resources, mobilising manpower and coordinating policy with sympathetic MPs at Westminster. Doubtless, exclusion from the party leadership further accentuated the creation of a group with structures, policies, parliamentary patrons, grass roots campaigners and a journal. This situation follows the normal rule that ideological Conservative factions are products of schools excluded by a hostile leadership regime. The readiness of Tory Reform activists to pitch from the outside highlighted their post-Heath exile, and, not surprisingly, they re-grouped and formalised their organisation outside Parliament.

In view of the displacement of many Heathites by Mrs Thatcher, it was inevitable that the TRG would contain considerable Westminster input from former front benchers. Giles Marshall, TRG journal editor and TRG Vice-Chairman in 2004, recalled a significant cast of supportive MPs who included Willie Whitelaw, Jim Prior, Ian Gilmour, Robert Rhodes-James and Douglas Hurd.*(52) The Group also contained many sympathisers from the Federation of Conservative Students, as well as Tory Europeans and Tory trade unionists. Essentially TRG facilitated paternalistic Tories of the Whitelaw/Gilmour ilk and Progressives drawn by the appeal of Europe, enlightened capitalism and social justice within a free market system. Others were drawn to the TRG out of embarrassment at the reactionary tone of Mrs Thatcher and fellow travellers, while others still feared that a Conservative Party run by the Right would fare badly with the electorate.

There was also the issue of policy. Essentially, this meant challenging the Right's control of many familiar causes that lately had made a comeback to Conservative orthodoxy. They included race and immigration along with Conservative support for the controversial Grunwick proprietor, George Ward. Additionally, Mrs Thatcher's rejection of Scottish and Welsh devolution, and the revived rapport between her Northern Ireland Spokesman, Airey Neave, and Ulster Unionists … all contributed to the alienation of Tory Progressives. This had the effect of boosting the TRG profile within the party.*(53)

A TRG journal, *Reformer*, first appeared in June 1977, predictably, carrying a support message from Edward Heath. Perhaps less predictable was the welcoming message from Margaret Thatcher.*(54) It was edited over its first few years by Roger Hayes, assisted by an advisory panel of Conservative activists (none ever reaching Parliament), namely Jimmy Gordon, John Harben, Lindsey Addison, Neil Winton and Oliver Netherclift.*(55) Significantly, the *Reformer* offered a platform for various non-Thatcher perspectives on contemporary issues, with most writers being MPs. For example, the first issue carried reflections on devolution from Scottish Tory, Alec Buchanan-Smith, along with Peter Walker's endorsement of the TRG.*(56) The journal was published quarterly, and over time assumed an enhanced status as a focus for Tory Progressive perspectives on race and immigration, the economy, industry and labour relations, public welfare, constitutional issues, Northern Ireland, Europe, the Commonwealth and foreign affairs.

Other parliamentary contributors over the next three years included Reginald Maudling, Hugh Dykes, Robert Rhodes-James, Peter Bottomley, Tim Sainsbury, David Knox and William Van Straubenzee.*(57) Among the contributing talents drawn from outside Westminster were Gerry Wade (TRG National Chairman after 1978), Ronald Butt (*Times* political editor), Gordon McLelland (leader of the militant junior hospital doctors) and Scottish TRG activist, Helen Miller.*(58) The journal avoided an overtly hostile line towards the Thatcher regime, instead adopting an independent approach epitomised by coded critical tones. These were in such stark contrast to the shrill, right wing agenda much favoured by Mrs Thatcher and her lieutenants seeking new direction.

The Tory Reform Group operated an office from 9 Poland Street in West London. In the difficult circumstances of Mrs Thatcher's accession, it was essential for TRG to maintain a visible presence among party activists and parliamentarians if only to keep up morale among their own "faithful". Finance, according to Giles Marshall, was always in scarcity, with revenue generated internally through periodic subscriptions from supporters and occasional 'one-off' large donations.*(59) No finance was forthcoming from established social, educational or political trusts, and nor did TRG receive aid from public sources, directly or indirectly. Yet there was enough revenue to employ an administrator from 1978, while publishing many policy papers over the ensuing decade. All this indicated a reasonable budget along with not-entirely impoverished sources of revenue.

Membership was a less straightforward matter. There emerged a retinue of some 500 supporters around the country, spread among constituency associations along with the Federation of Conservative Students, Conservative Europeans, trade unionists and women.*(60) This figure ebbed and flowed at various times, with a consistent trend of support among Conservative Students in the late 1970s where there existed a distinctive coolness towards the Right.*(61) Additionally, a hard core of about 20 MPs backed TRG from within Westminster. They included the MPs previously mentioned, while others lent support, e.g. Malcolm Rifkind, Michael Heseltine, William Van Strubenzie and William Waldegrave. Interestingly, Edward Heath's own backing was spasmodic; after his fall in 1975 Heath's willingness to support Progressive causes waxed and waned.*(62)

Giles Marshall recalled that TRG did not encourage local groups or anything smacking of "… a party within a party". Nor was a hostile line encouraged in constituencies where there was a rightist MP or parliamentary candidate.*(63) Instead activists were more keen to argue ideals on issues like taxation, labour relations, the economy, Europe and constitution. Those themes were reflected in the Group journal and policy pamphlets, as well as being reiterated at the various TRG conference fringe meetings.

After Mrs Thatcher's election victory in May 1979, TRG gradually drifted towards the margins. Although consistently sponsoring the Progressive cause through the 'highs' and 'lows' of the Thatcher years, it became increasingly estranged from the party mainstream and was constantly cast – by critics and pundits alike – as a monument to the Heath era. Yet somehow TRG and its One Nation cause have managed to survive the last 40 years, and as will be shown later, during the Cameron era underwent a transformation.

13. Conclusions

Many contemporary historians like Dennis Kavanagh view Mrs Thatcher's accession to the Conservative leadership in February 1975 as a seminal event ending 'Consensus' politics and ushering in the era of the New Right. The latter is especially synonymous with a culture of free markets, deregulation, lower taxes, reduced public spending, legal curbs on trade unions and renewal of British/American special relations. Given that Kavanagh's view is sustainable, the inevitable prelude to wider change in the country would have been a transmutation of the Conservative Party, as indeed happened over 1974/75. The latter set of events allowed Seyd to view the Conservative leadership as responsive to grass roots politics, more so than was earlier acknowledged by learned observers like R.T. Mackenzie writing over 40 years ago.*(64)

The failures of the Heath government meant final death for an already-faltering post-war Settlement, with the ensuing right-wing rebellion that forced his exit. In turn, this meant organisations of the Right undergoing rehabilitation in Mrs Thatcher's party. The likes of the Monday Club, NAFF, Centre for Policy Studies and others similar achieved a level of tolerance, if not endorsement, unforeseeable five years earlier. Those groups were publicists for the new Thatcher regime, symbolising her direction, promoting her cause and hooked to her star. Yet it is significant that because leadership ballots were restricted to Conservative MPs alone, none of those groups were in any position to directly shape February 1975 contest. All they could do was to lobby and HELP fashion a climate conducive to Heath's removal in favour of a rival from the Right. In Mrs Thatcher, the Right had found a champion, and one to whom they were stoutly pledged.

Publication of her first policy document, *The Right Approach* (1976), pledging to "... roll back the frontiers of the state ..." served notice of things to come. This programme highlighted the growing confidence of Thatcherites who were then gradually stamping their imprimatur on the party at all levels: organisational, ideological and policy wise. Yet Thatcher's cautious approach to front bench appointments and policy changes represented the prudent exercise of party management, not to mention political discretion.

It is also noteworthy that no sooner had Mrs Thatcher attained the party leadership than several lobby organisations went into slow decline. Although party factions generally – as Rose observed – experienced limited lifetimes, in this instance those right wing groups had served their role in agitating against Edward Heath's leadership. Thereafter their raison d'être changed to become publicists of the New Right, and in that respect some etched out a more successful existence than others. In any case, though fulfilling a lobbyist role, actually several in fact operated as outside pressure groups with independent structure, membership, specific policy goals and funding sources.

While it is possible to view the Monday Club and Centre for Policy Studies as essentially pressure groups, noting that most have as their de facto aim winning over the Tory Party, and with the bulk of activists being card-carrying Conservatives, clearly they were policy campaigners. While precise boundaries between pressure groups and party factions are not clearly defined, the primary purpose of those bodies was to win the Conservatives to their various causes. Moreover, some groups proved sufficiently effective to defy Conservative traditions of deference and compliance in order to market their agenda.

As for the defeated and displaced Heathites, their 'opposition' role meant a more meaningful existence through the revamped Tory Reform Group. Utilising the latter and freed from front bench duties, they were able to mount an independent profile in the Thatcher-led party. Yet the Conservatives were moving in a free market direction, something highlighted by successive Daily Telegraph editorials and Bow pamphlets after 1976.*(65) By May 1979, the scene was set for Mrs Thatcher's entry to Downing Street, an event holding major ramifications for the future direction of British Conservatives particularly and the British nation more generally.

FOOTNOTES and REFERENCES

1. Norton in P. Norton eds. (1996), Chap. 9, pp. 144-146.

2. See (i) M. Thatcher <u>The Path to Power</u> (1995), Chap. viii, p. 267.

    (ii) Norman Tebbit <u>Upwardly Mobile</u> (1988), Chap. 7, pp. 140-142.

    Also, interview Rt. Hon. Lord Tebbit/V. McKee, 9th July, 2001.

    (iii) Martin Burch in Z. Layton-Henry eds. (1980), Chap. 7, pp. 166-179.

3. Examples - Peter Temple-Morris and Michael Heseltine (earlier documented).

4. The election of October 1974 saw the Liberals gain 19% of the British vote, the SNP gain 31% of the Scottish vote, Plaid Cymru gain 10% of the Welsh vote and both major parties score a combined tally of under 72% of the total British vote..

5. (i) Kavanagh (1987), Chap. 4, pp. 107-111.

    (ii) Charmley (1998), Chap. 10, pp. 194-200.

    (iii) Blake (1985), Chap. x, pp. 322-325

6. See Barr - Draft of Bow Group history, Chap. 5, pp. 122-128.

7. Kavanagh (1987), Chap. 4.

8. See Heath autobiography (1998), Chap. 18, pp. 520-522.

9. Rhodes Boyson eds. <u>1985; An Escape from Orwell's 1984: A Conservative Path to Freedom</u> (Churchill Press, 1975).

10. See V. McKee - 'Conservative Factions', Contemporary Record, Vol. 3, 1, 1989.

11. I. Gilmour and M. Seddon <u>Whatever happened to the Tories?</u> (1997).

12. Behrens (1980) - Chap. 2.

13. Ibid.

14. See a range of Daily Telgraph editorials throughout January and February 1975, all lending weight to the free market and deregulation policies of the New Right.

15. See contributions by Patrick Cosgrave, Robert Moss and T.E. Utley to Rhodes Boyson eds. 1985 (1975). Also, McKee in Contemporary Record (1989).

16. McKee Contemporary Record (1989). Also, see P. Seyd, "The Monday Club', Government and Opposition (1972).

17. Ibid.

18. Interviews - Peter Temple-Morris, Lord Tebbit, Justin Powell-Tuck.

19. See Seyd - Chap. 10 on Conservative Factionalism in Layton-Henry eds. (1980).

20. John Barnes 'Ideology and Factions', Chap. 8 in Anthony Deldon & Stuart Ball (eds.) Conservative Century; The Conservative Party since 1900 (OUP, 1994).

21. Behrens (1980), Chap. 3, p.p. 37-41.

22. Behrens, Chap. 2, p.p. 8-12.

23. Interviews - V. McKee with Lord Tebbit and Peter Temple-Morris. Also, see Behrens, Chap. 2; Clark, Chap. 30; Ramsden, Chap. 15; Charmley, Chap. 10.

24. Rose - Political Studies (1964).

25. A view confirmed in the author's interviews with Lord Tebbit, John Townend, Mrs Teresa Gorman and Mrs Eila Bannister (a Monday Club activist):- all right wing protagonists of the period.

26. Ibid.

27. Behrens - Chap. 4, pp. 46 & 47, 62 & 63.

28. Author's interviews - Tebbit, Gorman and Temple-Morris.

29. Ibid. - Also, see a selection of literature from Monday World, Free World and the full range of rightist policy pamphlets of

the time, all supportive of Mrs Thatcher in expectation of major policy changes.

30. See Monday World, all issues 1978 & 1979. These addressed such issues as race and immigration, law and order, trade unions, the economy, Northern Ireland, Rhodesia and South Africa - all from a fundamentalist right wing perspective.

    Also, see 'Our Aims', Monday Club Statement of Aims, published 1976.

31. See Seyd - Government and Opposition (1972).

32. See Monday Club Statement of Aims (1976). Also, see John Stokes pamphlet, published by Monday Club, defending House of Lords against reform, 1979.

33. Lord Tebbit tacitly acknowledged that the Monday Club lacked major influence with the 1975-79 Thatcher front bench; - re. interview with V. McKee. Others from the centre expressed varying degrees of hostility towards the Club for their divisive activities of the period, notably Giles Marshall (Editor - Tory Reformer), Peter Temple-Morris, MP and Stephen Dorrell, MP - re. interviews with author.

34. In the early 1990s, the Monday Club experienced internal divisions partly of a strategic nature and partly due to personal rivalries, later splitting into three separate factions, none of whom achieved much profile. - Re. Discussions with Mrs Eila Bannister, 23rd October 1993 and 3rd January 1998.

35. Nigel Ashford's unpublished Ph.D. thesis (1983) - Chap. 4, pp. 177-179, and Chap. 5, pp. 241-250.

36. Ashford (1983), Chap. 5, pp. 243-250.

37. The author encountered little co-operation from officers of the Freedom Association (formerly National Association for Freedom) when conducting research. Information on membership and group structure was provided on a confidential basis by a middle ranking Association official; interview 9th October, 1998. This evidence squares with the Association's

activities which have been principally forthcoming from a base in the south of England.

38. Correspondence from Gerald Hartup of the Freedom Association, May 1984.

39. The NAFF/Freedom Association journal, Free Nation, in general proved to be a vociferous supporter of the Thatcher front bench throughout the late 1970s.

40. Interview George Ward/V. McKee, 3rd February, 2003. - Ward insisted that the Freedom Association's actual level of aid had been minimal.

See George Ward - Fort Grunwick, Chaps 10, 11 & 12 (Maurice Temple, 1977).

41. Information provided to the author by an unnamed Freedom Association officer, interview 9th October, 1998. - Also, see Kavanagh (1987), Chap. 3, pp. 93 & 94.

42. The author was among many 'candidates' threatened with a civil suit by the Freedom Association in respect of his article published in the Belfast-based Irish News, April 1984. That article mentioned the Freedom Association as a major lobby group on the Conservative Right. - No backtracking occurred at the paper and no civil action ever manifested from the complainants.

43. Interview unnamed Freedom Association officer, 9th October 1998. He confirmed that the Association had long ceased to focus its activities on the Tory Party, but had adopted a broader role as a free enterprise campaigning group.

44. Discussions- Mr Bernard Capel, former Coventry Conservative activist in 1980s, 29th October, 1999 and Mr Gordon Whiting, MBE (deceased), late Coventry Area Conservative full-time Agent/Secretary, 23rd October, 1983.

45. Kavanagh (1987), Chap. 3, p. 89.

46. Ibid.

47. Kavanagh (1987), Chap. 3, p. 87.

48. See Kavanagh (1987), Chap. 3, p. 89-91. - The CPS influence was also the subject of much comment in the press over the period 1975-79.

49. Kavanagh (1987), Chaps 3 & 4.

50. See V. McKee - 'Factions and Tendencies in the Conservative Party since 1945', Politics Review (Vol. 5, No. 4, April 1996).

51. Interviews with Giles Marshall and Justin Powell-Tuck.

52. Interviews - with Giles Marshall and Rt. Hon. Stephen Dorrell, MP. Also, this same information is contained Issue 1, Tory Reformer, June 1977.

53. Interviews - Giles Marshall and Stephen Dorrell.

54. Ibid.

55. Tory Reformer, p.1, Issue 1 (June 1977).

56. See Tory Reformer; issues 1 (Autumn 1977), 3 (Winter 1978), 4 (Spring 1978), 6 (Autumn 1978) and 7 (Winter 1978/79).

57. Ibid.

58. Interview - author with Giles Marshall.

59. Information provided in interviews with Giles Marshall and Stephen Dorrell.

60. (i) Information provided by Giles Marshall and Stephen Dorrell. Both were adamant that although a majority of TRG supporters were pro-Europeans, still this issue was definitely not an article of faith!

    (ii) Newsletter of the Federation of Conservative Students, Autumn 1978.

    (iii) Freshers Newsletter, Conservative Students Society (F.C.S.- affiliated), Coventry - Lanchester - Polytechnic (now called Coventry University), October 1978. This document carried a brief solidarity message from Edward Heath.

61. Interview with Giles Marshall.

62. Interviews with Giles Marshall and Justin Powell-Tuck.

63. Interview with Giles Marshall.

64. (i) R.T. McKenzie British Political Parties (second ed., 1963), Part 1, Chaps. ii & iii.

   (ii) Patrick Seyd - Chap. 10, pp. 231-234, in Zig Layton-Henry, eds. Conservative Party Politics (1980).

65. For detailed analysis, see Behrens (1980), and Barr's Bow Group history (1999).

CHAPTER 7

MRS THATCHER'S PARTY PROPER 1979 - 90

This chapter will examine and evaluate the character of Conservative ideological divisions and factional politics during Mrs Thatcher's premiership.

It will seek to establish how right wing political causes constituted the new orthodoxy and the degree to which right wingers manned a Thatcher-led party establishment that differed greatly from the previous three/four post-war decades. The profile and impact of right wing groups operating during those years merits special examination, as will their impact on fashioning the Conservative policy agenda. In particular, a distinction will be made between those rightist groups acting as ".. *government publicists* .." and those who operated as ".. *ideological radicals* .." promoting popular capitalism.

The dilemma of displaced Tory Progressives and other erstwhile supporters of the previous regime will also merit examination. Their adjustment from establishment advocates to opposition dissidents followed a painful and uncertain course, while this school was also riveted by the different strategies followed by diverse tendencies. Ironically, the Progressives were actually strengthened in group organisation during the Thatcher years, while paradoxically certain right wing groups went into decline. Those factors, plus the role of leadership, will form the basis for this inquiry.

1. Introduction

By May 1979, Mrs Thatcher was in Downing Street as Britain's first woman premier at the head of a rightist Conservative government. In June 1983, she won a second term, and four years later a third mandate. Yet by 22nd November 1990, after eleven years and seven months at the helm, it was all over. A poll of Tory MPs had denied Thatcher the necessary majority to continue, thus bringing down the curtain on, arguably, the most dynamic of Conservative post-war governments.

The key question was whether and in what form the so-called "Thatcher revolution" would survive? Was it a period of untrammelled nationalist renewal, accompanied by major deregulation of the British economy and society, such as re-fashioned the long term parameters of government? That was the view of academics like Kavanagh, Charmley and Blake, plus media commentators of the time, Peter Jenkins and Hugo Young.*(1) Yet other voices, like Ian Gilmour, wondered if Thatcherism had been an aberration whose real significance lay with having halted Conservative electoral decline rather than achieving a lasting transformation of public policy?

The Thatcher legacy is best debated elsewhere. What concerns this inquiry is the effect of Thatcherism on policy debates, ideological alignments and factional politics within the party. In particular, it is worth noting the impact of Thatcherism on various groups of the Conservative Right. That Mrs Thatcher dominated her party throughout the fifteen years and nine months of her leadership, especially during the Downing Street years, is well known. What is less well understood is how rightist groups fared over this period of hegemony. That several rightist groups actually emerged from the period weakened seems paradoxical. Equally ironic was the reality of the displaced Tory Progressives being forced into a modernising realignment that left their group structures – if not grass roots appeal – strengthened by the experience of prolonged exclusion and adversity. Such is the nature of internal Tory politics.

Another consideration is the extent to which factional alignments impacted on the 1990 Conservative leadership contest. There was certainly a factional input to issues aired in that seminal event, but impending evidence suggests factional politicking to have had scant effect on the outcome. Choosing a leader then was the exclusive prerogative of Conservative MPs, and they exercised autonomous choices. Yet it is significant that the battle of ideals preceding the ballot was of serious magnitude, and in that area rival group spokesmen each made their mark.

2. Impact of Thatcher

The impact of Margaret Thatcher on factionalism and alignments within her Conservative Party needs proper analysis. Such an evaluation must take account of Mrs Thatcher's programme, style, lieutenants and policy strategists. All those facts say much about the lady, while further enabling conclusions to be drawn about the nature of factional politics during her leadership term.

(i) *Mrs Thatcher's leadership*:- Under Mrs Thatcher, the party's shift to the right was marked by the adoption of distinctive causes, priorities and a personal style that contrasted sharply with what had gone before. Not only did she impact profoundly on her party, but so also did her agenda define Conservatives over nearly two decades, something variously acknowledged by biographers and historians.*(2) Yet Mrs Thatcher's Conservative Party was no place for dissidents or even the lukewarm. Plainly, she was a woman with a mission, who proved ruthless in harnessing her party in Parliament and beyond towards following her goals.

As already discussed, Mrs Thatcher's agenda coupled New Whig economics with revived nationalism. Her programme prioritised the free market and deregulation, which included a full scale assault on state-run enterprises, trade union power and high taxation.*(3) Additionally, she reasserted British sovereignty in Europe and world affairs while renewing the British/American alliance; the latter being specially valued for its effective counter to Soviet-led Communism.*(4) Hers was a very ideological ethos that relied less on tradition and what Philip Norton called the culture of "statecraft", and more on a specific programme for government.*(5) Thatcherism – as Dennis Kavanagh observed – was synonymous with a set of beliefs, whose very existence in Tory quarters was adjudged by some, mainly Paternalist grandees, as running contrary to the party's traditions and empirical wisdom.*(6)

Mrs Thatcher's trenchant style as prime minister – a trait more marked after 1983 – represented aggressive dogmatism, and eventually counted against her remaining in office.*(7) Yet until then the same trait had boosted her authority. Indeed in the halcyon days of electoral success, her "conviction-centred leadership" had been cited as being among her assets, but by 1989/90 this emerged as a depreciating asset. Subsequent events were driven by a fear among many Conservative MPs that their three-times election winner had become a liability. Thus followed an unseemly scramble to find a replacement; something conducted with an air of desperation. This told a clear truth about the Conservative Party and its obsession with holding office at all costs. Sentiment played second fiddle to the priority of power!

(ii) *Thatcher Establishment*:- It is noteworthy that the Thatcher manifesto for government was vigorously promoted by a close-knit fellowship of ideological disciples. They included mentors like Keith Joseph, Airey Neave and Ian Gow, 'young Turks' like the cerebral Michael Forsythe and such proponents then outside Westminster as David Willets (Centre for Policy Studies) and Dr Madsen Pirie (Adam Smith Institute). There were also fellow parliamentarians like Nicholas Ridley, Cecil Parkinson and Norman Tebbit, all of whom held office under her. Those 'Thatcher lieutenants' proved crucial to the effective propagation of Thatcherism throughout the period, and by their positions and influence ensured the prevalence of a Thatcher establishment.

It is significant that many official organisations of the party, as well as informal groups, were headed or at least patronised by people from the Thatcher circle. Keith Joseph's Centre for Policy Studies gained in stature as a source of policy initiation, especially after the disbandment of the Conservative Research Department. For a while, so did the Freedom Association, while the Bow Group also moved to the Right.

Central Office also recruited right wingers to its research and organisational departments, mostly dedicated New Whigs and/or career-minded Tories who opted to work with the Thatcher regime. Moreover, placing ideological soul mates like Cecil Parkinson, John Selwyn-Gummer and Norman Tebbit at the head of Conservative Central Office throughout the 1980s, Mrs Thatcher ensured that the new orthodoxy was pursued at all levels of the party. This meant a plethora of policy papers emerging throughout the 1980s stamped with the New Right imprimatur. It also ensured the parliamentary candidates' panel being weighted to the Right, leading to the selection of pro-Thatcher figures by a majority of constituency associations in winnable seats.

An example of the Thatcher grip on the party occurred in the case of Conservative Charter Group leader, Eric Chalker (a One Nation Tory), who had long campaigned for European integration and democratic reforms within the party.*(8) He was refused elevation to the Westminster candidates panel in the mid-1980s due to differences with the Thatcher leadership. Norman Tebbit – then party chairman – candidly acknowledged to the author that the exclusion resulted from Chalker's history of dissent.*(9) A growing number of such cases were aired in the 1980s by Tory Progressives and Europhiles, indicating that centralisation of the Conservative Party effectively minimised figures from outside the Thatcher fold. Significantly, this authoritarian trait had the effect of revitalising the revived Tory Reform Group.*(10)

Nor were ironies limited to Heath people. Interestingly, Central Office under the leadership of Norman Tebbit, was forced to exert control over right wing groups whose activities had a destabilising effect on certain constituency associations and ancillary organisations. Actually, most such groups involved were broadly pro-Thatcher in alignment, but were on the party margins rather than mainstream, and projected an image of aggressive dogmatism that got prominent coverage reported in broadsheet newspapers, plus BBC news.*(11) Examples included the ultra-Whig Libertarian Alliance, who were mainly youth and student-led, but whose activities caused disturbance within some associations, e.g. Coventry South East and Coventry South West, Leamington, Stirling and St Andrews.*(12) This group was organised at the universities of Warwick and St Andrews, and contributed to an ongoing fracas in the Federation of Conservative Students, whose rowdy 1985 Loughborough Conference led to Tebbit disbanding the organisation.*(13) The Freedom Association also operated an intense lobby which demonised party centrists, while the Monday Club strayed ever further to the right during the Thatcher era to the point that its appeal was restricted to a shrill group of hard line activists with much volume but minimal influence.*(14) Such were the dynamics of alliances conjured by the New Right for exerting dominance of the Conservative Party during those years.

Whatever his rightist leanings, as Tory Chairman, Norman Tebbit felt a duty to deal firmly with internal groups who damaged his party's image. He made clear to this author an unwillingness to see Toryism discredited by the aggressive tactics of student fanatics. Hence came Tebbit's crackdown on the hard Right over 1985/86!*(15)

(iii) *Why was Thatcherism acceptable to the Conservatives?* Margaret Thatcher's domination of her party for 16 years, was largely due to electoral success. Conservatives, after all, demand victory at the polls as the gauge by which a leader is measured, and under Mrs Thatcher the electoral slide was reversed. From losing three out of four elections 1965-74, Conservatives proceeded to win three consecutive general elections (1979, 1983 and 1987) with her at the helm. This record strengthened her hand over policy-making and personnel appointments at all levels of the party and government to the point of near-absolute authority. Only in 1989/90 when electoral prospects looked less promising did that hegemony come to an end, along with Mrs Thatcher's leadership. As will later be shown, lobbyist groups helped fashion the climate leading up to the event, but played no direct part in determining the MPs poll result that displaced Mrs Thatcher or affected the choice of successor.

Over the previous dozen years as a result of electoral resurgence, Conservative morale was greatly revived. Notwithstanding the scepticism of many figures from the ".. old establishment", Thatcher's new ideological direction had restored the party to government, and in the process demolished previous political orthodoxy based on trade union power, high taxation and a large public sector, all anathema to the Tories. The party was now back in power and dictating a new free market agenda based on popular capitalism and a revived nation state. While there remained much scope for debate between right and centrist wings, crucially the Conservatives by 1983 had become a party of office who would not be easily shifted by a divided opposition. For that delivery Thatcher was lauded by her fellows. Moreover, the same success made her contentious New Whig programme palatable to a majority of party colleagues.

One clear sign of how far Conservative morale had been revived was the immense confidence displayed by various right wing groups throughout 1987-90. In particular, there was the heady tone adopted after the 1987 election victory by certain Whig 'think-tanks' like CPS and the Adam Smith Institute, along with the Libertarian Alliance, all of whom actively propagated rightist causes like the poll tax and school vouchers. Equally significant were the tenth anniversary celebrations of Mrs Thatcher's premiership. That occasion involved a triumphal spectacle among vocal, flag-waving Young Conservatives, whose attachment to her free market and nationalist beliefs appeared close to fanatical. Generally, the Conservative Right showed an appetite for confrontation at a time when some academics considered Socialists and Liberals to be in long term decline.*(16) In fact such misplaced notions were to ultimately rebound on Mrs Thatcher and her party within 18 months.

3. Conservative Right

Perhaps the biggest change for the Conservative Right after Margaret Thatcher's accession to the leadership was the manner in which its standing altered. From being an erstwhile refuge for dissenters and traditionalist cranks under previous leaders, rightist groups overnight became adjuncts to the new Thatcher establishment. So too were they assumed to be proponents of its radical orthodoxy. The days of continual opposition to leadership and expounding an "extreme" policy agenda were over.

After February 1975 the Conservative Right was associated with the leadership, and thus their activists in the Monday Club, Freedom Association, '92 Committee', Centre for Policy Studies and others had to act with regard for the success of their patroness and her front bench team. When the party returned to government in the election of May 1979, the need for caution was even greater. Yet that did not inhibit a full-blooded campaign for the adoption of free market and nationalist policies by groups on the inside, while seeking their acceptance among voters on the outside.

Essentially, the Right divided into two broad camps during the Thatcher years. One camp acted as *defenders* of the Thatcher crusade, while the other exercised the role of ongoing *ideological revolutionaries*. Groups in the former category proved to be pro- government publicists, and viewed their role as promoting the government's cause to party and public. They were not willing to embarrass the government by making radical demands through the Conservative Conference, pamphlets or other platforms, and were positive about government achievements through media and their literature. As for the ideological revolutionaries, though supporting the Thatcher government, this was conditional on its advocacy of their aims. In the main, they did not hesitate to criticise if there were shortfalls in government policymaking. Generally, 'outsider' groups fared rather less successfully during the Thatcher years, and like the Monday Club and Bruges Group were later forced to either wind up or realign.

(i) *Thatcher Defenders*:- There were several groups in this category, many of them being 'think-tanks' who had previously postulated a New Whig economic programme. They included the Centre for Policy Studies (CPS), Adam Smith Institute (ASI), Selsdon Group and Institute for Economic Affairs (IEA). To the latter may be added the Bruges Group and No Turning Back Group (NTBG), the latter chaired by John Redwood. All had campaigning records, and from their ranks were drawn some of Mrs Thatcher's most influential allies at all levels of the party. It is significant that several Thatcher 'defenders' had either been spawned or resuscitated by the New Right's rebellion against Edward Heath, with examples including CPS, ASI and the Selsdon Group.

They produced policy papers and commented on government plans, while running meetings and conferences to enable ministers to meet with policy specialists from the groups. These organisations were patronised by parliamentarians and ministers, and had Mrs Thatcher's ear from the beginning.*(17) Indeed it was a measure of their influence that the Adam Smith Institute and Centre for Policy Studies sponsored key policies like privatisation, school vouchers and the poll tax. So also did many leading figures from those groups proceed to Parliament and the party front bench, like David Willets (CPS) and Michael Forsythe (Adam Smith Institute).

At the same time, support from those 'think-tanks' lent respectability to the 'Thatcher revolution'. The leader was sustained by a creditable body of economists, policy specialists and philosophers, all helping to define her direction while offering mentors on whom she could rely when challenged by critics. Those groups also provided a body of 'Young Turks' promoting Mrs Thatcher's crusade in the universities, press, boardrooms and other centres across the country whose persistence was matched by pugnacity. Yet it was to those zealots – numerous among Young Conservatives – that Mrs Thatcher turned when her support declined elsewhere after 1989.

The Thatcher zealots maintained a degree of common purpose. It was clear that their prominence would only last while Margaret Thatcher remained Prime Minister. She committed to the same programme as they propagated, but hers was a contentious profile, and while breaking with the old post-war settlement, no new policy consensus had emerged in its place. Accordingly, a high likelihood existed of Mrs Thatcher's demise spelling concomitant decline in the influence of her allies. Thus the strong resistance that groups like CPS and Adam Smith mounted in her defence was driven by necessity, though ultimately it failed to ensure her survival at the party helm.

In organisation, the groups had minimal corporate structures, a specialised graduate membership, usually a paid director and budgets variously generated by donations from business and professional patrons, membership subscriptions, literature sales and grants from sympathetic trusts.*(18) The groups measured their success by the impact of their pamphlets, as well as support given by party establishment figures. Besides, in Mrs Thatcher's party, there was a special welcome for the litany of free market 'think tanks' campaigning in the party. In the late1980s, Thatcher came to rely on those groups for ideas and battle troops as her judgement and leadership came under critical scrutiny both from within and beyond the Conservative Party.*(19)

(ii) *Whig and Nationalist ideologues*:- The other category of rightist groups proved no less committed to the New Right programme, but showed a primary concern with ideology rather than Mrs Thatcher's regime. Significantly, many of those ideological groups had been around for some time prior to the New Right's emergence, while others peaked during the Thatcher era. In any case, they proved obdurate campaigners regardless of the shifting fortunes of Thatcher, and, significantly, their aims transcended her premiership.

They included such nationalist organisations as the Freedom Association, Monday Club, Western Goals Institute, Olga Maitland's Women and Families for Defence, the Anglo-South African and Anglo-Rhodesian Friendship Societies, various Euro-sceptic lobbyist groups, along with the ultra-Whig Libertarian Alliance and the Conservative Family Campaign. Other names included the Bow Group and '92 Committee', both of whom experienced lengthy tenures before and beyond the Thatcher era.*(20) With the Bow Group, its pronouncements and policy papers assumed an increasing free-market tone after 1975, while the '92 Committee' under George Gardiner had a lengthy track record of asserting the Right's cause in the party at Westminster.*(21) The '92 Committee' and No Turning Back Group (Founded in 1985) were dominated by Tory MPs, but also provided a platform and facilities for ambitious lobbyists and policy analysts. Moreover, there existed an overlap between members of the two groups.

Elsewhere existed the Ulster Unionists' London lobbyist group, Friends of the Union. It was established in the late 1980s in order to propagate the Unionist cause after the failure of disruption tactics in protest against the 1985 Anglo Irish Agreement. In reality, Ulster Unionists, despite their formal break with the Conservatives in 1973 (over Heath's abolition of Stormont), had kept open contact channels with former allies at Westminster, tending towards the Right in sympathies and supporters.*(22) The platforms of rightist groups like the Monday Club and '92 Committee' facilitated that process, while the Unionists' own 'Friends' lobbyist body ensured a continuation of contacts between the two parties.*(23) At the same time, it was Margaret Thatcher whose desire for a settlement in Northern Ireland had led to the historic accord with Garret Fitzgerald's Fine Gael/Labour coalition in Dublin – much to the pleasure of moderate SDLP nationalists – that so alienated Unionists.*(24) Yet Belfast Unionists provided a critical partner to the Conservative right wing alliance that supported Margaret Thatcher throughout her Downing Street years, albeit one that steadfastly opposed her prime policy centred on the Hillsborough agreement.

Patrons of the Right were many and varied. Senior parliamentarians like Keith Joseph and Norman Tebbit lent instant weight to their organisations, but others like George Gardiner, Ronald Bell, Jill Knight (all 92 Committee) and John Biggs-Davison (Monday Club and 92 Committee) and Julian Amery (Anglo-South African and Anglo-Rhodesian Friendship societies) operated on the fringes of the Conservative Right.*(25) The same was true of 1980/90s figures like Teresa Gorman and Bill Cash (European Foundation) and Dr Adrian Rodgers, Ann and Nicholas Winterton of the Conservative Family Campaign. Like other bodies, the ideological rightist groups were self-financed by donations from supporters, as well as literature sales, grants from sympathetic trusts and contributions from patrons in the business world.*(26)

Overall, this category of Conservative groups produced incessant campaigners and publicists who opened ranks to Conservative grass roots and middle management activists. These ideologues proved to be constant advocates, but their shrill tactics forced them to operate from the outside. They lacked the 'insider' connections of Thatcher defenders, and though enjoying the ear of Mrs Thatcher and soul mates such as Tebbit, Ridley, Baker and Joseph – who spoke on their conference platforms – actually their real impact was minimal. Examples include the Monday Club and Freedom Association, both of whom went into decline and irrelevance during Mrs Thatcher's Downing Street years.*(27) Yet those groups articulated different causes to the Conservative grass roots, and their profile enabled a longevity of existence that rather exceeded any useful purpose. Also, influence was decidedly marginal.

It must be added that the ideological Right included groups whose formal aims were neither nationalist nor free market, but concerned with other issues like defence and social questions. Examples included Olga Maitland's nominally independent Women and Families for Defence and Disarmament, Coalition for Peace and Security and the Conservative Family Campaign. There was also the Conservative Life Campaign, sponsored by parliamentarians like Norman St John Stevas, Nicholas and Ann Winterton, David Amos and Jill (now Baroness) Knight, but closely directed by the National Life Organisation from its head office in Leamington Spa, Warwickshire. Inquiries by this author showed a majority of leading members of all four organisations – and others similar – identifying with the Conservative Right and supporting the leadership of Margaret Thatcher.*(28) Indeed it was the emergence of Mrs Thatcher with her right wing programme that spawned a reawakening among so many fellow Conservatives of the broad Right ilk.*(29)

(iii) *Moral Campaigners*:- Significantly, members of Mrs Thatcher's front bench openly lauded the aims of social conservatives, as for example with Keith Joseph's endorsement of the 1960/70s anti-pornography campaigner, Mrs Mary Whitehouse. There were also the determined campaigns against pornography, abortion and homosexuality waged by Nicholas Winterton, Jill Knight – both ardent Thatcher allies – and other right wingers. Aside from general sympathy on the Right at that time for a revival of family and Christian causes, many moral campaigners shared the Right's devotion to the free market and national revival, and to that extent were compatible fellow travellers.

Significantly, Kavanagh's view of pro-life, anti-pornography and anti-libertarian moral campaigners as fellow travellers in a broad New Right alliance looks questionable.*(30) It overlooks the fact that moral revivalism enjoyed a wider appeal than the Conservative Party which extended to supporters – and some MPs – of the Labour and Liberal parties, as well as Celtic nationalists. Indeed the cross-party membership of organisations like the Society for the Protection of Unborn Children, Life and the National Viewers and Listeners Association suggested there to be a fair cross-section of working class and middle class personnel, with the predominant strain being active Catholicism, especially in the pro-life movement. This input of active Catholicism to Conservative politics was noted – though, regrettably, not fully developed – by Dennis Sewell in his recent treatise on British Catholicism*(31), a publication on which this author made a considered commentary.*(32)

Paradoxically, according to Tim Bale, the various liberal reforms initiated by Conservative governments of the 1950s and 60s set a definite phase in place.*(33) These included the 1960 Betting and Gaming Act that licensed gambling shops, the introduction of commercial TV (ITV, 1954), creation of Premium Bonds (1964), establishment of the Wolfenden Committee to explore the prospects of legalising homosexuality, the 1957 Homicide Act that restricted hanging to specified murder kinds along with Butler's other penal reforms, and general phasing out of theatre and literary censorship, all of which combined to lay foundations of the Permissive Society against which a later Tory generation so objected.*(34) This view was also prominently articulated by Mark Jarvis in his recent study of Conservative governments of that same period and moral changes in British society.*(35)

It was only in the 1980s that there emerged a more secularised rightist tendency – which was either uninterested or hostile to family and pro-life causes – symbolised by Teresa Gorman and grass roots activists of the

Libertarian Alliance. Their goals were a sovereign British nation state and untrammelled free market, and did not include the Christian fundamentalism programme on which America's Moral Majority coalition actively promoted Ronald Reagan's 1980 election to the White House.*(36) Needless to add, Christian moral campaigners got seriously alienated by David Cameron's Same-Sex Marriages Act of 2014 that followed some three decades later.

Yet Thatcher's appeal to the nascent British Christian Right had clear rationale, as outlined by Rob Behrens.*(37) Her agenda targeted the "permissive society" as symbolic of a failed socialist era, where the state had abrogated support for family and discipline, allowing hedonism, amoral relativism and sheer irresponsibility to supplant the Judo-Christian social order. It was a trend, she maintained, needing swiftly reversal in order to facilitate a revival of Victorian values of family, self-reliance and thrift – rooted in Christian thinking – so beloved of her political vision. This clarion call though vague, nevertheless evoked much sympathy among pro-lifers, family campaigners and Conservative educationalists like Dr Rhodes-Boyson worried at the permeation of decadent influences in British society.*(38) It also generated much support for the Conservative Life Campaign and the Conservative Christian Fellowship, both of which, predictably, experienced membership overlap.

The Tory pro-lifers were funded by the Leamington-based organisation, Life, but run by Conservative pro-life campaigners. They targeted Tory MPs and the party leadership, and were patronised – among others – by Norman St John-Stevas and Jill Knight. The group produced a small amount of literature, ran a letter writing campaign, organised fringe meetings at the Annual Conference each year from 1976-84 and had around 700 activists on its register in the peak year of 1979. After the second election victory of 1983, the group's profile diminished and it went through various realignments, before becoming effectively mothballed. It springs to life in one form or another with each recurrent pro-life debate, but in recent years has had to rely on a reducing number of committed pro-life Conservative MPs.*(39) Mrs Thatcher's sympathetic sentiments also encouraged groups like the Society for the Protection of Unborn Children to openly back pro-life Conservative candidates in parliamentary by-elections, such as Jeremy Handley –

against Labour's Tessa Jowell – at Ilford North in March 1978. Handley's unexpected victory there was put down to the vigorous campaigns of SPUC, which later finished up in the electoral court.*(40)

In reality, Margaret Thatcher was always lukewarm about certain moral causes.*(41) Although personally supporting the private member pro-life amendment bills of John Corrie (1979) and David Alton (1988) – both seeking to reduce the abortion time limits – along with Enoch Powell's Unborn Children Protection Bill of 1985 (barring embryo experimentation), Mrs Thatcher did not impose a three-line whip on her MPs. As a result, a significant minority of Tory MPs voted against the bill (including many from the Heath camp), while the Thatcher government declined to rescue any of the pro-life initiatives as each in its turn ran out of Commons time.*(42) So also did she decline to intervene in 1985 when pro-life Conservative, Victoria Gillick, battled in vain all the way to the House of Lords with the Department of Health to stop doctors prescribing contraception to under-16 girls without parental knowledge or approval.

Overall, hopes of an American-style moral revivalist programme under Mrs Thatcher proved misplaced. There were few advances beyond the legislation of Section 28 of the Local Government Act banning the promotion of homosexuality by local councils. Yet this outcome was as much indicative of secularisation casting its shadow on the Conservative Party and wider British society by the 1980s as any specific weakness on the Right.*(42) The Conservatives being a broad coalition of the political Right could not afford to get drawn closely to the Christian Right, lest other groups be alienated. At the same time, it was during the Thatcher era that this lobby wielded some influence and key leadership allies, albeit with limited results in respect of policy gains. Such advantages had never been available in Heath's day, and fell away during the respective terms of John Major and his successors.

(iv) *Publications*:- Journals, newspapers and texts played a major part in what Thatcher convert, Professor Stephen Haseler, called ".. the battle of ideals".*(43)

A number of media outlets facilitated the New Right's campaign. Additional to the Daily and Sunday Telegraph(s), Times, Mail, Express and Sun, there was also The Spectator, the Bow Group journal,

Crossbow, and a string of magazines published by rightist groups ranging from Monday World and its successor magazine, Salisbury Review, to those of the Libertarian Alliance and Young Conservatives. Even the centrist journal, Tory Reformer, engaged regular debates with the Right over policy and goals. Additionally, the right wing 'think-tanks' – e.g. CPS, Adam Smith Institute, IEA and others – produced a litany of policy pamphlets such as offered ideological succour to the government. They were both chief proselytisers and cerebral architects for the Whig school from which Mrs Thatcher drew her major policy initiatives.

Throughout most of the Thatcher years at Downing Street her profile among party grass roots and even middle rankers was positive, while her policy agenda was largely credited with having restored the Conservatives to government. This reputation ensured that policy debates were conducted within the Thatcher mould, and it was her ideals which defined the party and its programme, while providing stimulus for critics to respond. As was demonstrated separately by Peter Jenkins and Hugo Young, in the absence of a dependable establishment, she relied upon ideological allies in the policy institutes and among fellow Whigs at Westminster for support.*(44) Accordingly, during her leadership years, the Right mobilised its platform and ground troops for promoting the Thatcher agenda in the party and to the country at large.

4. Impact of the Conservative Right

Assessments of the Right's impact may be made on several fronts. These include the extent of the party's ideological conversion to right wing causes, especially the New Whig economic programme, along with the Right's effects on rank and file, its impact on the electorate, and consequences for the party throughout the country.

As has already been shown, the Right's domination of the Conservative Party under Mrs Thatcher was facilitated by the election victories of 1979, 1983 and 1987, which established her credibility with the mainstream in parliament and at grass roots. She had rescued the party from electoral decline, restored it to government, revived internal confidence and offered a fresh policy programme based around a revival of parliamentary and national sovereignty and renewal of the free market.

It was not to everyone's liking, but the party's resurgence at the polls generated a concomitant rise in the overall fortunes of the Conservative Right. This new-found self confidence was particularly evident following the third electoral victory of 1987.

In any major political party, it has always been the place of campaigning groups who support the leadership to promote their policies. At the same time, convivial 'think-tanks' will laud policy while pushing it further forward. This is a strange condition, because in effect these types of groups in the 1980s Conservative Party acted as leadership publicists, a position which rather compromised their independence. So too did they appear connected to the leadership regime. Generally, independent groups thrive in the more combative climate of "opposition" to the leadership regime, and will acquire the traits of a functional movement within their party. Such factors were missed by several academic observers of factionalism, but the efficacy was reinforced on this author as a result of various studies of party groups (see bibliography).

When considering the experiences of so many rightist groups during the Thatcher years, it seems that they came into their own under a friendly regime. Yet their impact should be weighed against antagonisms generated within and beyond the party. It might be noted that right wing think-tanks, e.g. CPS, Adam Smith Institute and IEA, along with campaigning bodies like the Freedom Association and Monday Club were independent of Central Office authority. This meant these groups had a profile beyond the party – some indeed acquired a high profile – and attracted variable reactions to their policies and campaigns from press and opponents alike. Even ideological campaigners like the '92 Committee and Bruges Group (the latter having emerged in 1988) found their campaigning priorities defined by the Thatcher agenda.

One effect of the groups was to reinforce domination of the party by Mrs Thatcher's regime at Central Office headed variously by Cecil Parkinson, John Selwyn-Gummer*(45) and Norman Tebbit throughout the 1980s.*(46) They lauded Mrs Thatcher in front of the cameras, especially at Annual Conference and other media occasions, while also berating her critics to the press. Indeed a marked feature of fringe meetings organised by the Monday Club, CPS, No Turning Back (NTB) and Freedom Association were the hostile gestures directed at Edward Heath and his allies by right wing activists. Also, from those same groups several younger Thatcher allies emerged as Conservative parliamentarians, such as David Willets (CPS Director) and Michael Forsythe (Adam Smith Institute) being examples in point.

It has been said by several commentators that the adulation of her supporters was a primary reason why by 1990 Mrs Thatcher failed to realise the extent to which her stock had declined throughout the nation, and, increasingly, her own MPS.*(47) She had become cocooned by flatterers, shielded from the unpopularity of key policies like the Poll Tax, and impervious to a growing public perception of her leadership as dogmatic and authoritarian.*(48) In short, by 1990 Mrs Thatcher had lost contact with the wider political world, for which she later paid the ultimate price.

With the benefit of hindsight, it can be said that the Right maintained its ascendancy for the duration of the Thatcher term, but gradually became a liability to its own cause. It had grown disconnected, divisive and increasingly aggressive while using tactics that proved embarrassing to the party. So too did the Right appear synonymous with extremist politics, given their opposition to Europe, hostility to the Anglo-Irish Accord (which ironically Mrs Thatcher had negotiated with Irish Taoiseach, Dr Garret Fitzgerald), backing a poll tax and opposing Nelson Mandela's release from prison in South Africa.*(49) It was hard not to see the hand of the Monday Club, Freedom Association and their allies bidding for the loyalties of Conservative grass roots.

An example of rightist impact was the fracas erupting at the Federation of Conservative Students conference at Loughborough University in Spring 1985. This affray was widely blamed on the activities of various right wing groups, one of which was the Libertarian Alliance and another being Monday Club activists. In any case, the events generated negative media publicity, which in turn caused much embarrassment to Conservative Central Office; hence Tebbit's decision to close the FCS forthwith.*(50) The turbulence had emanated from a right wing clique led by ideologues like David Hoyle and Marc-Henri Glendenning from the University of Warwick. These groups had earlier ousted the centrist regime running the organisation at the beginning of the 1980s decade, and sought to impose their agenda on FCS.*(51) Although a student organisation was subsequently revived, it was done under close monitoring of Central Office, including vetting of officers and spokesmen.*(52)

Another area of reaction to the Right was Scotland. Scottish Conservatives did not share in the Thatcher political success to the same degree as their English brethren, having been reduced to 10 Westminster seats and 24% of the Scottish vote in the 1987 election, a decline accentuated by the Scottish Nationalists and Liberals each competing for the main opposition mantle against a then-dominant Labour Party.*(53) This position was further reduced to near collapse a decade later when the Scottish Conservatives lost all remaining Westminster seats, plus the Home Rule referendum of September 1997, before managing a minor comeback in 2001.*(54)

One prime feature of the Scottish party was Mrs Thatcher's dogmatic insistence on a straight Unionist line against any form of devolution or home rule. This proved a very divisive position. According to Lynch, it highlighted her ".. innate Britishness .." in line with traditional Conservative beliefs in the Union and Empire.*(45) At the same time, it caused much dissension among Scottish Tories, many of whom viewed Thatcherism as a principal reason for the sharp decline in their vote and overall marginalisation. In his evaluation of recent Scottish political developments, James Kellas noted the extent to which Scottish Conservatives had become isolated from the mainstream of Scottish political life as a result of Thatcher's implacable unionism.*(56) That legacy remained for nearly two decades after Mrs Thatcher departed the political stage.

Many tensions among Scottish Tories were generated by competing cliques – with varying degrees of affinity to the Thatcher leadership – rather than formal groups. Yet evidence did emerge of influence being exerted by among others the Monday Club, Adam Smith Institute and a couple of short-lived Scottish unionist action campaigns – originally spear-headed by the 1970s Union Flag Group at Westminster – aimed at challenging the growing tide of sympathy for home rule.*(57) Right wing group activity was especially marked in two Scottish universities, St Andrews and Edinburgh, both of whom attracted large numbers of

English students, and from those same places emerged student activists who played a part in disrupting FCS. Also, in certain constituency associations based around Stirling and Edinburgh small bands of ideological activists operated from the right.*(58) They campaigned for the selection of rightist candidates, adoption of rightist motions on Europe, nuclear weapons, and the economy and defending the Union. Moreover, their guiding star was none other than Margaret Thatcher, whom they adulated to a degree bordering on a personal cult, and in a fashion most uncharacteristic of British political culture.

Additional to a lingering divide left by the 1970s devolution debate – when some Tories led by Malcolm Rifkind backed a limited home rule package, while others like Teddy Taylor and Bill Walker remained resolutely opposed – Scottish Conservatives clearly possessed rival right and left wings. The former was centred on Michael Forsythe, a 'guru' to neo-Whigs and unionists, while notwithstanding their services in Mrs Thatcher's cabinet Rifkind and Ian Lang spearheaded One Nationites both in Scotland and throughout the wider British Conservative Party.

Overall, the Right's influence in Scottish Tory politics while pronounced in the 1970s and '80s proved of doubtful value to the party's wider appeal, and rather waned following Mrs Thatcher's demise. Although the Scottish Right had pitched from a minority vantage point, their influence rose and fell concomitant with that of their heroine. Accordingly, the Right's hegemony in the party across the country and its limits can be traced more or less directly to the rise and fall of Mrs Thatcher.

5. Tory Progressives

While the Right thrived during the Thatcher era, conversely those were lean times for the displaced Tory Progressives. Their fortunes were at a low ebb in two respects.

First, was the party's obvious electoral recovery under Mrs Thatcher, culminating in three successive victories at the polls. This turn-around proved inspiring for the party faithful who had previously watched Conservative fortunes sink to their post-war nadir under Edward Heath in the two elections of 1974. Second was the apparent success of Mrs

Thatcher's 'political revolution', specifically an ending of state-run industries, high public spending, trade union power and other traits of the post-war 'Consensus'. Those achievements and Mrs Thatcher's accompanying authority contrasted starkly with the economic stagnation and policy failings of the Heath years. Yet it is in the nature of factionalism to facilitate dissenting tendencies, and thus in the halcyon mid-1980s when Mrs Thatcher's fortunes were at their height that centre-left Conservative critics were best organised in the party.

Actually, this diverse strand of Heathites, Euro-zealots, One Nationites, old-style Tories, single issue social reformers and party reformers changed little throughout the Thatcher years. Moreover, their organisational structures acquired new impetus from the re-emergence of the Tory Reform Group (see Chap. 6) after 1975. TRG activities brought a steady stream of recruits who – as one leading TRG activist recalled – "... were heartened by the visible presence of a rallying standard for Tory centrists, One Nation folk and others alienated by Mrs Thatcher's regime."*(59) At the same time, there was a dilemma for the Tory Progressives in that they were forced to operate within a party led from the Right and winning power continuously.

(i) *Tory Reform Group*:- Like other sections of the Conservative Party, the centre-left was also led by front benchers. Most pivotal was Peter Walker who proved the lead personality behind the launch and growth of the Tory Reform Group.*(60) Others included Jim Prior, Michael Heseltine, Stephen Dorrell, Malcolm Rifkind, Ian Gilmour and later Ken Clarke, all of whom to a greater or lesser degree helped keep the flickering Tory centrist torch burning. It was a lonely furrow that they ploughed, but they persevered.

What is interesting was the diversity of strategy that prevailed among the Progressive forces and lead figures. Such was especially true of those accepting positions in the governments of Mrs Thatcher. Some Progressives like Heseltine, Prior and Rifkind favoured limited co-operation with Thatcher governments, so long as they contained Progressive ministers. Others like Edward Heath and, initially, Peter Walker were less keen, believing the Thatcher regime to be of limited duration and likely for defeat at the general election following its first term; hence Tory Progressives did not want to be sullied by association with the hard Right.*(61) This strategy took no account of the Falklands war or Opposition divisions that characterised the 1979-81 parliament, both of which ensured Mrs Thatcher's victorious re-election in June 1983. Later, Walker amended his line, and by 1985 he, Heseltine, Clarke and William Waldegrave were among the only Progressives remaining in the Thatcher administration.

Only Heath remained aloof, becoming an increasingly isolated figure even among Tory Progressives.*(62) Other leading Progressives like Ian Gilmour, Robin Rhodes James and Hugh Dykes (later to defect to the Liberal Democrats) maintained a clear distance from the party establishment, while also showing basic loyalty.*(63)

Thus while Mrs Thatcher enjoyed near hegemony for much of her Downing Street tenure, her writ never ran totally throughout the party. Significantly, the assorted collection of centrist critics assembled on Westminster's backbenches and throughout the party organisation provided a nucleus for opposition that manifested periodically at various stages of her premiership. In Thatcher's final days, TRG did not exercise a direct impact on events leading to the Heseltine challenge or John Major's succession, but provided a platform for anti-Thatcher malcontents and centrist Tories. Its publicist function proved as important as any lobbying undertaken by activists.

Given TRG's publicist role, it is instructive to examine the nature of its publications and their impact on party opinion. So also are several of the contributors significant.

Andrew Rowe, Tony Baldry, Michael Welsh, Nigel Forman, John Maples and Geoff Lawler were among the MPs/MEPs writing articles for the *Reformer*.*(64) So did Peter Walker, Michael Heseltine, Ken Clarke, Stephen Dorrell, Chris Patten, Malcom Rifkind and Norman Fowler contribute to the journal throughout the Thatcher decade.*(65) The journal was led by parliamentarians, though contributions from non-Westminster figures like Stephen Parker (TRG executive), journalist Nigel Moore and social researcher/TRG activist, Robbie Gilbert, indicated some grass roots input.*(66)

The TRG journal, *Reformer*, developed a profile, as much for the tone of its material as the range of contributors. Throughout the Thatcher years at Downing Street, this quality journal carried many coded criticisms of government policy presented by familiar Westminster Tory Progressives, several of them front benchers and former ministers. Such causes as European integration, an interventionist economic policy, curbs on public spending cuts and challenging the government's general ideological policy ... all figured quite prominently in its pages. The journal offered further heart to Tory Progressives variously battling within the Cabinet, Parliamentary Party, Central Office, Tory Trade Unionists, Federation of Conservative Students (FCS), Young Conservatives and in the constituency organisations.

Of particular significance was the grim, and ultimately failed, battle waged by Tory Reform supporters to keep a majority on the FCS national executive during the early and mid-1980s. Then, prominent TRG student figures included Anna Soubry (now at Westminster) and Nick Robinson, former BBC political editor. The TRG also sought to exert an influence in the running of the Young Conservatives, which brought it into battle with the Right.*(67) As always, the problem was one of scarce ground troops, and a diminished strength outside of the South of England. Nevertheless, the journal gave generous coverage to TRG efforts, positions and activists.*(68)

At the same time, TRG causes were further obvious from the range of pamphlets it published. They included 'Tax Credit Report' (1979), 'Signing on at 16' (1980), 'Reversing the Trend?' (1981), 'Young, British and Black' (1982), 'The Case Against Student Loans' (1983), 'Imprisonment in the 1980s' (1983), 'Flat Out – A Study on the Right to Buy as it affects flats in London' (1983), 'High Noon in the National Health Service' (1984) and 'Prisoners on Remand – A real crisis of penal injustice' (1985).*(69) This concern with issues of social justice characterised TRG at a time when such causes were frowned upon by Mrs Thatcher and Central Office. To that extent, TRG acted as an opposition tendency counterpoising official leadership orthodoxy and drawing upon social causes drawn from One Nation traditions. After 1989, with prompting from Norman Fowler and Michael Heseltine, the British/E.U. integration cause assumed greater prominence, especially after Mrs Thatcher had openly inveighed – as at Bruges – against further E.U. involvement in UK affairs.*(70)

The Group was openly despised by assorted figures from the Right, who viewed them as misguided and potentially disloyal.*(71) In particular, several prominent right wingers denounced TRG's agenda and its lead figures, implying that their loyalties lay with the displaced Heath regime rather than Margaret Thatcher. Some more extreme pro-Thatcher groups had no hesitation about attacking TRG and other centrist groups (e.g. Tory Europeans and the Charter Movement) in the most aggressive terms, often using intemperate language.*(72) Whether this penchant reflected critics' insecurity, intolerance or was in fact an unwitting acknowledgement of the Tory Reformers continuing appeal is unclear. What is clear was that TRG's profile as a long standing and potent critic of Mrs Thatcher was played to the full during her crisis-ridden final 14 months of office from September 1989 until November 1990.

In terms of organisation, TRG developed greater corporate structures – while at the same time realising more resources – after 1983. This development represented something of a paradox, because otherwise 1983 ushered a dark era for Progressives following Mrs Thatcher's electoral landslide and ensuing domination of the British political agenda. Yet a faction is nothing if not a safe refuge for dissidents, and such a quarter was desperately needed then by anti-Thatcher forces within the Tory Party.

TRG's active supporters never numbered more than 500 during those years, a majority of whom were based in London and the 'Home Counties'.*(73) Although the Group encouraged gatherings of its members, in fact only in London, Birmingham, Cambridge and Hampshire did short-lived local groups emerge; otherwise for the most part the organisation was led from London.*(74) Students, young professionals and some businessmen were among TRG backers but significantly, all the evidence points to few grass roots activists or a grass roots base. Its 1980s executive was headed by Iain Picton as Chairman, Alistair Burton MP and David Grayson as Vice Chairmen and Liz Spencer as editor of The Reformer.*(75) At the same time, the principal moving force was Peter Walker, while Stephen Dorrell, Michael Heseltine, Andrew Rowe and Tony Baldry all took an active interest in TRG development.*(76) Funding came from various supporters inside and outside Parliament, few if any who would be named, but about whom the author was reliably advised there was no question about their legitimacy.*(77) Literature sales, occasional donations and collections at rallies also helped meet administrative costs, as well as running TRG's London office.

Overall, TRG was the principal organisation on the Conservative Right. It enjoyed a degree of overlap with others such as the Conservative Europeans and the Charter Movement. However, TRG spokesmen were at pains to stress there was no automatic link between Europeanism and the One Nation cause and pointed to Peter Walker's own earlier Euro-scepticism as an example.*(78) Equally, the Charter Movement spokesmen maintained that their group avoided ideological affinities.*(79)

Actually, given the Tory Progressives broad association with Europe and party reform, beyond certain idiosyncratic exceptions, pro-Europeans and party reformers (the latter driven by principled opposition to centralisation of power under Mrs Thatcher) were natural allies for the Tory centre-left school. After all, Europe was a defining cause of the Macmillan and Heath schools, and was vigorously carried on into the 1980s generation. As for Mrs Thatcher's opposition to the European integration cause, her stance after 1988 forced Euro-zealots into the Tory Progressive – and ultimately Tory Reform – camp. Such are the exigencies of politics!

(ii) *Conservative Europeans*:- As earlier indicated, though the Conservative European Group operated independently of TRG and other ideological tendencies, in reality from the mid-1980s onwards it emerged as something of an adjunct to the Tory Progressives.*(80)

It had become aligned with Tory centrists due to dogged opposition by Mrs Thatcher towards further European integration – specifically the E.M.S., later the Social Directive and single currency. There was also the principled support given to the European cause by many leading Conservative One Nationites – including Kenneth Clarke, Malcolm Rifkind, Michael Hesltine, Stephen Dorrell and Edward Heath – as well as several Thatcher ministers unconnected to the Tory Reform camp, specifically her two chancellors, Geoffrey Howe and Nigel Lawson. Also, there had been a group of unconnected pro-European middle rankers who included John Selwyn Gummer, Mark Carlisle, Christopher Soames, Norman Fowler, Kenneth Baker, Norman St John Stevas and

Edwina Currie. This combined group operated an influential lobby, and one that Mrs Thatcher found difficult to stem even at her strongest point.

Europeanism never caught the imagination of Tory rank and file activists, and indeed anti-Europeanism remained popular at grass roots.*(81) Nevertheless, the abundance of so many Westminster Euro-patrons – within and beyond the Tory Progressive camp ensured this was a platform where they could offer meaningful resistance to a key policy of the Thatcher government from within the party. Moreover, as the fraught circumstances of Mrs Thatcher's downfall in 1990 indicate, Europeanism had a stronger appeal to the Westminster party than she appeared to understand. It proved a rude awakening for the Conservative Right at large and Mrs Thatcher in particular. Meanwhile, the constant Euro-proselytising task had been carried on relentlessly by Tory Progressives; hence they were entitled to claim some ownership of that cause.

(iii) *Tory Charter Movement*:- This movement was formed in June 1981 by a group of Home Counties-based activists with a commitment to democratising the Conservative Party. Their aim was to achieve a radical shift in the balance of authority away from the Westminster leadership and its appointees to a system of electing the major party functionaries by the mass membership. In particular, they sought to clip the powers of the Leader as well as establishing some form of democratic accountability for the running of Central Office and the party's funds and administration.*(82)

"The object of the Charter Movement is a democratic Conservative Party owned by its members, a Conservative Party in which the conduct of affairs at all levels is in the hands of democratically elected and accountable officers, and a Conservative Party in which the members are fully able to participate at all levels."*(83)

This statement of purpose made conflict with leadership inevitable. The movement was after all challenging a power structure that had been in place since the party's modern evolution under Disraeli. It sought new structures that would transfer power away from the leader to the members, a prospect that had not been welcomed by Edward Heath and was resented even more by Mrs Thatcher and her lieutenants.*(84)

It might also be said that though the democratisation campaign was in keeping with trends experienced by centre-right parties across Europe, actually the Charter agenda confronted more than just the structures of the party. Chartists also challenged the very essence of Conservative tradition of enlightened and effective leadership. For sure, the Charter Movement's vision differed starkly from that of Philip Norton's view of the Conservative Party which essentially was about accommodating itself to a democratic world, but nothing more than that.*(85)

Yet interestingly, as Chartist spokesmen repeatedly asserted, the movement's roots lay in the radical democratic leanings of the Greater London Young Conservatives of the 1960s. In 1968 the latter body had published a document called 'Set the Party Free' which demanded elections for the major party offices, financial accountability and the general empowerment of rank and file members. This programme had been eagerly propagated by many Young Conservatives at the time and those who formed the Charter Movement had drawn strength from that era.

The lead figure in the Charter Movement was Eric Chalker. He had been an active Young Conservative in the 1960s, subsequently a councillor in Harrow and constituency officer, as well as serving for a lengthy period on the Board of Finance of the National Union. Chalker (ex-husband of Thatcher's Overseas Development Minister, Lynda Chalker) had also been a vociferous supporter of European accession in the 1960s. He was twice refused entry to the approved list of parliamentary candidates in the late 1960s and was further debarred in the 1980s. Despite a recent silence on policy issues, his Tory Progressive profile made campaigns on party reform doubly antagonistic to Central Office and the Right generally.*(86) Chalker variously held different positions within the Charter Movement, but as far as can be established he was the principal policy maker and strategist in the organisation.*(87)

Charter literature insisted on the ideological neutrality of their campaign and support from all wings of the party. While right wingers like Edward Leigh spoke at their Conference meetings, actually in what was a relatively small, London-based and self-financed organisation (containing fewer than 300 active supporters) the predominant character was centre-left. One of the few prominent supporters was the centrist

MP, Robin Squires (a pronounced One Nationite who also backed electoral reform), while Piers Marchant from the centre right also lent open support. Otherwise there were few right wingers and no Thatcher allies, and Westminster patrons generally were scarce (even from the centre), which rather limited the Charter Movement's appeal to a cross-section audience.*(88) At the same time, the Movement stubbornly persisted with its campaign throughout the Thatcher years and into the era of John Major and William Hague, while battling the party establishment. Its campaigning achieved some progress in the decade after Margaret Thatcher's departure with the adoption of the party constitution and full member vote for choosing the leader. For that purpose, the Charter Movement teamed up with another body called the Reform Steering Committee – launched 1990. However, as evidence presented in subsequent chapters indicated, the major democratic changes sought in respect of financial accountability and member representation on the party's national boards never quite materialised.

(iv) *Other Tory Progressive Groups*:- They included Centre Forward Group (launched in 1984 by Francis Pym) and the Blue Chips, both of whom were dining clubs confined to parliamentarians drawn from a reducing Tory centre. While cooperating with leadership and producing occasional policy pamphlets, neither group developed links outside Westminster and offered little effective challenge to the strident free market and Euro-sceptical direction of Margaret Thatcher's regime. Most importantly, neither of those groups made any headway with winning over grass roots, Conference or other rank and file elements.

In 1989, William Van Strubenzee set up another body called the Lollards Group, which was not confined to the Conservative Parliamentary Party. This body operated from an office owned by the Anglican Church commissioners, was avowedly pro-European and argued for a revival of the party's One Nation traditions.*(89) Significantly, the Lollards was funded by a grant from the Rowntree Foundation so as to aid research and fund the publication of centrist policy pamphlets on Europe and the economy.*(90) Later, the Lollards merged around 1991 with another centrist campaigning body, Macleod Group, to found Conservative Mainstream operating from a central London office near to Westminster, and functioning on an enhanced Rowntree grant.*(91) More later!

6. Summary

Throughout this chapter, it has been shown that the Conservative Party of Margaret Thatcher's premiership was more or less dominated by the Right at all levels. Yet, paradoxically, the evidence presented here indicates that a rightist regime did not lead to a mushrooming of influence across the party by right wing groups.

In fact, rightist factions played only a marginal role in party affairs. While right wing groups managed a voluble profile, actually their importance was far less crucial than had been the case in the five/six years prior to Mrs Thatcher's accession to the premiership. The principal role of the rightist groups was as cheerleaders for Mrs Thatcher and her policies at party conferences and in the wider political sphere. Also, there was an offering of new policies from the expanding range of 'brains factory trusts' that emerged over the same period. Plainly the Right's groups made no major impact over candidate selections or influencing MPs or peers in policy matters. Nor did the Right impose their agenda on the party. Indeed it is indicative of their relative weakness that rightist groups were unable to prevent Mrs Thatcher's removal from power in November 1990 or quiet scuppering of certain key policies that followed.

Conversely, the centre-left having lost control of the party, was forced onto the defensive throughout the Thatcher years. This meant generating group structures for ensuring their own survival. As was shown throughout the chapter, the Tory Reform lobby, European integrationists and party reformers developed their own agendas and accompanying organisations, primarily for the purpose of reaching out to elements of the Conservative party who were sceptical of the Thatcher crusade. It proved a non-salubrious mission over more than a decade of right wingers in power, but they persisted. While the centre groups made no pretensions of wielding influence in party politics in respect of candidate selections and other dynamics, and had no impact on the leadership struggle of November 1990, nevertheless they contributed to a climate of policy debate within and beyond the party. That role was in itself noteworthy.

Following Mrs Thatcher's fall, the Conservative Party's factional arena underwent yet another change in which group dynamics were refashioned along new lines.

FOOTNOTES and REFERENCES

1. (i) Peter Jenkins - <u>Mrs Thatcher's Revolution: The Ending of the Socialist Era</u>, Chapter 13, p.p. 326-333 (J. Cape, 1987).

   (ii) Hugo Young - <u>One of Us</u>, Chapter 22, (Macmillan, 1989).

2. (i) Dennis Kavanagh & Anthony Seldon (Eds.) - <u>The Thatcher Effect: A Decade of Change</u> - Chap. 6, 'The Changing Political Opposition', D. Kavanagh, (Oxford University Press, 1989).

   (ii) J. Enoch Powell - Chap. 5, 'The Conservative Party', Kavanagh & Seldon (Eds.), 1989.

   (iii) Anthony King - 'Margaret Thatcher as a Political Leader', Chap. 2, Robert Skidelsky (Ed.), Thatcherism (Blackwell, 1989).

3. Margaret Thatcher - <u>The Path to Power</u>, Chaps. X, X1 & XV, (Harper-Collins, 1995).

4. Thatcher (1995), Chap. X.

5. Norton in Norton Eds. (1996) Chap. 4, pp. 69-71.

6. Kavanagh (1987) - Chap. 4, pp. 102-107.

7. Alan Watkins - <u>A Conservative Coup: The Fall of Margaret Thatcher</u>,

   See Chaps 1 & 2 (Duckworth, 1991).

8. Interview Eric Chalker/V. McKee, 23rd February, 2000.

9. Interview Rt. Hon. Lord Tebbit/V. McKee.

10. This impression was conveyed in separate interviews with Giles Marshall, Justin Powell-Tuck and Rt. Hon. Stephen Dorrell, MP.

11. Visiting the 1989 and 1990 Conservative Annual Conferences, I was struck by the plethora of youthful rightist groups campaigning for more deregulation and tax reform along the free market lines whose doctrinal Whiggery was matched by open adulation of Margaret Thatcher's leadership. Chief among

these groups were the Libertarian Alliance, Conservative Students and the CPS.

12. Interviews - Bernard Capel and Cllr Francis Lancaster, plus a past executive official of Coventry South West Conservative Association who asked for anonymity, 6th June, 1998.

13. Interview - Tebbit.

14. Interview - Tebbit.

15. Interview - Tebbit.

16. See successive issues of Monday World and Salisbury Review; also interviews with Mrs Eila Bannister (a former Monday Club activist) and Giles Marshall.

17. See Robert Skidelsky's Introduction to Thatcherism, Ed. R. Skidelsky, (Blackwell, 1988) and Kenneth Minogue, Chap. 7, 'The New Right' (Skidelsky 1988).

18. (i) Interviews with Peter Temple-Morris, Lord Tebbit.

    (ii) See Kavanagh (1987) - In Chap. 4, the author sets out list of groups with their respective patrons.

19. Interviews with James Barr, Lord Tebbit, Lord Heseltine, Giles Marshall,

    Peter Temple-Morris and Justin Powell-Tuck - all of whom confirmed the practice of funding and recruitment of group officers.

20. Interviews - Lord Tebbit and Iain Duncan-Smith.

21. See Barr's Bow Group history and Grant's unpublished M.A. thesis (1998).

22. (i) See Grant thesis (1998), Figure 2, Section 3, pp. 9-11.

    (ii) Interviews - Mrs Eila Bannister (Monday Club London activist) and un-named Friends of Union activist from London with Belfast connections.

23. See consecutive Monday World issues 1972-75; the tone is explicitly pro-Unionist and devotes substantial attention to the Unionist cause.

24. Friends of the Union briefing papers, - Patricia Campbell, London 1996-98. Also, the organisation staged fringe meetings at successive annual Conservative conferences and operated briefings to Conservative MPs.

25. Martin O'Brien - <u>Margaret Thatcher and Northern Ireland,</u> Chap. 2, pp. 17-33, Unpublished M.A. thesis (1993), Queen's University, Belfast.

26. Grant thesis (1998), pp. 9-11.

27. Interviews -Cash, Gorman and Townsend. Also, the author attended the fringe meeting of the Conservative Family Campaign at the Conservatives' Annual Conference, October 1998, Bournemouth.

28. Interviews with Lord Tebbit, Iain Duncan-Smith and John Townend; all agreed that the Monday Club had failed to keep up with the pace of events in the Conservative Party.

29. Conclusions drawn from a study of the journals of the following groups, as well as the author attending their Conference fringe meetings:- Women and Families for Defence and Disarmament, Conservative Family Campaign, Conservative Life Campaign, Coalition for Peace and Security.

30. Kavanagh (1987), Chap 4, pp 104-106.

31. Dennis Sewell - <u>Catholics: Britain's Largest Minority</u> (Penguin 2001)

32. For critical commentary of Sewell's book, see Vincent McKee, Reviews, Catholic Times, 3rd September 2002.

33. Tim Bale   <u>The Conservatives since 1945: Drivers of Party Change</u> (OUP, 2012), Chap 2, pp 70-73.

34. Bale (2012), p. 73.

35. Mark Jarvis <u>Conservative Governments; Morality and Social Change in Affluent Britain, 1957-64</u> (MUP, 2005); pp 72-75, 109-110, 165-170.

36. See Nigel Ahford - 'The American New Right'; Social Studies Review, November 1987.

37. Behrens (1980), section on 'Die-Hards'.

38. Rhodes Boyson   <u>1985: An Escape from Orwell's 1984</u>
    (Churchill Press, 1975), Chap. 7 on Standards and Choice in
    Education; eds. Rhodes Boyson.

39. Discussions with Mr Peter Garret, Political Co-ordination
    Officer with Life and a former Conservative Councillor, 28th
    November 3003.

40. (i) News reports, Times, Guardian and Daily Telegraph, 4th
    and 11th March 1978.

    (ii) Also, see coverage in Catholic Herald and Catholic
        Universe, issues 27th Feb, 5th and 12th March 1978
        respectively.

    (iii) In the event, Mrs Phyllis Bowman was censured by the
        Electoral Court for her intervention - urging support for the
        victorious Conservative candidate, Vivien Bendall, on
        account of his pro-life sympathies - a sanction which she
        openly scorned in a speech to a SPUC rally at Hyde Park,
        London, 29th April, 1979. Author's recording of event,
        plus previous interview with Mrs Bowman - now, sadly,
        deceased. (iv) Also, see SPUC newsletter issues March
        -July 1978 and April 1979, and Life News Spring 1979.

41. Discussions with Mrs Bowman, SPUC Director; Mr John
    Smeaton, SPUC General Secretary; Professor Jack Scarisbrick,
    National Chairman, Life, and Lord (David) Alton (February
    23rd 2010).

42. The Cory, Powell and Alton bills all fell due to overrunning
    Commons time.

43. "The battle of ideals" was a constant theme of Professor
    Stephen Haseler's in various texts - see bibliography. Also, he
    repeated this view in two separate interviews with this author.

44. (i) Peter Jenkins (1986), Chap 8, pp. 200-212.

    (ii) Hugo Young (1998), Chap. 11, pp.200-208.

45. Parkinson (Central Office Chairman, 1981-83) and Tebbit (1985-87) were both ideological supporters of Mrs Thatcher, whereas Selwyn-Gummer (1983-85) had been more centrist-inclined prior to Mrs Thatcher's accession, and subsequently had a non-distinguished term as party Chairman.

46. Tebbit candidly acknowledged having used his chairmanship of the party to promote the leadership agenda of Margaret Thatcher:- interview with author.

47. See Alan Watkins (1991) - Chap. 6, p.p. 124-156.

48. Ibid.

49. See - Conference issues (Autumn 1989 and Autumn 1990) of the Monday Club news letter as well as Salisbury Review (editorials - Autumn 1989 and Autumn 1990). Both journals carried a consistent right wing theme.

50. Interview with Lord Tebbit.

51. Discussions with Lord Tebbit, Giles Marshall, the late Gordon Whiting (Agent - Coventry S.W. Conservative Association), Bernard Capel, plus Warwick Boar and Coventry Evening Telegraph throughout May 1985.

52. Discussions with Lord Tebbit.

53. In June 1987, Scotland voted: Labour 42.4 of vote (50 seats), Conservatives 24.0 (10), Liberal/SDP Alliance 19.4 (9), SNP 14.0 (3). Richard Parry-Scottish Political Facts, pp 2-3, Fig.1.1 (T.&T. Clark, Edinburgh, 1988).

54. 1992 General Election, Scotland - Labour 39.0 (49), Conservatives 25.7 (11), Liberal Democrats 13.1 (9), SNP 21.5 (3).

55. Lynch (1999) - Chap. 3, p.p. 51-59.

56. James Kellas - 'The Scottish Political System', Social Studies Review, May 1988.

57. (i) See Kavanagh (1987), Chap. 3, p.p. 87-88.

    (ii) Interviews -Lord Tebbit, John Townend and a Libertarian Alliance activist who requested anonymity.

58. Gerald Warner - <u>The Scottish Tory Party: A History</u>, Chap. 16, p.p. 218-221, (Weidenfeld & Nicolson, 1988).

59. Interview - Giles Marshall, Editor (2000)- Reformer.

60. The lead role played by Walker in TRG's launch was confirmed in interviews with Lord Heseltine, Giles Marshall and Stephen Dorrell.

61. Walker was recalled to office by Mrs Thatcher in 1981; a year in which she cleared the Cabinet of several so-called 'Wets' (Progressives), including Norman St John-Stevas, Mark Carlisle, Ian Gilmour and Christopher Soames.

62. Heath – as recalled in his memoirs – indicated clearly that he was not interested in any ministerial or patronage preferment from his successor. So also did he decline to take an active part in the Tory Reform Group and its various sister groups. Interviews -Stephen Dorrell and Giles Marshall.

63. Information imparted by Rt. Hon. Stephen Dorrell and Mr Giles Marshall in separate interviews with the author.

64. Reformer (TRG journal), Issue - Summer 1985 - Ed. Liz Spencer.

65. See successive issues of Reformer 1979-90 for contributions from various lead figures.

66. See Reformer, special European issue, May 1984 - Ed. Liz Spencer.

67. See 'Destruction of a Movement' by Giles Marshall; Tory Reformer, Autumn 1996.

68. Information supplied by Mr Giles Marshall, one time TRG journal editor.

69. Information supplied by Giles Marshall.

70. Interviews - Dorrell, Marshall and Heseltine.

71. Rightist hostility towards TRG was acknowledged variously in interviews with Mrs Teresa Gorman, Lord Tebbit, Mr John Townend, Mr William Cash and Mrs Eila Bannister. The common theme appeared to be their general ideological outlook

that was so opposed to Mrs Thatcher's agenda. Interestingly, Mr Cash acknowledged to the author that his hostility towards TRG was based purely on the Group's pro-European preference.

72. Newsletter of the Libertarian Alliance (September 1985) and the Conservative Students magazine, University of Warwick (Spring 1985), displayed open hostility towards the TRG in common with others of the centre.

73. Information supplied in interviews with Giles Marshall and Stephen Dorrell.

74. Ibid.

75. See successive issues of Reformer, 1984-87.

76. Information given at interviews by Heseltine, Marshall and Dorrell.

77. Information supplied by Marshall, Dorrell and Heseltine.

78. This point was particularly stressed by Dorrell and Marshall in interviews with the author.

79. Eric Chalker denied all Tory Reform alignments to the Charter Movement - interview with author – and in subsequent correspondence dated 13th April, 2000. In fact Chalker's earlier track record was as a pro-European advocate at Conservative conferences in the 1960s. He was a casualty of Norman Tebbit's discouragement of centrists from Conservative Central Office's approved list of parliamentary candidates, and had twice been refused in the 1960s.

80. See a consistent plethora of pro-European articles appearing in Reformer, 1983-90 by a succession of authors.

81. The now-defunct 1970s/early '80s grass roots magazine - published by Central Office - Conservative Newsline, frequently ran readers letters that postured hostility towards the European (Community) Union.

82. (i) Interview with Mr Eric Chalker.

(ii) Successive issues of Charter News, monthly newsletter of the Charter Movement.

83. Charter Movement, Statement of Aims.

84. Almost all right wingers interviewed by the author were either uninterested or, more usually, plain hostile towards the Charter Movement's campaign.

85. Philip Norton - <u>The Conservative Party</u>, Chaps. 8 & 9, (Prentice Hall/ Harvester Wheatsheaf, 1996).

86. Lord Tebbit – in an interview with the author – expressed particular opposition to the Charter Movement's campaign, and also the ideological credentials and track record of Eric Chalker.

87. Author's discussions with three principal participants (all of whom requested anonymity) in the Charter Movement confirmed Chalker's leading role. Also, much of the media profile centred on Eric Chalker.

88. Eric Chalker was the most public face and articulate spokesman of the Tory Charter Movement.

89. William Van Strubenzee was a long standing supporter of the Tory Reform Group, as well as being a Commissioner of the Church of England.

90. Information supplied in interview with Peter (Lord) Temple-Morris.

91. Information supplied in separate interviews by Lord Temple-Morris and Mr Justin Powell-Tuck.

CHAPTER 8

CONSERVATIVES DURING THE JOHN MAJOR ERA

1990 - 97

This chapter will examine Conservative factionalism over the seven years of John Major's leadership of the party and nation. It will include evaluations of sharpening ideological conflicts occurring within the party, plus new issues arising like Europe, taxation, the evolving Irish peace process and the perennial question of leadership. Further consideration will be given to the effects of Mrs Thatcher's political demise on the Conservative Right, while also examining the changing fortunes of the Tory Progressives in light of the re-emergence of political fellow travellers as Michael Heseltine, Stephen Dorrell, Malcolm Rifkind and Ken Clark in Major's Cabinet. Finally, the chapter will consider the ongoing question of whether a spell on the outside actually strengthens dissenting factions, and if so, whether Tory Progressives were adversely affected by increasing connections with Major after 1994.

1. Introduction

The fall of Margaret Thatcher in November 1990 presented the Conservative Party with a dilemma about future direction. In the first instance, the primate of the British political right for the previous fifteen years had been overthrown, in big part by the efforts of one who had earlier confronted her in Cabinet and the parliamentary party, Michael Heseltine. On the face of it, that might have suggested a bright new dawn for the displaced party centre. However, in an ensuing contest to succeed Mrs Thatcher, it was John Major, the Right's candidate, who defeated Heseltine and Douglas Hurd to emerge winner, thereby suggesting continuity with the past. Yet over the seven years that followed, conditions proved very different for leader and party alike, and in subsequent turmoil ideological alignments experienced substantial changes.

As John Major headed the Tories from November 1990 until losing office in the crushing election defeat of May 1997, that era is synonymous with his policies and leadership style. Major's programme represented a balance between a New Right Whig and yet one who also recognised that Mrs Thatcher's dogma had divided the country, split Conservatives, caused public unrest and alienated many voters. As for style, Major found himself caught between warring camps in a divided party. It was an impossible position, and though wishing to consolidate Thatcher's policies, he was also keen to hold the party together so as to present an effective electoral appeal. In fact Major was undermined at every turn, not least by a mixture of dissident MPs and campaigners on the Right. They believed him to be an apostate who had betrayed the Thatcher legacy, and plotted his removal while also challenging his policies over Europe, the economy, transatlantic relations and the Irish peace process.

As Conservative Leader and Prime Minister, Major could not formally hold factional alignments, but his style encouraged perceptions of ideological vacuum and uncertainty over direction. It was said in his defence – among others, by his biographer, Anthony Seldon – that having led the Tories to unexpected victory in 1992, the narrowness of his 21 seat majority facilitated dissidents, rebels and other disloyal elements whose attacks and defiance made Major's task impossible.*(1) This argument while containing much merit overlooks the primary fact of the Conservative Party's disarray of the 1990s going rather further than just leadership style.

Actually, by June 1992 the party had emerged from the New Whig era without clear direction and indeed, debates over sovereignty and the role of the market reflected that uncertainty. This issue will be examined later in the chapter. Yet certain key questions must be addressed. Did the Right really lose outright control of the Conservative Party after Margaret Thatcher's fall, and if so why did its forces become ever more trenchant in a manner that clearly imperilled the party's electoral appeal? Was there a coordinated strategy on the Right to destabilise the government of John Major, and if so why and how? Were any ministers involved in the Right's campaign? How was the Tory Centre affected by key figures from its own ranks like Heseltine, Dorrell and Clarke in senior Cabinet roles? Why did factionalism permeate the party throughout the 1992-97 Parliament? Was that factionalism symptomatic of ideological struggle, or was there another reason for the fragmentation characterising the party during the final two years of Major's administration?

Those questions will be pursued throughout the chapter. While precise answers may be difficult to establish, plainly the intensity of Conservative factionalism over that period suggests the party's turbulence to have been linked to a desperate internal struggle, itself a recurrent trait associated with the party ever since 1945.

2. Principal Events and Preliminary assessments of Major's leadership

Initially, it is necessary to examine the troubles besetting John Major's premiership. Not only did the party sustain itself in government, but it was in the manner of electoral battles and key policy debates that factional politics manifested at their rawest and most implosive. Quite simply, by the time of their crushing defeat in May 1997, the Tories had descended into a fragmented, ill-disciplined and barely creditable rabble whose removal from office had looked a near certainty for much of the previous five years.

The consensus of opinion among various commentators is that Major exercised a steadying influence on the party following the grave turbulence that accompanied Mrs Thatcher's overthrow.*(2) Though coming of the political Right, John Major was his own man; he avoided involvement with rightist organisations and quickly resolved to keep right wingers – who had previously supported Mrs Thatcher – at bay.*(3) He had been mandated to lead a Conservative Party that under his predecessor was palpably faltering and heading for electoral defeat; hence he acted to avert political disaster.*(4) Leading his party to an unexpected fourth win in April 1992, it seemed to many that Major had snatched victory from the jaws of defeat. Yet with hindsight, that victory now looks to have been more of a stay of execution than the stemming of a political tide.

In his memoirs, Major acknowledged that after acceding to the premiership he realised policy reappraisal to be essential for securing his party's survival. While elected with the votes of the Right*(5), he was never going to be dominated by the Right or its policy agenda.*(6)

Among the issues that would divide the party over the ensuing seven years were Europe, taxation, the Irish peace process and continuing debates over his own leadership. All generated intense debate between the Centre and Right, provoking dissension with leadership, rebellions in Parliament and general unease among grass roots over policy and ideological direction. Moreover, debates produced rival lobbies, along with rival spokesmen operating from different platforms, and with disunity channelled to the voters. Factionalism thrived in this atmosphere of uncertainty and conflict between leadership and internal critics. As a result, Conservative appeal to voters was damaged by the in-fighting, with its effects embedded in the Conservative political orbit long after Major's leadership tenure had ceased.

It is tempting to view Major as a weak and vacillating figure, and dismiss his leadership as characterised by misjudgements, lost chances and a show of poor authority at all levels of the party, thereby causing the electoral catastrophe of May 1997. Several right wingers interviewed made such accusations.*(7) Among Centrists a more mollified view was taken. They viewed defeat as inevitable given the consequences of the fall-out over EMS withdrawal, the Maastricht Treaty and further European divisions as well as the prime minister's failure to regain authority with his party or the voters despite his re-election over right wing challenger, John Redwood, in 1995. All these troubles were accompanied by an improving economy characterising the last two years in office.*(8)

Major's troubles took five principal forms:

First was the divided state of the Conservative Party after Thatcher's removal. The Right resented their heroine's fall, and though mollified by Major's victory over Michael Heseltine and Douglas Hurd, nevertheless support was conditional on his continuing Mrs Thatcher's programme.*(9) Seldon makes much of Major's refusal to be photographed jointly with Thatcher outside No. 10 Downing Street on the evening of his election, suggesting early awareness of dangers emanating from expectations of him as a Thatcher protégé.*(10) Indeed the refusal was viewed with suspicion by Thatcherites, not to mention the displaced 'empress' herself.*(11)

Second, was the narrow 21 seat majority attained by Conservatives in the general election of April 1992, an advantage eroded by deaths, defections and by-election defeats that by 1995 had left Major heading a minority government and depending on Ulster Unionists and rebels at Westminster for survival.*(12) It also rendered him vulnerable to their demands.

Third, was the cruel impact of divisions wreaked by the 1990s European integration drive on the party. Opt-outs from the Maastricht treaty (specifically the Social Directive) were followed by moves towards federalism, including a common currency, foreign policy and even talk about a European defence force. Such ideals emanated from the Euro-federalist regime of 1990s Commission President, Jacques Delors, and aroused the interest of a Tory Europhile tendency variously spearheaded by Edward Heath, Michael Heseltine and Ken Clark. However the resentment of other Tories was aroused; they viewing Euro-federalism as a threat to British sovereignty, a prime Conservative cause. As with other dilemmas, Major relied on support from the Centre, and was at odds with the Right who were demanding principled resistance to federalism.

Fourth was the track record of Major's first Chancellor, Norman Lamont (his campaign manager in November 1990), whose performance left the government looking inept in its economic management. The chaotic uncertainty leading up to EMS withdrawal in September 1992 haunted Lamont right up to his dismissal the following Spring and plagued the Prime Minister for the next five years. His troubles were compounded by incessant demands from the Conservative Right for a veto on British accession to the Euro over the next decade, something Major felt unable to agree. The result was a state of virtual civil war which left the Conservative Party disunited and barely electable.

Fifth, Major endured many embarrassing incidents involving the private lives and business ethics of Westminster colleagues, ranging from extra-marital peccadilloes (Tim Yeo and David Mellor) to financial irregularities (Neil Hamilton and Tim Smith) to the death of Stephen Milligan following an irregular sexual liaison. Subsequent revelations about the teenage sex partners of Piers Marchant and Jonathan Aitkin's conviction for perjury compounded the embarrassment. Paradoxically,

Major's much-vaunted 'Back to Basics' campaign – launched at the 1993 Conservative Conference, reaffirming traditional moral values – was undermined by the conduct of many Tory ministers and MPs. While no blame attaches to the Premier for colleagues' behaviour, still his judgement in choosing so many reprobates for high office looked questionable. Doubtless 'sleaze' troubles contributed to the magnitude of the Tory defeat in 1997.

Major was essentially a 'reconciler' drawn from, but not driven by, the Right. His goal was to sustain Conservative governance and his readiness to welcome prominent One Nationites like Heseltine, Clark and Stephen Dorrell to key Cabinet positions (Deputy Premier, Home Secretary/Chancellor and Health Secretary respectively) highlighted a desire to heal past divisions and maximise the party's broad church appeal. Another key centrist appointment was that of Chris Patten to head Conservative Central Office in the run-up to the general election of April 1992. Overall, Major's emphasis was put on holding the party together. He declined to follow a right wing agenda, believing that to be a recipe for electoral defeat, and as shown by his axing of the poll tax, he displayed a willingness to jettison whatever baggage looked likely to antagonise the voters. Such a strategy made conflict with the Right inevitable.

Given the Conservatives spectacular loss of power in 1997, it may be argued that John Major's was a failed premiership that offered no direction, split the party, generated poor discipline, encouraged factionalism and left the Tories defeated, depleted and out of office for 13 years. However, such a view is over-simplified and takes scarce account of the longevity of the party's occupancy of government. After three full terms in office, the fourth term was always likely to be troubled and difficult to convert to a fifth. Major's style differed from that of Thatcher, but so also did he face different challenges to those of his predecessor. Accordingly, his responses took their own form.

3. Thatcher's enduring influence on the Conservative Right

Assessments of John Major's term and its impact on factional politics term must necessarily take account of Mrs Thatcher's continuing influence on the Right. After all, this was a force which plagued his premiership for all its seven years, and whose roots clearly emanated from the legacy of his predecessor.

(i) *Damaged Morale:* In Chapters 6 & 7, Thatcherism's influence on the 1970s and 1980s Conservative Party was evaluated. She ushered in a distinctive school of New Whig ideologues committed to free markets, tax and public spending cuts and revived British nationalism which overturned public policy making of the previous 45 years. It was therefore fanciful to believe – as some centrist Tories hoped – that Thatcherism would perish in the wake of its "empress's" fall from power.

Instead displaced Thatcherites retreated to a factional base, from which they mounted a strident campaign in promotion of the New Whig values that she epitomised. This base numbered key organisations whose combined platform ensured the Right's voice continuing to be heard, as was Mrs Thatcher's for several years into her successor's premiership. The organisations included the pro-sovereignty Bruges Group, the newly-formed Conservative Centre Forward movement, Selsdon Group and 92 Committee, plus a range of outside 'brains trusts' like the Centre for Policy Studies (whose founding guru, Lord Keith Joseph, died in Autumn 1994), Institute for Economic Affairs and William Cash's European Foundation. Together those groups mounted a defence of the Thatcher legacy with a high media profile, pamphlets, intensive lobbying of constituency associations and staging conference fringe meetings. In effect, the Right challenged Major from the beginning to demonstrate fidelity to the Thatcher agenda, and demanded nothing short of full scale continuity of its core policies.

Yet the fact was that Thatcher's fall had left the Right leaderless and displaced. Their long hegemony had neared its end, and notwithstanding the succession of Major there was no great confidence that the new prime minister possessed either the ideological purpose or commitments of his predecessor. Thatcher had confronted more than just her opponents! As noted in previous chapters, throughout the previous twelve years she had brought about major political, social and economic changes to British society which would outlive her premiership. Major was a different kind of leader. His priority was for consolidation rather than innovation. He wanted to heal divisions manifesting over the previous twelve months, but at the price of reducing right wing influence in Cabinet. Specifically, there followed a curtailment of right wing ministers, a re-introduction of centrists like Michael Heseltine (Deputy Premier) and Chris Patten (Party Chairman) to key Cabinet positions and ditching of certain Thatcher policies, e.g. Poll Tax. Major's insistence on advancing his agenda put him in conflict with dedicated right wingers who, with tacit encouragement from the lady herself, persistently undermined his leadership and imperilled the party's cohesion for the duration of his time at the helm.

The psychological damage done to the Right's morale was palpable. Confidence was dented by the realisation that Mrs Thatcher's fall meant their long ideological hegemony was passed. Such a recognition came with pain, and caused much soul-searching about the appropriate direction to follow.*(13) From previously acting as government publicists and the leader's 'praetorian guard', after November 1990 the combined forces of the Conservative Right faced an uncertain future where they could no longer expect to dominate the party, far less be chief publicists of its policy-making.

(ii) *Defence of the Thatcher Legacy:* The likelihood was that the Right would act as a defender of the Thatcher legacy within the Conservative Party, but even that role was tempered by two pivotal factors. First, was clear evidence from opinion polls and public protests that certain Thatcher policies like the Poll Tax were unacceptable to a majority of British voters, and would have to be replaced. Second, the effects of Thatcher economics had divided the country, as with employment and economic regulatory policies. Taken together, there was a desire among many mainstream and centrist Conservative MPs and activists to shed parts of the Thatcher legacy in order to make the party acceptable to voters with an election looming.*(14) Never did Thatcherism seem more divisive than in the aftermath of its leader's fall, and with a new leader at the helm.

Against this background of political reversal, accusations by fellow Tories of dividing the party, alienating many Conservative voters, and a fallen leader whose loyalty to the new regime was at best suspect, did the Right brace itself for the Major years. It was to prove a testing time for both the Right and Centrist sections of the party.

As for Margaret Thatcher herself, she continued to fashion events within her own party. Now freed from the restraints of high office, no longer encumbered by the restrictions of leadership, and more than a little vexed by the manner of her removal, she resolved to continue promoting the New Whig doctrines that had driven her policy agenda. Yet it was the nature of her profile and campaigning style that characterised her input to debates from one whose purpose seemed as much personal as ideological.

Additional to the publication of her memoirs in 1993, Mrs Thatcher established an office in West London which produced a litany of pamphlets and press releases. The Margaret Thatcher Foundation – as it was named – liaised with foreign leaders, parties, overseas universities and policy institutes so as to arrange speaking tours and other promotional engagements. Media liaisons were conducted vigorously, as was Mrs Thatcher's sponsorship of select campaigning groups like the anti-integrationist Bruges Group, various Conservative defence bodies and the rightist Conservative Centre Forward movement. Inevitably the former Prime Minister's lingering presence on the Commons back benches made for a poignant spectacle. Her organisation bore the hallmarks of a court in exile, which was unwelcome to many Major ministers, who saw it as undermining her successor and encouraging disaffection within the party.*(15) There was also serious concern about the impact her personal presence at the 1991 Conservative Conference might have on activists morale, not to mention encouraging media efforts at projecting splits between centrist and right wings of the party.

Another concern centred on the many senior figures at Conservative Central Office who owed their appointments to Mrs Thatcher, including policy advisers. In general, most of those individuals came of the ideological Right, and their loyalties looked uncertain in the ensuing era of John Major.*(16) While Major himself had no reason to doubt the cooperation of Central Office officials, the same presumptions could not be made for those centrists he had appointed to his Cabinet, several of whom like Heseltine and Clarke had played a substantial part in the previous leader's fall.

(iii) *Countering Destabilisation*: Major's appointment of Chris Patten as Chairman of Conservative Central Office – in preparation for the 1992 election campaign – reflected a balance of calculations. It was the same Patten who had served in Mrs Thatcher's government, and thus had the benefit of ministerial experience, not to mention a record of cooperation with the Right. Yet Chris Patten – a discerning and social-minded Catholic with green sympathies – was also a One Nation Tory who had previously headed the Conservative Research Department during Edward Heath's time. His accession at the organisational helm marked a pragmatic, if conciliatory, gesture to Centrists whose allegiance Major desperately needed in order to rejuvenate Conservatives ahead of the election. While never demonised by the Right, nonetheless they viewed Patten with suspicion; a position only partly ameliorated by his contribution to the election success of 1992.*(17)

It is important to clarify that notwithstanding widespread press speculation about Thatcher-led conspiracies over the years 1990-97, no evidence emerged in interviews undertaken with key right wingers or from their literature to support such a proposition. While such figures as the late Teresa Gorman, William Cash, John Townend and Iain Duncan Smith, all acknowledged an affinity with the ideals and legacy of Mrs Thatcher, each specifically ruled out suggestions of the former leader's direct hand in their campaigns.*(18) Nor, despite Anthony Seldon's commentary, has any reliable evidence been adduced to corroborate claims that Thatcher directly incited the turbulent events leading to John Major's tactical resignation and re-election in July 1995.*(19)

Actually, it seems that Thatcher had no interest in de-stabilising the party which over the previous two decades she had led back from opposition to government. However, she valued the essential policies of her legacy, and was concerned not to allow them to be displaced for the sake of temporary electoral gain or any other expedience. Causes like Euro-scepticism and British sovereignty, deregulation and lower taxes she hailed, and these were consistently propagated by right wing groups often at odds with the Major government. Thatcher supported those campaigns, but without formally aligning with most of the groups involved or financing them.*(20) Overall, she remained a consistent voice on the Right, frequently addressing fringe meetings and issuing pamphlets, but keeping a tactful distance from most factions.

4. Effects of Thatcher on rightist groups, post-1990

It is now worthwhile to evaluate the impact of Mrs Thatcher's changed fortunes upon her ideological brethren among the Conservative rightist groups.

In Chapters 6 & 7, it was shown that groups on the Right had become less important during the Thatcher years of government due to a right wing regime at the party helm. Groups are primarily the stuff of opposition, and with the Right in charge from 1975 until 1990 there was little scope for independent rightist activity. However, with a new leader and uncertain future, the Right's confidence wilted, thereby generating fresh purpose for those ideological campaigners who previously had backed Mrs Thatcher. Their zeal was re-energised in defence of what they saw as the Thatcher legacy, and while some hitherto established organisations re-emerged, others were born out of the new policy debates that engulfed the Conservative Party during the John Major era.

The Monday Club had long been in decline, and despite attempting a revival - as a clarion platform for the outside Right - in reality it had long lost any real influence at Westminster and Central Office. Its adoption of such causes as immigrant repatriation, repeal of race relations legislation, backing the beleaguered regime in Pretoria and the Ulster Unionists (against any deal with Irish nationalists, including the 1985 Anglo-Irish Accord) put the Club beyond the pale of front bench sponsorship.

At the same time, the Club experienced internal turbulence. With membership having slipped to under 600 by 1987, the new regime headed by Deputy Chairman, Dr Mark Mayall, and Gregory Lauder-Frost (already discussed in Chapter 7) had by 1992 revived membership to over 1,600.*(21) At the same time, several moribund branches were revived. So too was a key figure of the founding dynasty forced out; in January 1991 Cedric Gunnery was stripped of his salaried position as Club Director. Equally significant was the move to new premises –

owned by a lead figure, W. Denis Walker, a former Rhodesian education minister – opposite Higham Park Railway Station, central London.*(22) On 17th January 1991 Chairman, David Story, lost an almost unanimous vote at the Club's Executive Council, and was forced to quit. Three weeks later, Story was expelled from the Club for allegedly ".. engag(ing) in behaviour prejudicial to the best interests, reputation, objects and other members of the Monday Club; by abusing his position as Chairman in encouraging members to leave the Monday Club and join a new political grouping".*(23)

Despite the changes, the Club's fortunes failed to lift appreciably. Only a handful of backbench right wing Tory MPs continued their sponsorship of the Club, while there followed an intense debate between those wanting close ties with the Conservative Party and others favouring the role of an independent rightist pressure group. Output of policy pamphlets declined, while the energies of lead figures got ever more drawn into a furious internecine battle. A series of personal and legal problems forced the exit of Gregory Lauder-Frost on 31st May 1992. Thereafter, problems mushroomed, with more resignations, failed expulsion attempts, litigation and large legal bills, etc. Amidst this internal chaos, which left the Monday Club marginalised and rather irrelevant, control passed to Denis Walker's group in late 1992. As a result, Walker refashioned the Club as a campaigning group within the Conservative Party, in the process bringing in a new rule requiring that all members must first be members of the party, something that the previous regime had steadfastly opposed for over a decade.*(24)

Yet the Club's post-1992 Conservative affinities counted for little in the party. A dearth of MPs and peer sponsors, accompanied by embarrassing press reports of splits and divisive litigation, ensured that the Monday Club was kept at arms length by the broad majority of ordinary party members. Even its much-vaunted support of the Party was viewed suspiciously at Westminster and Central Office. Given the Club's reputation as a harbinger of rightist causes, its position within the party was believed to be as a legion of the right, hostile to the leadership of John Major and encouraging disaffection.*(25) For that reason, the Monday Club was viewed with bemused hostility on the centre, while among right wingers it was considered an embarrassing anachronism.*(26) It was eventually proscribed in 2002 as a legitimate organisation of the Conservative Party by the-then Leader, Iain Duncan Smith; a move widely supported by a cross section of opinion on centre, left and right.*(27) Thereafter the Club dwindled to the periphery.

***Centre for Policy Studies*:** This organisation maintained an autonomous existence over the period discharging its principal function as a 'brains trust' for propagating ideas and policy proposals. The demise of Mrs Thatcher and fluidity of John Major's policy direction re-awakened the zest among right wingers for promoting the Right's continuing New Whig agenda, especially given the party's election victory in the general election of April 1992.

Nevertheless, despite the election in 1992 to Westminster of CPS Director, David Willets, the organisation remained primarily a think-tank. It did not partake in rightist lobbying or encourage organised dissent against the Major government. Indeed Willets, who was appointed Paymaster General in 1996 – a post from which he subsequently resigned after criticism from the Standards and Privileges Committee in the aftermath of the Neil Hamilton 'cash for questions' scandal – proved a moderating influence on colleagues of the political right. Also, notwithstanding his preference for a free market agenda, he remained a loyal member of the government right up until its demise. Willets also debated the merits of Whig economics and continuing the Thatcher legacy with the centrist-leaning Professor John Gray, a political scientist of Oxford University, in an erudite publication emerging during the Major era at Downing Street .*(28)

CPS specialised in producing books and policy pamphlets, and generally championed economic liberalism both within the party and the wider political community, a role bequeathed by its principal founder, Keith Joseph. Its publications followed that theme, and by virtue of their associations with the most Whig-leaning school on the Right acquired a reputation as "keeper of the Thatcher legacy". The organisation was run by a Board of Directors whose membership included a collection of familiar right wing 'heavyweights' from the worlds of politics, business and academe. Michael Forsythe, Lord Saatchi, Professor Kenneth Minogue and Willets's successor, Ruth Lea, were among the CPS directors, and augmented by a circle of kindred soul mates. Other prominent figures appeared among the membership of CPS Council, including MPs like Oliver Letwin, David Heathcoat-Amery and Graham Brady, *Daily Telegraph* editor, Charles Moore, political scientist, Dr Stuart Ball and economists, Professors Patrick Minford and Nick Bosanquet. Those names lent further cerebral respectability.

CPS was entirely funded from the donations of supporters, especially business and City corporate backers.*(29) Such generosity was needed in order to operate a viable publishing budget, as well as running a central London office with three full time staff. While shy about publishing details of its finances, in reality CPS was enabled to meet its role through the donations of business supporters who valued its commitment to deregulation and private enterprise. Also, the closeness of CPS to the Conservative leadership ensured further respect for its role in policymaking.*(30) To that extent, CPS which had operated as an establishment force during the Thatcher years but, thereafter as an independent policy lobbyist, survived the Tories' transition. It was and remained a campaigning force for free market economics and social policies.

Bruges Group: This group was founded in 1988 by an Oxford University student, Patrick Robertson, in response to the nationalist sentiments expressed by Mrs Thatcher in her Euro-sceptical Bruges speech of that same year.*(31) Though the group was established to promote ideological dialogue among Euro-sceptics of all parties (it was never formally aligned to the Conservatives), in practice it quickly emerged as a campaigning group of the Conservative Right.*(32) In particular, the group assumed fresh momentum following Mrs Thatcher's downfall, and by 1992 Mrs Thatcher had become its Honorary President, followed after 1993 by ex-Chancellor, Norman Lamont, as Vice President.

Among its lead figures were – and remain – co-Chairs, Barry Legg and Brian Hindley, both with a long record of campaigning rightist causes among Conservative activists, while in early days the contemporary historian, Dr Alan Sked, was another prominent figure. Sked's zealous anti-Europeanism caused him to clash with group colleagues, with the result that he left around 1991 to form the Anti-Federalist League (seeking UK withdrawal from Europe) that later emerged as the UK Independence Party.*(33)

The Bruges Group operated primarily as a platform for the Conservative Right, most particularly its liberal Euro-sceptical wing, and was centred on Westminster. It was not a Conservative grass roots organisation. Its conference platform and many pamphlets argued the case for British independence within the European Union, a cause that assumed growing prominence as the 1992-97 Parliament progressed. The inability of Prime Minister, John Major, to achieve a unified policy acceptable to the broad stream of his parliamentary party meant that the Bruges Group acted as a focus for Euro-sceptics and other right wing malcontents who strained Tory unity to the limits. Its finances were boosted by donations from right wing supporters, many of whom were disturbed at the growing Cabinet influence of Michael Heseltine and the Major government's general drift towards electoral disaster, as indeed happened in 1997.*(34)

Selsdon Group: Another Whig tendency whose profile was revived was the Selsdon Group. This body founded in 1973 by the late Nicholas Ridley but lying semi-dormant for most of the Thatcher years, experienced a political rebirth in the eighteen months after her downfall. Its principal role was as a publicist for the Right's Euro-sceptics and free market lobby, but was confined in scope to Parliament and the London-based policy making elites. In no sense did the Selsdon Group attempt to mobilise grass roots support.

The Selsdon Group – as its literature emphasised – saw its role as to defend the place of free enterprise and property interests in the wake of Mrs Thatcher's political fall.*(35) Having been inactive for the previous decade and a half, the group found itself dashing to the rescue of the Thatcher legacy especially given the Right's general unease at the Major Cabinet's abandonment of the poll tax principle in Spring 1991. Thereafter, the group published pamphlets arguing for a continuation of

Mr Thatcher's free enterprise policies, rather than risking their displacement by a government whose principal thrust was in the opposite direction. Following Nicholas Ridley's retirement from the House of Commons in 1992 and subsequent death in 1995, the group presidency passed to former Welsh Secretary and 1995 rightist challenger to Premier Major, John Redwood.

Like other groups of the kind, Selsdon continued to be funded by a mixture of pamphlet sales and supporters donations. Revenue was forthcoming from supporters in politics, the City and business sources uneasy about John Major's direction. There was nothing sinister about funding, though general coyness about finances rendered suspicions in centre-leftist circles about the exact sources of revenue.*(36)

Other right wing organisations ..... like the Coalition for Peace and Security and Olga Maitland's Women for Families and Defence fizzled out due to their cause having been achieved and thus being low on the Conservative battle agenda.*(37)

On the other hand, the Conservative Family Campaign was given a medium life booster from John Major's 'Back to Basics' Campaign that ultimately failed so dismally – much to the party's embarrassment – over the course of his premiership. Though Mrs Thatcher had always studiously avoided formal alignments with the pro-family and pro-life politics of the religious right, she had made no secret of her general sympathy with their aims and personal admiration for figures like Dr Adrian Rodgers, and Mrs Mary Whitehouse. To that degree, with support proffered by right wingers like the Wintertons (Anne and Nicholas), David Amos, Jill Knight, William Cash and later, Iain Duncan-Smith, rightist family campaigners got drawn into battle during the Major years, as much in disgust at revelations of sexual deviance by numerous Conservative front benchers as actual policy lobbying.*(38) At the same time, the religious Right's influence had noticeably waned by the time of Major's retirement in 1997, and even more so a decade later. The extent of the latter's decline was manifest by their failure to stem David Cameron's mission to legalise same-sex marriages after 2011.

5. How did Major's Leadership Affect Factionalism?

The general nature of Major's impact on the party has already been considered, and it now remains to evaluate his impact on factionalism. Specifically, was his style a stimulant or cause of group activity, and in which areas was it most pronounced?

Given the Right's swift disaffection that had become obvious even ahead of the 1992 general election, available evidence points to a rebirth of right wing factionalism. Throughout his period of office, Major found himself counterpoising erstwhile allies on key issues like Ireland, the economy, local taxation and Europe to the extent that some challenged his strategy and leadership. Although the Centre also had their own agenda, they avoided open conflict with the Prime Minister and did not undermine his authority, far less encourage revolts. To that degree, John Major started off as the Right's man, but later became dependent on the Centre whose lieutenants – Heseltine, Patten, Clarke, Dorrell etc. – figured prominently in his cabinet. Moreover, the revival of Conservative factionalism after 1992 was right wing driven and focused on the causes of rightist disaffection that have been previously listed. In any case, Major always professed an interest in One-Nation Tory principles, and by virtue of his support for the European Union was drawn ever further away from the Right towards the Centre to the extent that in later years, after quitting office, he became President of the Tory Reform Group.

Perhaps the crucial test of shifting allegiances manifested with the 1995 leadership contest. The challenge of right winger, John Redwood, gave vent to a series of rightist grievances on Europe, Ireland, the economy, transport, privatisation and the general direction of John Major's government. Redwood was supported exclusively by the Right, both at Westminster and in the country. Conversely, whatever misgivings Tory One Nationites may have had with Major over European integration and the state of British society, their MPs and peers loyally backed the Prime Minister, as much from a pragmatic desire to curb the Right as any feelings of political kinship.*(39) Significantly, the 'Tory Reformer' did not inveigh hostilities against the Premier.

From the beginning, Major steered clear of factions and put his emphasis on party unity. Indeed in a fashion not unlike Jim Callaghan's management of the Labour government some twenty years earlier, Major trod carefully, mindful of the sharp tensions between left and right, nurturing figures from all sides of the party, making tactical concessions here and there, and – like Callaghan – leading a minority government for some three years. What he lacked in charisma was compensated by the adroit skills that held his administration and party together for the duration of the parliamentary term.

In the end, the Conservatives under Major drifted towards an overwhelming election defeat, and thereafter banishment to the opposition benches for 13 years. Also, in the electoral lead-up, there were implosions from within, especially over issues like European integration, economic management and standards in public life. There was also the embarrassing spectacle of Tory ministers and MPs either disregarding the official line or being unmasked in assorted forms of sleaze and sexual peccadillo.

Actually, the perceived lack of integrity among parliamentarians proved less of a spur to factional revival than the Major government's aimless drift. To the Right, it was all symptomatic of a weak successor to Margaret Thatcher, while on the Centre some wondered aloud if there really was any place for liberal Tories in a Right dominated party.*(40) Also, with the question of Europe being fundamental to both Centre and Right, albeit from different vantage points, it was thus inevitable that Major's insistence on not ruling out British accession to the European currency for the life time of two parliaments was not going to please anybody from either wing. It also left open the door to a renewal of ideological battle as soon as the party found itself in opposition, which was precisely what happened in the aftermath of the party's catastrophic defeat to Labour and the resurgent Liberal Democrats in the general election of 1st May 1997.

As was shown by the experiences of Conservatives immediately after the election defeats of 1945, 1964 and 1974, factionalism manifests when ideological direction is unclear and a rebellion is being staged against official policy. Such happened again in 1997, and indeed over the preceding three years, when the party appeared to drift without firm leadership. Hence old tensions between Centre and Right revived at all levels of the party – at and beyond Westminster – as indicated by the intensive battles fought over Europe, taxation, the economy and political progress in Northern Ireland.

The lead had been set by the Tory Euro-rebels, while elsewhere a plethora of mainly short-lived groups – previously highlighted – confronted the Prime Minister from within his own ranks on so many policies such as highlighted the disunity of the Tory party as its 18-year term of office drew to a close. For this state of affairs, John Major must take some responsibility as his leadership and programme dictated events from 1990 until 1997. His willingness to hold the party together for the sake of bolstering electoral credibility is understandable, but it was a strategy for which the Conservatives paid a high price after 1994 and even more so following the defeat of 1997. The 1995 Summer leadership contest may have settled doubts about Major's own position, but by virtue of the cogent challenge of John Redwood, it fairly lit up all the ideological divisions prevalent within the party and left a clear impression of disunity with the electorate. This legacy undermined Major for the remainder of his term, and weakened his entire calibre of authority, while encouraging fragmentation on the inside.

6. Tory Centre

It has to be asked how the Major leadership tenure impacted on the reviving fortunes of the Tory Centre? Specifically, after 15 years of Rightist dominance under Mrs Thatcher, did John Major's appointment of key Tory Centrists like Michael Heseltine, Ken Clarke, Stephen Dorrell and Chris Patten to his Cabinet spell a realignment of One Nationism with the party leadership? Equally significantly, why did Major come to depend on the support of Centrists in the Cabinet, parliamentary party and wider party organisation as his relations with the Right deteriorated, especially after the dismissal of his right wing Chancellor, Norman Lamont, in Spring 1993? If that was true, how did realignment of political alliances impact on groups and causes of the Centre?

In order to address those questions, first it is necessary to view the state of the Centre after the fall of Margaret Thatcher and accession of John Major in November 1990.

Plainly, as was confirmed in most interviews with Centrist figures of the time (not least Heseltine and Dorrell), there were few regrets either at Thatcher's demise or the manner of its happening. In their eyes, she had imposed a right wing agenda that was now backfiring in the form of rising inflation, economic instability and an unpopular poll tax that had cost the party dearly in by-election losses and council seats, and looked likely to lose the Conservatives the next Westminster election. Therefore, she was in a weak position with the party faithful generally, and like those predecessors who had paid the price of electoral failure, so was she felled by the same sword. Yet by November 1990 the Tory Centre itself had been severely truncated by a right wing establishment that had flourished over the previous fifteen years. With the exceptions of Ken Clarke and Chris Patten, few other Centrists held senior positions, while Central Office was almost bereft of Centrists in research or administration.

Among centrist groups and causes, little progress had been achieved under Margaret Thatcher. European integration had been stoutly resisted, so had constitutional reform in Scotland and Wales, while curbs on local government and deregulation of public utilities had been pursued with ideological fervour. The latter figure had proved impervious to Tory Reformer's concerns about maintaining a balance between private enterprise and social cohesion, not to mention Centre-Right unity in the party.*(41) It was the Centre who had felt the sharp end of New Whig zeal, and thus the Centre whose people felt the greatest relief at the political demise of the Right's principal icon.

As the evidence shows, it was in Cabinet that the Centre exercised its greatest influence. This was attributable to two factors. First, the various centrist lobby organisations – e.g. Tory Europeans, Tory Reformers, Charter Movement, etc. – emerged from the Thatcher era in a weakened state; their influence among grass roots was limited, membership reduced to a hard core, and with appeal greater among non-party than party sources. Second, the Centre did not lack front line advocates in parliament and the government; it was a measure of Major's gradual disavowal by the Right that he came to depend on Centrist lieutenants like Heseltine, Clarke and Dorrell especially after 1992. Some of the Right's principal Westminster activists of the time acknowledged Major's close alliance with the Centre, and while berating his alleged apostasy over issues like free market economics and European sovereignty, nevertheless grudgingly agreed that the Centre had gained much ground from Major's obligated favour.*(42)

In fact the re-emergence of Tory Centre organisations was neither immediate nor automatic under Major. The Tory Reform Group had long maintained a dignified if also low key existence during the Thatcher years; membership remained constant, finances durable and activities creditable, if more directed at sustaining rather than proselytising the Progressive cause. Its magazine, Tory Reformer, remained a voice for relevant Centrist causes, and despite being a platform for party dissidents still managed to stay both solvent and marketable. Contributors were drawn from a cross section of the party, including rightists, and the journal's editorial line while propagating the One Nation agenda also avoided challenges to the party leadership.*(43) During the Major years, Tory Reformer maintained a position of broad critical support, and directed its fire at the "... wrecking tactics ..." of the Right's Euro-rebels whom it accused of leading the Conservatives towards certain electoral defeat.*(44) This position was stridently pursued during the Redwood leadership challenge of Summer 1995 and over the final two years of the government's lifetime. Such a strategy rendered the Prime Minister's travails all the more acute by effectively highlighting his break with the Right.

Conservatives in Europe proved most vulnerable to Rightist hostility. The organisation that was at various points headed by Norman Fowler and Stephen Dorrell, and openly supported by former Premier, Edward Heath, was positioned on the Euro-centred wing of the party, but kept at arms length by Central Office and the party leadership. Its Eurointegrationist agenda proved embarrassing to a Prime Minister who wanted to avoid commitments either in favour of or against accession to the Euro currency, and it was thus sidelined as far as any endorsement or preference went. The group was forced to lobby its cause by a series of pamphlets, Conference fringe meetings, debates and the usual retinue of Westminster supporters like Heath, Hugh Dykes and others. While little appeared in the memoirs of relevant leading Tory politicians about the group, actually its lobbying was real and coordinated in Parliament and on the outside.*(45)

The Conservative Charter Movement also enjoyed a mini revival during the Major years. Its campaigns were low key, its mainly Home Counties membership remained active, and its general profile was sustained. Yet Charter campaigns were directed at the party leadership and policy makers and, in reality, held little interest for many activists at grass root.*(46) Its programme ran against party traditions, especially its power structures, and thus was never likely to wrestle many concessions from a reluctant party establishment of the Right, Centre or otherwise. At the same time, the Charter Movement raised issues about the lack of democracy in the Conservative Party that proved timely, and additionally prefaced the introduction of a party constitution under Major's successor, William Hague.*(47) That initiative owed less to Charter campaigns as more the party's modernisation and regularisation following unseemly events that preceded the electoral devastation of 1st May 1997 – see Chapter 9. *(48)

Other Conservative centrist campaigning groups also emerged in the Major years. These included the Conservative Campaign for Electoral Reform, Tory Campaign for Gay Rights and the Tory Greens, all of whom were policy lobbyists aiming to challenge the traditional political culture of the Conservative Party. While not significant in size or mobilising large numbers of activists, favourable exposure in newspapers like the Guardian and Independent, plus having influential patrons at Westminster, gave those groups a profile well beyond their position in the party.*(49) Significantly, the libertarian nature of those tendencies showed a gradual change in the character of the Conservative Party that became more marked over the next decade.

7. Conclusions

Overall, the Conservative Party divided profoundly over the seven years of John Major's leadership. While the balance of power at Westminster shifted towards the Centre, conversely evidence produced here points to grass roots activists having preferred the politics of Mrs Thatcher and her Rightist school.

Put simply, Thatcher, by virtue of three consecutive electoral victories, won over the hearts and minds of her rank and file, whereas Major never reached that stage. Instead, as indicated by a litany of figures from across the party spectrum in interviews and articles, he became synonymous by 1995 with a party that was visibly losing its grip on power as well as public confidence. In those conditions, and given the Conservatives historic penchant for faction fighting when facing or immediately following electoral defeat, factional politics were revived during and as a result of the Major era.

With the benefit of hindsight, while John Major's succession to Margaret Thatcher gave the appearance of continuing New Right dominance at the party helm, in fact Mrs Thatcher's departure from Downing St meant a concomitant decline in the fortunes of her ideological brethren. Over the previous decade, she had come to epitomise not just an agenda for government, but also policies that no longer commanded widespread public support. Chief among those were the Poll Tax which threatened to cause public unrest and dislodge her party from office and which was swiftly – and painlessly – buried by her successor. Other issues generating public unease included further privatisation, economic recession and European integration. In each instance, Rightist zeal, as represented by Thatcher and some in Major's Cabinet (Portillo and Redwood), plus the Parliamentary Party, appeared to have run its course by the mid-1990s.

It was left to Centrist pragmatists like Heseltine, Clarke and Fowler to keep the Prime Minister on course for adapting Conservative policies to a climate less conducive towards (and an electorate less eager for) New Right ideological assertiveness. Indeed the revival of the One Nation Tories occurred more by stealth and evolution than any serious ideological crusade. However, after Major's defeat of John Redwood in the party leadership contest of Summer 1995, the New Right were a spent force as far as influencing public policymaking was concerned. Yet this had occurred at the cost of continuing factional conflict in the party; something that lingered on right up to and beyond the catastrophic Conservative electoral defeat of May 1997. It also played a big part in the choice of Major's three short-lived successors, William Hague, Iain Duncan-Smith and Michael Howard, and the policy debates that accompanied each of their elections in 1997, 2001 and 2003 respectively. Such was the price of ideological mutation!

FOOTNOTES and REFERENCES

1. Anthony Seldon - with Lewis Baston - "Major: A Political Life", Chap. 20, p.p. 290-300 (Phoenix, 1997).

2. This view has been articulated by Seldon (1997), Clark (1997) and Charmley (1996), with an affirmation from John Major in his own memoirs (1999, see Chaps 8 & 9).

3. John Major The Autobiography, Chap. 9, p.p. 214-217 (Harper Collins, 1999).

4. Ibid.

5. (i) In the first ballot – declared on 20th November, 1990 – Thatcher scored 204 votes (3 less than what was needed for outright victory), with Heseltine winning 152 and 16 abstentions. Thatcher withdrew after two days, leaving the field open. The second ballot result declared on 27th November 1990 was:

    John Major: 185   Michael Heseltine: 131   Douglas Hurd: 56

    With Major 2 votes short of the total required for outright victory, Heseltine and Hurd withdrew, thereby allowing Sir Cranley Onslow, Chairman of the 1922 Committee, to declare Major the new Conservative Leader and Prime Minister.

    (ii) For a list of the MPs backing particular candidates, see Appendices 2 & 3.

6. (i) Major outlined his hopes for a distinctive premiership and policy programme throughout Chapter 9 of his autobiography.

    (ii) Also, see Seldon biography (1997), Chap.11, p.p. 132-134.

7. This view was confirmed to a substantial degree in interviews with a number of right-wingers, namely: Lord Tebbit, Iain Duncan Smith, Teresa Gorman and William Cash. There was no personal animosity towards John Major, but rather disappointment at what they saw as the "..missed chances.." of his government over the years 1990-97. Also, several felt he had abandoned key tenets of Thatcherism in order to appease the Centre in Parliament and his

Cabinet (lead by Heseltine and Clark), plus non-Conservative forces elsewhere.

8. Interviews - Heseltine, Dorrell and Temple-Morris.

9. This view was made clear to the author in interviews with Teresa Gorman, William Cash, Iain Duncan-Smith and Lord Tebbit.

10. Seldon (1997), Chap. 10, p. 128.

11. Major admitted in his memoirs that he regretted snubbing Thatcher, explaining that he was responding to opposition taunts that a joint photograph would risk appearing as though she were pulling the strings over his premiership – see Major (1999), Chap. 8, p. 199.

12. Early in the 1992-97 parliament, the Conservatives lost by-elections to the Liberal Democrats at Newbury and Christchurch, both safe seats whose loss was acutely felt throughout the party.

13. A point acknowledged in interviews with Tebbit, Gorman and Cash.

14. Acknowledged in interviews with Heseltine, Dorrell, Justin Powell-Tuck and Peter Temple-Morris.

15. A view confirmed in interviews with Heseltine and Dorrell.

16. Ibid

17. A view confirmed in interviews with John Townend, Teresa Gorman, William Cash (all Westminster-connected) and Mrs Eila Bannister of the Monday Club.

18. Interviews - Cash, Townend, Gorman and Duncan Smith.

19. See Seldon (1997), Chaps 17 & 22.

20. Baroness Thatcher spoke on platforms arranged by the Bruges Group and Conservative Centre Forward, to name but two, but without proffering any direct financial aid to those or any other similar groups.

21. (i) Interview - Mrs Eila Bannister.
    (ii) Monday Club News, January 1991.

22. Ibid.

23. Minutes of Monday Club Executive Council, 11th February, 1991.

24. Monday Club News, June 1992 and August 1992. Also, interview with Mrs Eila Bannister.

25. Interviews - Dorrell, Temple-Morris and Giles Marshall.

26. A view confirmed in interviews with Tebbit, Gorman, Townend, Temple-Morris and Dorrell.

27. Interview with Iain Duncan Smith.

28. John Gray & David Willets "Is Conservatism Dead?" (Profile Books, 1994).

29. Information supplied by a CPS administrator (requesting anonymity), but generally available from CPS profile literature and website of the 1990s.

30. Interviews - Tebbit, Dorrell, Gorman and Powell-Tuck.

31. Given 28th September, 1988.

32. Bruges Group - Information gathered from interview with Group London-activist who wished to remain anonymous; interview 15th March 2006.

33. Times, Daily Telegraph, Independent and Spectator reports January - July 1991.

34. Interview - Bruges Group activist, 15th March 2006.
    Also, interview with Powell-Tuck.

35. See Selsdon Group publications and website, all carrying a Statement of Aims.

36. Discussions with Lord Tebbit (July 2001).

37. The Coalition for Peace and Security was a prominent organisation in the 1980s when countering CND on university/polytechnic campuses. Its links to the Conservative Party were never formal, though nearly all activists were card-carrying Tories usually of the Right. The organisation faded by the 1990s after the end of the Cold War when defence debates assumed less passion or profile. Such was also true of Olga Maitland's Women for Families and Defence which had all but gone by the time of her loss of Westminster seat in May 1997.

38. Interviews with Iain Duncan Smith and William Cash. Note too this author's article, 'The American and British Right; comparisons of tactics and impact', Church Times, 15th October, 2007.

39. Interviews with Stephen Dorrell, Lord Heseltine, Giles Marshall, Justin Powell-Tuck and Peter Temple-Morris.

40. See Iain Gilmour and Mark Garner - "Where have all the Tories Gone?" (1997, Palgrave).

41. Tory Reformer, Spring and Summer issues 1990.

42. A view repeated in interviews with Heseltine, Dorrell, Temple-Morris and Marshall.

43. See Tory Reformer, issues Summer and Autumn 1992, Spring 1993, Autumn 1993, all issues 1994 and 1995, Spring 1996.

44. See Tory Reformer, issues Summer and Autumn 1995.

45. Interviews - Dorrell, Heseltine, Temple-Morris and Marshall.

46. Interview - Eric Chalker and Charter News, issues 43 (1996) and 49 (1997). Also, observations of Lord Tebbit shared in interview.

47. Ibid.

48. See Eric Chalker's article - 'The Stalinist Tories need purging', Independent, 25th June, 1997.

49. It was noticeable that liberal Tory groups like the Gays, Europeans, electoral reformers and Environments were treated generously by newspapers like the Guardian and Independent. See press coverage of Conservative Annual Conferences 1992, 1993 and 1996 in both papers.

CHAPTER 9

CONSERVATIVES IN OPPOSITION 1997 - 2007

THREE SHORT-TERM CAPTAINS!

This chapter aims to evaluate the nature of Conservative factionalism after 1997 when the party returned to Opposition. It will examine issues like Europe, Celtic devolution and the economy which divided the party, as well as the different styles, impact and agendas of four separate Tory leaders over 13 years. Specifically, the chapter will make assessments of how far factional politics were affected by the travails of opposition. In particular, did any or all of the three leaders – i.e. Hague, Duncan-Smith, Howard or, later, Cameron – consort with or sponsor particular groups? What consequences did leader-led ideological crusades, e.g. Hague's 1999 party plebiscite that ruled out UK-European currency accession, have for groups adversely affected by official policy? Finally, the chapter will consider the extent to which leadership changes and evolving ideological direction were assisted by factional politicking in the constituencies and at head office.

All the questions raised by this chapter relate to a party experiencing the cyclical phases of government and opposition. As was shown in earlier chapters, Conservatives are usually restless in Opposition, and the most recent experience proved to be no exception.

1. Introduction

U.K. General Election - May 1997

Labour: 418 seats (43.2% of national vote, + 8.8%)
Conservatives: 165 seats (30.7% of national vote - 11.2%)
Liberal Democrats: 46 seats (18% of vote share, but with seats more than doubled.)

Whatever the many views to have been expressed about the causes of defeat, there can be little doubt about the consequences of the 1997 election for the Conservative Party. First, by lunchtime on 2nd May the defeated Prime Minister, John Major, announced that he was resigning the Conservative leadership. Second, Major was leaving a party in turmoil, reduced to a rump in the Commons, and whose losses figured a string of outgoing ministers including Michael Portillo, Ian Lang, Malcolm Rifkind and Michael Forsythe. Third, the Conservatives were left without a single seat in Scotland or Wales, and none in the cities of Manchester, Liverpool, Sheffield and Newcastle upon Tyne, with just one in Birmingham. This acute weakness raised serious questions about the party's ability to achieve recovery in the short or medium term. Fourth, electoral catastrophe produced the inevitable blow to morale at all levels of the party from Westminster to the grass roots. This demoralisation further extended to Conservatives in the media, City of London, education, the law and public sector, all of whom were forced to taste the bitter fruits of defeat and the likelihood of a prolonged period in Opposition.

As events over the ensuing decade showed, Conservatives did not respond positively to Opposition. The story of their party during the ten years of Labour leader, Tony Blairs's premiership (1997-2007) was one of political restlessness resulting from three successive Westminster election defeats, four leaders in eight years (after Major), a generally limp Commons performance by the majority of shadow spokesmen/women, intermittent embarrassments from press disclosures about the private lives of key figures and continuing divisions over key issues like Europe, taxation, civil liberties and the constitution. Additionally, there was the ongoing whiff of financial scandal arising from the business dealings of key Conservative business supporters, as well as occasional defections by parliamentarians (e.g. Shaun Woodward and Peter Temple-Morris) to Labour and former Harrow MP and Europhile, Hugh Dykes, to the Liberal Democrats. Additionally, there were lingering troubles about effective leadership, with those troubles haunting Major's three immediate successors.

As was shown in 1964 and 1974, Conservatives are most prone to implode in the aftermath of losing power, with factionalism manifesting from political disarray and leadership uncertainty compounding the dilemma. The experience of 1997 followed the same pattern, with Major's three short-lived successors each failing to stamp authority on the 'brethren' and a consequent drift that left the party disconnected and rather irrelevant.

As for the election of new leader, William Hague's victory was predictable given the Right's dominance of a depleted Conservative Westminster force. Yet the contest was not without its bizarre moments.*(1) In what turned out to be the last election determined solely by Conservative MPs before the new constitution took force, giving final voice to ordinary members, an unholy alliance briefly emerged between the Rightist, John Redwood, and Tory Progressive, Ken Clarke. Having been eliminated at the penultimate round, Redwood reached an arrangement with Clarke whereby the former – with whom he shared little ideological ground – openly endorsed the latter in the run-off. Not that it benefited Clarke much because he was roundly defeated by Hague – who was endorsed by among others, Baroness Thatcher – in the final vote. It is also significant that as soon as the result was announced by the 1922 Committee Chairman, Clarke announced that he would not be serving in his victorious rival's Shadow Cabinet. Though avoiding displays of sour grapes, the former Chancellor's absence from the Hague and Duncan Smith front benches had a weakening effect on both, while his open campaigns in favour of European integration heightened the impression of deep divisions at the party helm.

Tables 1, 2 and 3 below show the figures all too clearly in what was to prove the party's last leadership contest decided by the remaining 164 Conservative MPs alone.

Table 1	First Ballot (4th June 1997)
Kenneth Clarke	49
William Hague	41
John Redwood	27
Peter Lilley	24
Michael Howard	23

Howard was eliminated and Lilley dropped out.

Table 2	Second Ballot (11th June 1997)
Kenneth Clarke	64
William Hague	62
John Redwood	38

Redwood eliminated

Table 3	Final Ballot (18th June 1997)
William Hague	90
Kenneth Clarke	72

Hague elected.

As events were to demonstrate, Hague, though later a consummate figure on the Conservative front bench (not least as shadow foreign secretary under David Cameron), nevertheless had the misfortune in July 1997 to assume leadership of a party that was unelectable as a government for at least a decade thereafter. That he failed to make a significant impact on his party's weak electoral position was probably less of a personal failing than was projected by critics, as more an indication of the serious crisis of voter confidence which afflicted Conservatives over the first eight years of Opposition.*(2)

2.   Conservatives under Hague

William Hague's leadership was never fully established from the very beginning, nor throughout the entire four years of his captain's tenure. He struggled to reverse the Conservatives low voter appeal in the wake of their gravest defeat for over a century, and to revive morale among activists and parliamentarians who counterpoised a formidable Tony Blair and his New Labour government from an enfeebled Opposition bench. A succession of unfavourable opinion polls, negative perceptions of the young Conservative leader, plus criticism of his policies by former

Tory ministers, Anne Widdecombe, Ken Clarke and others contributed to a diminution of his credibility with Conservative voters. Even his one-time mentor, Margaret Thatcher, was not always supportive.

Over the same period, Hague depended heavily on the loyalty of backroom aides like Sebastian Coe and Amanda Platell, plus a small coterie of loyal backbenchers. As Simon Walters's account testifies, Hague's authority was regularly undermined at Westminster not so much from One Nationites like Ken Clarke or Stephen Dorrell *(3), but rather from right wing rivals, specifically John Redwood, Francis Maude and, later, Michael Portillo.*(4) Following his return to Parliament in a by-election in 1999, Portillo proved to be the most venomous of "..disloyal knaves.." with his constancy of negative gestures, media leaks and damaging comments.*(5) Frustrated ambition is the most likely guide to Portillo's conduct, and did not stop with Hague either, as Iain Duncan Smith recalled.*(6)

Party morale, already rock-bottom following the electoral drubbing by Labour in the General Election, took a further dip when Hague, against advice from many pragmatists in the Scottish Party, opted for a vigorous campaign against Scottish and Welsh Home Rule in the constitutional referenda of September 1997. Given that the Tories were without seats in either nation, this unionist gesturing by the English leader of what looked increasingly like an English party seemed to begrudge the Scottish and Welsh peoples recognition of their historic rights to self-rule, albeit within the United Kingdom. The results (i.e. overwhelming endorsement in Scotland and majority endorsement in Wales), highlighted the marginalisation of the Conservative Party and its seeming electoral crisis before even the party had met for its post-election conference. To add to the latter went the limp performances of several Conservative front benchers – of which Andrew McKay was probably the gravest handicap *(7) – that contrasted so starkly with those of Blair, Gordon Brown, David Blunkett, Peter Mandelson, Robin Cook and other Labour titans. With Heseltine recovering from a heart attack, Clarke, Dorrell and Widdecombe all unavailable, and others like Ian Lang, Malcolm Rifkind, Michael Forsythe and the defeated Portillo outside the Commons, there simply was not the talented manpower in place for Hague to even begin to match the Labour government in Parliament.

When the Tory annual gathering finally occurred, Hague found himself presiding over a raffish assortment of battling Euro-sceptics and Europhiles, free marketeers, One-Nationites, social liberals, traditional social conservatives, Thatcherites, old Heathites and many more grass roots activists baffled by the ideological divisions. Hague himself, an economic Thatcherite, Eurosceptic (but not anti-European) and social conservative chimed with many, but by no means all of his grass roots. He was counterpoised by the Europhile Clarke, himself committed to UK accession to the Euro-currency, and the mischievous Portillo on the outside – until his return to Westminster from a by-election Kensington in 1999 – who had lately devised a new "inclusive" agenda that embraced homosexuals, and increased women and non-whites in contrast to the social conservatism of the Thatcher era. In practice, all were posturing so as to boost their ambitions.*(8)

Overall, William Hague's inheritance was lacking in potential. His party was devoid of discipline, purpose and direction, and as far as polls could be taken seriously, his prospects looked doomed from the beginning. Against this ominous background, Hague made his pitch to turn things around, but for all his ingenuity, it was never likely to achieve major results. Significantly, Hague knew this to be the case from an early stage, but nevertheless persisted with what he considered his overriding constitutional duty as Leader of Her Majesty's Loyal Opposition in Parliament.*(9)

3.   Dominant challenges of the Hague years, 1997-2001.

Broadly speaking, four major issues defined Hague's four years at the Conservative helm.

First, was Home Rule in Scotland and Wales, which under Hague Tories had opposed. Having sustained big defeats in the constitutional referenda of September 1997, Hague opted – in classical Conservative tradition – to gracefully concede that which he could not prevent. However, grudging acceptance of the new Scottish Parliament and Welsh Assembly rather undermined Tory prospects in elections – held in 1999 under variable preferential rules – to both institutions. The latter saw the party reduced to a rump in Edinburgh and Cardiff respectively, something that reflected the weak Tory profile in both countries where it was devoid of even a single Westminster MP. Moreover, as Philip Lynch showed, recovery came very slowly over the ensuing decade.*(10)

Second, was the 1997/98 Northern Ireland Peace Process, where Conservatives were rendered irrelevant. The Conservative Northern Ireland Spokesman, Andrew McKay, aside from questionable choice of priorities (earlier mentioned), proved to be a weak and poorly informed figure whose interest in Irish affairs was modest and partisan. That said, there was no repeat of the 1985 post-Anglo Irish Agreement, when hard line Unionist factions had aligned with their brethren in Belfast against the Hillsborough Accord, and the party gave its formal support to the Good Friday Belfast Agreement of April 1998. Yet attempts at introducing the Conservative Party to Northern Ireland proved to be an embarrassing failure, when candidates failed to win above 2% in elections of the time. For the record, a later accord between the British Conservatives and Ulster Unionists – initiated between David Cameron and the Belfast leader, Sir Reginald Empey, for the 2010 Westminster election – proved an even greater disaster, producing no seats and defeat everywhere to the rival Democratic Unionist Party (DUP) of Dr Ian Paisley.*(11)

Third was the issue of European integration. Hague, along with a majority of his diminished Westminster force and grass roots, resolutely opposed further European integration, and was particular hostile towards the Euro currency. Among his supporters were remnants of the European rebels – the so-called "bastards" – who had lost the whip, albeit temporarily, during the previous administration of John Major. Yet there was also a dedicated Europhile tendency centred on the Tory Reform Group, which contained key patrons like Michael Heseltine, Ken Clarke, Nick Scott and Stephen Dorrell. A party plebiscite in 1999 produced a substantial endorsement of Hague's Eurosceptical policy, supposedly binding on all Tory parliamentarians, but openly rebuked by Clarke and TRG.

Overall, the European issue simmered beneath the surface, and while divisive in terms of its effect on the party membership, nevertheless it did not cause any open rifts. The TRG journal, *Reformer*, continued to offer a platform for Europhiles, but without posturing hostility towards the party leadership.*(12) This European rift reflected a sobering reality with which successive party leaders had to deal over the next twenty years.

Fourth, was the reform of party organisation, which emerged as a positive legacy from Hague's leadership term. There was the merger in 1998 of Conservative Students, Conservative Graduates and the Young Conservatives to create an official youth organisation, Conservative Future, with the aim of rejuvenating the party's appeal among younger voters. With declining membership – down from 2.8 million in 1951 to under 250,000 by 1997 – and widespread dissatisfaction with outdated practices and decision-making procedures, Hague's new chairman, the veteran Cecil Parkinson, managed to produce a revived organisation and constitution that sought to modernise party structures. Its main features included: a written constitution with clear definitions of the titles and authority of various party bodies ranging from constituency associations to annual conference to the national and regional executives, a national membership, rules for the selection of parliamentary and local council candidates, provisions for party plebiscites and the election of leaders, inclusive of a full member ballot for the final run-off between two lead candidates. Although putting up a quasi-democratic constitution in place of a somewhat ramshackle predecessor, the reality was that it concentrated power in the hands of MPs and the central cabal. This reality was borne out by the clinical manner in which Iain Duncan Smith was supplanted as leader by Michael Howard in 2003.

Hague's reforms certainly did not satisfy either of the two campaigning organisations, Tory Charter Movement or the Conservative Campaign for Party Democracy, both of whose leading spokesmen confirmed suspicions of a window-dressing exercise that altered power balances very little.*(13) Already there had been the 1993 Feldman Report - commissioned by the then-Chairman, Norman Fowler – which had accepted the case for greater membership involvement in leadership elections and policy input, followed by Hague own endorsement after assuming the party leadership. However, the Hague constitution as it emerged fell far short of the reformers hopes. Both groups were particularly unhappy at the party establishment's refusal to concede elected national offices, plus the failure to separate the party central office from its pivotal role in approving a parliamentary candidates panel.*(14)

Given that, for the first time in over half a century the party rules and institutions were overhauled, Hague left an efficient organisation as his most enduring legacy. His reforms were endorsed by most sections of opinion within the party, and were not altered by any of his successors. However, attempts by Hague to popularise his appeal by appearing less formal at the Notting Hill Carnival and admitting to having consumed high levels of beer during student days, fell on barren ground. With the onset of the 2001 general election, few people gave much for his chances of achieving a recovery, much less a breakthrough. This sober prediction, according to Walters, exercised rivals like Portillo and Maude with plotting a succession which it was assumed the impending election would facilitate.*(15) Evidently, Hague was blessed with few loyal parliamentary colleagues at any level!

4. Factional Activity during the Hague Era

All evidence points to factional dominance by the Right throughout the Hague years. It was not that the party looked likely to make an early return to government or that the writ of Margaret Thatcher continued to brim a decade after her departure, although from the Lords the elderly Baroness gave mixed signals to her supporters not all of which oozed loyalty to Hague, whom she had earlier endorsed. Actually, the recognition of Hague as something of a stop-gap leader unlikely to survive was accepted by a consensus of opinion on all sides of the Conservative Party. This instinct encouraged various rightist tendencies to fight for their party to be led from the Right in terms of emergent parliamentarians, leadership and in policy agenda.*(16) There was no way the Right would willingly facilitate any return of the One Nation cadre in their time.*(17)

The leading rightist faction embracing parliamentarians and grass roots was Conservative Way Forward. This organisation – with Parkinson and Tebbit as its co-presidents – at its high point commanded the active allegiances of over 1,000 activists and was something of a Thatcherite ideological crusade that worked in collaboration with fellow travellers of the Right. The latter included the Libertarian Alliance, Bill Cash's European Foundation, Bruges Group, 92 Group and the No Turning Back Group, all with the combined aim of defending the

Thatcher legacy.*(18) Various figures of the Conservative Right testified to the pivotal role of the No Turning Back Group as the Westminster organisation which largely controlled the plethora of rightist campaigning groups operating at Westminster and throughout party grass roots. Most importantly, it was the NTB which coordinated the right, facilitated its Euro-sceptical and free market agenda, and encouraged its financial sponsors.*(19) So also did the NTB liaise regularly with Baroness Thatcher.

Much has already been said about most of the previously-listed groups in terms of numbers, activists, leaders, agenda, activities and sources of sponsorship. So much of the membership overlapped from one group to the next, and there existed common purpose in holding the line against European integration and in support of free markets and deregulation – all established rightist causes. However, with Tory Commons numbers so depleted and the polls showing little indication of an early recovery, as Guy Walters's observed, it was in social issues that the Right's façade of unity first cracked.*(20) Significantly, the return to Westminster by by-election in 1999 of Michael Portillo, with his new-found zest for 'Gay' rights and equal opportunities, sparked off a wave of personal battles within the parliamentary party that reflected an innate ambition to succeed Hague.*(21) In the process, Portillo was counterpoised by John Redwood, whom Hague had removed as Shadow Chancellor to facilitate his great rival, as well as Francis Maude, Iain Duncan Smith, Michael Howard and Ann Widdecombe, none of whom took gracefully to his new policy conversions or the manner with which he undermined Hague. Ultimately, Portillo was to pay a high price for perceived disloyalty in the 2001 contest.

Portillo did not operate through the mechanism of an established group, either inside the parliamentary party or beyond Westminster. He had many admirers, but no structure for mobilising supporters; a factor that was to work against him when came the 2001 leadership contest. Instead, rather like Enoch Powell from a previous generation, Portillo exuded an agenda of identifiable causes which he updated after 1997 to embrace the secularisation of the post-Thatcher/Major Conservative Party, and which he hoped would be embraced by a broad stream of supporters at Westminster and beyond, enough to carry him to the leadership after the anticipated drubbing of Hague in the coming election.

In terms of the party's changing social direction, his judgement was not entirely off-beam, but embracing multi-culturalism, women's extended representation, equal opportunities and same-sex marriages were causes slightly ahead of their time for Tories at the turn of the millennium. As events were to show, it was a subsequent leader, David Cameron, who a decade later successfully tapped into this underlying stream among the changing and ever-secularising Tories for producing new legislation and practice.

As for Conservative Centrists/One Nation forces, though depleted by a mixture of lost parliamentarians, policy defeats, deaths and retirements, actually they congregated in the Tory Reform Group. Unquestionably, the Tory centrists had lost control of the party, but notwithstanding grave misgivings about Hague's Eurosceptical agenda they did not posture hostility towards leadership. Instead TRG provided a platform for pro-Europeans, party and constitutional reformers, environmentalists and other progressive causes. These causes were addressed in their journal, Reformer, and through conference fringe meetings and independent seminars in collaboration with like-minded campaigns, including Charter Movement, Conservative Europeans and Centre Forward Movement.*(22)

Additionally, TRG activists sought to defend vulnerable centrist MPs and councillors in constituencies where the Right were active. While deselections were exceptional, at the same time TRG figures noted that the centrists generally stood little chance of getting selected as parliamentary candidates in winnable constituencies.*(23) The earlier-documented experience of Eric Chalker, lead figure in the Charter Movement, was a monumental example in point, but there were others.*(24)

Prominent Westminster sponsors included Stephen Dorrell, Michael Heseltine, Malcolm Rifkind (after his return to the Commons), Hugh Dykes (who lost his Harrow East seat in 1997) Peter Temple-Morris, Sean Woodward and Ken Clarke – all of whom spoke on TRG platforms. However, in the cases of Dykes, he defected to the Liberal Democrats, while Temple-Morris and Woodward quit the Conservatives for Labour – thereby weakening the centrist cause and its credibility among Conservative grass roots.

There was also the publication just after the 1997 election of a seminal text by prominent One Nationite politician, Ian Gilmour, in collaboration with Conservative academic, Mark Garnett, *"Whatever happened to the Tories"*. To a greater or lesser degree, Gilmour and Garnett's thesis was of similar status among Tories to that of Anthony Crosland's 1956 treatise among Labour, *"The Future of Socialism"*.*(25) The pair noted accurately the slow decline of Tory ideology and values in a party that had been increasingly transformed by aggressive Thatcherite liberalism into a movement more akin to a hard right faction of the American Republican Party. Nor did they hold out much hope for the future of One Nation ideals in the party bequeathed by Margaret Thatcher.*(26) It was a grim look-out for One Nation Tories, and the success of Hague and even many of his rivals boded poorly for their chances of surviving as a major force in the party.

5.   Hague/IDS Transition

As expected, the general election of June 2001 proved to be a disaster for Hague and his party. The Conservative vote share rose by just 1%, with no signs of any recovery; six seats lost to the Liberal Democrats and one to Labour, and a net overall gain of just one seat.*(27) Hague resigned immediately the results were confirmed, thereby facilitating the process for electing a successor. Press and pundits widely expected this to be Portillo.

In the event, things turned out differently. Actually, in what was the Conservatives first-ever direct leadership contest, from a pool of five candidates (Michael Ancram, David Davis, Ken Clarke, Michael Portillo and Iain Duncan Smith) Portillo failed to make the postal ballot, being eliminated at the third ballot – gaining just 53.2% of votes behind Clarke and IDS, who went forward to contest the members postal ballot. The result, announced on 12th September, gave IDS, with 155,993 votes (60.7%) a clear victory over centrist, Clark, with 100,864 votes (39.3%). Euro rebel, IDS, had triumphed over the former Chancellor and Health Secretary to become the first Roman Catholic Leader of the Opposition since the Reformation.*(28)

Evidently Portillo's rebuff by his Westminster colleagues was due to a lack of trust, even on the Conservative Right. His dithering back in

1995 before declining to challenge John Major for the party leadership (leaving the task instead to John Redwood) had not been forgotten, while his disloyalty towards William Hague from his shadow front bench position after 1999 had also been noted. It was for those reasons that rightist loyalties transferred to IDS, whose track record had been rather more consistent. This reality was augmented by the absence of any formal Portillo lobbyist organisation either at Westminster or among the wider party faithful. Accordingly, Portillo's assumption of lead role in the 2001 leadership contest proved seriously misplaced.

Over the next four years, Portillo proved to be an equally disloyal colleague to IDS as he had been to Hague before him. With no prospect of securing the top job, he later opted out of Westminster for a media career after 2005.

Significantly, the 2001 leadership contest generated little in the way of overt factional activity. Although the emergence of leading standard bearers from right and left gave the various ideological campaign groups no difficulty in determining where their support was best directed, especially in the full membership ballot, those groups played a minor role in the actual debates and outcome. For one thing, IDS and Ken Clarke, while enunciating their respective causes on Europe, the economy, foreign affairs, taxes, social affairs etc., were each eager to avoid being seen as closely tied to particular groups. Each was eager to broaden their appeal to all sections of the party.*(29) For that reason, appeals to members were made through media outlets and official mechanisms, rather than utilising the energies of groups activists, who were seen by many rank and file as divisive, and counterproductive to their particular candidates in the long run.*(30)

6. The Brief Era of IDS

The first ever directly elected Tory leader, Iain Duncan Smith, experienced the shortest tenure of just two years and nineteen days, and one beset by a combination of mishap, treachery and the cold winds of political revenge. His credentials were based on a solid record of Euro-scepticism, defence of free market economics and a misplaced initiative in favour of married couples and heterosexual social structures in which he failed to carry a reluctant and increasingly mutational

Conservative Party. In the end, it was his inability to make a positive impact on opinion polls and the low key nature of his captaincy that persuaded a sufficient number of parliamentary colleagues that under him the party was heading straight for an iceberg at the impending general election. Following from the latter, IDS bowed out to a killer 'no-confidence' motion at an emergency meeting staged under party rules by the 1922 Committee on 31st October 2003.

The irony of IDS's short tenure was that at no point was he out of step with Conservative mainstream opinion. IDS was a dedicated champion of the Right, having previously supported numerous Commons rebellions against John Major over Europe; he supported the free market line of Thatcher and Hague, and also backed the Blair government in its 2003 military assault on Iraq. The Conservative leader proved a stern opponent of same-sex adoptions, and, notwithstanding Portillo's dissent (doubtless fuelled by admissions of homosexual liaisons during student days), insisted on all Conservative MPs backing the same line in a Commons vote, itself a measure provoking hostile media comment.

The same IDS sought to make his party credible in that unacceptable actions by front benchers were swiftly censored. Perhaps the most poignant manifestation of the latter occurred in Autumn 2002 when Shadow Cabinet member, Ann Winterton, was sacked for injudicious racial comments at a constituency rugby club dinner.*(31) So also did IDS move against far Right groups operating on the Conservative fringes. Most famously, he proscribed the Monday Club, which by then had descended into a hostile right wing institute posturing overt hostility towards the Conservative leadership and was devoid of any parliamentary or even middle ranking Conservative supporters. All the same, IDS's actions were brave given his dependence on rightist support. The proscription was done out of embarrassment at the extreme tone of Monday Club literature and its utter contempt for the One Nation wing of the party. IDS explained to this author that the Club had become an embarrassment to the Conservative Party image, and he had to force remaining Tory members to choose between Club or Party.*(32)

The principal cause of IDS's brief and failed tenure at the Conservative helm was an inability to communicate policies and values to the wider electorate such as might give the party some chance of staging a recovery at the polls. Plainly, he failed to inspire public confidence either as head of the alternative party of government or himself as a shadow prime minister in the wings. Performances in local elections in 2002 were poor, and while there appeared a modest resurgence in 2003, it was wholly inadequate to give grounds for any serious confidence about winning the next election. Additionally, IDS's personal rankings in opinion polls dragged well behind Prime Minister, Tony Blair, as well as those of the ebullient Liberal Democrat leader, Charles Kennedy. This in turn led to a growing crisis of confidence in his leadership, such as was voiced by a succession of Tory backers, several of whom threatened to pull funding while IDS remained in charge. The hapless Tory leader's profile was rendered further negative by constant media suggestions of splits in his shadow cabinet and parliamentary party. It has since been established that much media comment was encouraged by hostile briefings on the part of Michael Portillo, Archie Norman, Francis Maude and other hostile elements.*(33)

The crisis escalated further when certain key Tory donors threatened to withdraw funding, thereby increasing the pressure on the party to ditch its leader. So also did Tory middle level campaigners like Ian Dale, writer, founder and manager of Politicos Bookstore of central London, turn openly against the increasingly embattled IDS.*(34) As could be expected, the broadsheet press brimmed with negative commentary, all of which fed a heightened climate of insecurity and uncertainty about leadership.

In terms of factionalism and direction, with the party being led from the right, there was surprisingly little input to the leadership debate from ideological factions of either right or centre. IDS was not being criticised for his views as more the manner of his leadership, which was widely believed to be too low key, moralistic and unimaginative. It was making little positive impact on the opinion polls or at local or Westminster by-elections, and as a result the Conservatives seemed likely to be heading for electoral decimation. There was little in the way of overt factional activity that weighed on the power balances at Westminster, Annual Conference or even in the party organisation. IDS's optimism was briefly revived by a modest improvement in the 2003 English and Welsh local elections, and at Conference promised that the so-called "quiet man" would become more assertive over the months ahead.*(35)

Significantly, IDS's efforts at achieving a more positive projection were not criticised by the Tory centre, least of all TRG's journal; with the latter having endorsed his electoral strategy if not his Euroscepticism.*(36)

In the aftermath of the conference, IDS was forced to bear the indignity of having his wife and political aide, Betsy, accused of receiving a salary for no meaningful work.*(37) Although she was later cleared, the effect was to torpedo the nascent Tory revival, and raise existing backbencher concerns to crisis level. In the end, the 1922 Committee's 'No Confidence' vote was inevitable, a vote that IDS lost by 90 votes to 75.*(38)

The irony of the party's first directly-elected leader having been ditched so swiftly and unceremoniously highlighted the weakness of his position. Notwithstanding IDS's full member mandate, the reality of power was that it continued to rest with the party's parliamentarians, not its membership. IDS did not fail an ideological test nor fall foul of an ascendant school of factions like Heath in 1975. Instead IDS failed to give sufficient evidence of his capacity to lead the Conservatives to victory, and rather like Thatcher in 1990 it was the nervousness of MPs worried over electoral omens that forced his exit.

7.   Conservatives under Michael Howard, 2003-2005.

In the immediate aftermath of IDS's resignation, Michael Howard emerged unopposed to succeed to the Conservative leadership. Indeed the ease with which Howard took over the party reins suggests that preparations were afoot for a successor long before IDS fell in that crucial Halloween confidence vote. Previously, Howard's name did not figure greatly among dissenters, and though he did not lend his name to major petitions that challenged IDS's tenure, there can be little doubt that he waited in the wings ready to seize the main chance when it came. His uncontested election amounted to something of a coronation that highlighted the party's distaste for yet another leadership battle, not to mention its desperation for achieving some kind of electoral recovery.

What is significant about the IDS fall and Howard succession is that it was rather devoid of ideological overtones. The Right after all was in full control of the Conservative Party at Westminster and at head office, and both figures were men of the Right. Each was a Euro-sceptic, an economic free marketer, and conservative on law and order and social issues. Each in their own ways was anxious to keep the Conservatives firmly entrenched on the Right, and each took a strident tone of support for the government over Iraq and Afghanistan; neither had any sympathy with the Europhile or interventionist lines being argued by Ken Clarke and his declining school of Progressive One Nation Tories.*(39)

Factionalism remained low key with no attempts made at upstaging leadership or mounting challenges in the constituencies or at annual conference. The party was entrenched firmly on the right, and while the One Nationites and their Europhile allies maintained a base around the Tory Reform Group and Conservatives in Europe, otherwise most political discussions were conducted within official structures. What little impact waged by factions came through the growing plethora of 'brains trusts', meaning nominally-independent research/lobbyist groups like the long established Adam Smith Institute and Institute of Economic Affairs who produced pamphlets and operated on the party fringes. Such organisations of the Right included Conservative Way Forward and the anti-federalist European Foundation, along with the Westminster No Turning Back Group and Bruges Group. On the centre, there was Conservative Mainstream, Lollards, the European lobby and TRG, all of whom published considerable amounts of literature that discreetly challenged the official line with its own alternatives.*(40)

One group feature noticeable during the Howard period was the growing profile of secular Conservative lobbyists. The increasing appeal of Tory 'Gay' and Abortionist lobbies was symptomatic of a trend in wider British society and reflected in the support accorded to both groups, whose sympathisers included Archie Norman, Francis Maude and David Cameron himself.*(41) The latter were to emerge at the highest party levels both during the Howard and subsequent Cameron eras. Conversely, the Conservative Family and Christian campaigns became marginalised and restricted to beleaguered figures like Ann Widdecombe, Ann and Nicholas Winterton, David Amos and Baroness Jill Knight, along with a diminishing number of fellow travellers in what had once been the 'church and state' party of bygone times. Moreover, it is significant that the secular Tories were just as likely to be found on the

Right as Centre; the latter there had always shown a residual sympathy for secular causes like abortion and 'gay' rights.*(42)

As was to be expected, the Conservatives under Michael Howard did not experience any fundamental policy changes, and the party manifesto for the election of 2005 bore few changes to that on which Tories had contested the 2001 election under William Hague. It was increasingly hostile towards Europe, rejecting the single currency and further integration, championed the free markets, supported – albeit more critically than under IDS – the government's Anglo-American military action in Iraq and Afghanistan and envisaged the creation of more prisons and admission of fewer immigrants.*(43) The issue was more about authority of the party leader, and the party's electability. Although a couple of pre-campaign spats occurred – with one rightist Tory MP, Howard Flight, losing his party's whip – otherwise there was relative harmony throughout the campaign. Moreover, Howard's position as Conservative Leader was not queried or undermined by either rebellious MPs or outside donors or other supporters.

While the Conservative performance in local government elections and opinion polls had experienced a modest increase over the previous 18 months, it fell a fair way short of serious expectations of winning an election. The paradox was that in the aftermath of the Iraq war and campaign in Afghanistan, a less than popular Blair government was reasonably assured of re-election due to perceptions of a Conservative opposition widely deemed unfit for resuming office.*(44) Significantly, the low turn-out of 61% (up by 2% from 2001) augmented the predictable result that followed.

Labour - 356 seats (-47), 37% of GB vote.

Conservatives - 198 seats (+33), 33% vote

Liberal Democrats - 62 seats (+10), 22% vote.

A decisive defeat for the Conservatives and win for the Labour government!

That said, the result marked a bottoming out of the Conservative electoral decline, and even a modest revival of prospects. What might have been the result had Iain Duncan Smith been still leading the party is open to speculation, but in so far as the tide of decline was stemmed, Michael Howard had done his party the most valuable service. It was now time for him to turn over the leadership to a new figure, and he acknowledged, preferably "… from the younger generation of Tories".

Hence following a reflective period over the Summer, Howard announced his impending resignation on 7th October, and indicated a time frame for the leadership selection and election taking its course over the next two months.

8.   Enter David Cameron!

In the contest following there were initially 7 candidates, namely Dr Liam Fox, David Davis (an arch-Brexiteer) and the youthful David Cameron, all of them right wingers to one degree or another, with Ken Clarke for the third time holding the torch for the beleaguered One Nation centrists and Europhiles. The other three candidates were ex-Transport Secretary, Alan Duncan, former Foreign Secretary, Sir Malcolm Rifkind and Environment Secretary, Tim Yeo, but all dropped out before any votes were cast. Yet the leadership contest was primarily about personalities, and for that reason the whole event was devoid of factional politicking, instead featuring the candidates and their machines. No major policy differences were enunciated by the candidates. So also did media focus intensify, but on candidates and their respective agendas without any hint of organised group activity along the lines of earlier contests of the 1970s, '80s and '90s.

In the MPs ballot first round held on 18th October, David Cameron got 56 (28.3%) votes, Davis 62 (31.3%), Fox 42 (21.2%) and Clarke 38 (19.2%).

A second ballot held on 20th October gave Cameron 90 votes, Davis 57 and Fox 51.

Hence the names of Cameron and Davis proceeded to a full member ballot, and with a clear momentum growing in favour of the Old Etonian against the veteran Davis.

The full campaign was conducted over a six week period, and on 6th December the result was announced as follows.

David Cameron 134,446 (67%)   David Davis 64,398 (32.4%).

A clear win for Cameron, and a mandate for change in style and strategy from his party!

Given the sober reality of the Conservatives having lost three consecutive Westminster elections, and fought off the harbingers of their own funeral lament, it was clear that the party membership had opted for a young man in desperation to secure their very survival. Ideology and strategy were secondary considerations behind securing the winning of public office and the wielding of actual power in managing the British state.

What followed was directed at reviving the Conservatives as a party of government. Cameron would be judged by the yardstick of whether or not he could restore his party to their long perceived historic mission. It was as simple as that!

FOOTNOTES and REFERENCES

1. See reports and analysis of the first, second and third ballots in Independent, Guardian, Times and Daily Telegraph - 5th June, 11th June and 18th June 1997.

2. Hague, to his credit, made no effort to blame other factors for the heavy Conservative defeat of June 2001, but instead resigned as Leader immediately after the election.

3. Dorrell maintained a silent profile about Hague, and specifically acknowledged his inclination to do so in an interview with this author (see bibliography).

4. Simon Walters 'Tory Wars: Conservatives in Crisis' (Politicos, 2001), Chaps, 11, 13 and 15. In those chapters, the author documents numerous instances of disloyalty by Hague's rivals on the Right towards their leader.

5. (i) Ditto.
    (ii) This author also picked up on the Tory briefings "war" from an enlightening interview in November 2000 with Peter Temple-Morris, MP who was at that time on his way out of the Conservative Party, and later joined Labour.

6. Apparently Portillo regularly briefed against Iain Duncan Smith, who had defeated him for the Conservative leadership in 2001. Ref. Interview IDS/author, October 2005.

7. McKay, the Conservative Shadow Northern Ireland Secretary, chose Holy Week, including Good Friday, 1998 – when the critical Irish Peace Talks were taking place at Belfast, under the watchful gaze of the world's media – to have a holiday in South Africa. What a curious judgement of timing and priorities!

8. See McKee V. 'Post-Conservative factionalism', Politics Review (April 1996). Although the article appeared the year before Hague came to the leadership, in fact the spectacle presented then bore a close likeness of what he had to deal with after taking the helm in June 1997.

9. Significantly, it was clear from the Walters text (2001), plus this author's recorded interviews with a cross section of Conservative figures, that there was no expectancy on the part of Hague or any of his parliamentarians for an early return to government, and that any mild hopes of a swift come-back were dashed within 18 months of Hague's accession. Rt Hon Stephen Dorrell MP told this author in 2000 that Hague's future at the party helm depended on his ability to win back a few seats (at least 30) at the forthcoming general election. If that did not happen, Hague would have to quit. Dorrell proved to be entirely correct.

10. Philip Lynch 'Conservatives: Britishness and the Nation State' (Palgrave, UK, 1999), Chaps 1 & 9.

11. In reality, the 2010 electoral alliance between British Conservatives and Ulster Unionists amounted to a pitch, albeit an unsuccessful one, for the Protestant middle class allegiances in Northern Ireland. The former Protestant establishment party that had previously governed Northern Ireland for half a century from its Belfast base was reduced to having no Westminster seats, and entirely outflanked and outperformed by its Protestant rival, the DUP, then led by Dr Ian Paisley's successor, Peter Robinson.

12. See successive issues of Reformer, 1996-2001.

13. Recorded Interviews: Eric Charter, Chairman of Tory Charter Movement (2000), and John Stratford, Secretary of Conservative Campaign for Democracy (2003), with this author.

14. (i) Ditto.
    (ii) Also, see copies of Charter News and the Conservative Democracy Campaign's newsletter 1999-2002, both of which struck the same note.

15. Walters (2001), Chaps 13, 15 & 16.

16. A view confirmed in recorded interviews with the late Teresa Gorman MP, Rt. Hon. Lord Tebbit, Rt. Hon Iain Duncan Smith, MP and John Carlyle.

17. This view was expressed very trenchantly by the late Mrs Gorman, MP and William Cash, MP – in recorded interviews with author.

18. Much corporate information supplied by the late Mrs Gorman and John Carlyle in recorded interviews with author.

19. Information confirmed in recorded interviews with Mrs Gorman and Messers' Cash, Carlyle, Iain Duncan-Smith and Lord Tebbit – plus informal discussions with the 92 Group history author, Mrs Lucy Grant.

20. Guy Walters (2001), Chap 15, p.p. 174-180, appropriately titled 'The Mummy Returns'!

21. Walters (2001), Chap. 18, p.p. 206-217.

22. (i) Information provided in recorded interview by Mr Giles Marshall, Secretary of the Tory Reform Group, and occasional editor of its journal, Reformer. This author was also granted access to select TRG documents and correspondence.

    (ii) Mr Marshall's information was confirmed in similar interviews by Rt Hon. Stephen Dorrell, Rt Hon. Lord Heseltine, Lord Peter Temple-Morris and Coun. Francis Lancaster.

23. A view confirmed in recorded interviews with Giles Marshall and Lord Temple Morris – and squared with the facts of selections in constituencies where the retiring Conservative Member had been on the centrist wing of the party.

24. Recorded interviews with Messers' Eric Chalker, Giles Marshall and Lord Temple-Morris.

25. C.A.R. Crosland The Future of Socialism (J. Cape, 1956, London).

26. See Gilmour and Garnett (1997) - Chaps 12 & 15.

27. See results of the June 2001 British General Election, Times, 9th June 2001.

28. See profile of Iain Duncan Smith by Vincent McKee; Irish Catholic (Dublin), 9th February, 2006, and Catholic Herald (London) April 2006 – based on two recorded interviews with author.

29. This message was emphasised clearly in recorded interview with Iain Duncan Smith. Similar sentiments were spoken by Clarke supporters.

30. Ditto.

31. Interview IDS/author. IDS admitted that this decision had troubled him greatly on account of a long running friendship with Ann and Nicholas Winterton, both MPS and ardent Christians, but was forced upon him by circumstances. Since both the Wintertons voted to support IDS in the 2003 1922 Committee Confidence vote, clearly the friendship survived.

32. Interview IDS/author.

33. Interview IDS/author. Significantly, IDS clarified that hostile leaks came from Portillo and his coterie, but not his defeated One Nation opponent, Ken Clarke, or any of the Tory Reform people.

34. Private discussions Ian Dale/author.

35. See reports of the Leader's October 2003 speech, Times, Daily Telegraph and Guardian.

36. See Tory Reformer, Conference issue, September 2003.

37. IDS blamed Portillo for the ".... poisonous media leaks ...", which helped to undermine his leadership in 2003. Interview IDS/author.

38. Reports – Times, Daily Telegraph and Guardian, 1st November 2003.

39. Clark was openly supporting UK accession to the Euro-currency while also opposing the British military intervention in Iraq.

40. (i) Interviews William Cash/author, Peter (now Lord) Temple Morris/author, John Carlyle/author, John Stafford/author and Giles Marshall/author.

    (ii) See successive issues of 'Tory Reformer', 2000-2006, kindly supplied to the author by Giles Marshall.

    (iii) Pamphlet – '<u>Associated, not Absorbed</u>', first published 2000, re-published 2003, by European Foundation. Author is most grateful to Mr William Cash, MP for so kindly making his Foundation's literature freely available.

41. See Tory Gay News newsletter of September 2004 to note the increasing numbers of overt supporters at Westminster and in the regions. The newsletter oozed a new-found confidence that would never have been asserted twenty years earlier.

42. In previous decades, the likes of Ian Gilmour, Edward Heath and even Ken Clarke and Stephen Dorrell had supported secular causes like abortion and homosexual rights. More recently, Theresa Gorman and other right wing populists had taken a similar line. Interviews: - Right Hon. Stephen Dorrell/author and Mrs Theresa Gorman/author.

43. See Conservative Manifesto for the British General Election of May 2005.

44. See a selection of election editorials and commentaries from the Guardian, Daily Telegraph, Times, New Statesman, Daily Mail and Spectator, April/May 2005.

Forty Shades of Blue

CHAPTER 10

CONSERVATIVES IN THE CAMERON ERA 2005 - 2016

The aim of this last chapter is to evaluate the major events defining the leadership of David Cameron as they related to factional politics and internal divisions, December 2005-June 2016. In that period the Conservatives returned to government, albeit as a transformed force rejuvenated by a mandate of economic free markets, Euro-scepticism and social inclusiveness. While preparing for office, Cameron's Conservative Party shed much outdated baggage in search of a more inclusive and progressive image so as to appeal to the widest sections of the electorate in a bid for power.

In the end, an inclusive agenda and new Tory backers proved adequate for restoring the party to government, albeit initially in coalition with the Liberal Democrats and, later, alone. However, Cameron proved unable to either unite his party or the country at large around the vexed question of Britain's relationship with the European Union. Notwithstanding the electoral success of 2015, the Conservative Party experienced grave divisions over whether to support reformed EU membership or Brexit. In the end, with his party and government divided, and a narrow Brexit verdict rendered by the referendum of 23rd June 2016, Cameron chose resignation from public office. In so doing, he ensured that the party bequeathed to his successor was every bit as fractured as that which he had inherited some 10½ years earlier.

It is important to note that like other chapters, this one will not be so much concerned with a chronological narrative of events and challenges as more evaluating their impact on Cameron and his party. A particular focus will be maintained on the extent to which factionalism and its alignments affected the party, and what part was played by factional groups.

1. Overview

The accession of David Cameron as Conservative leader in December 2005 appeared to mark the beginning of a new era. This 39 years old, Old Etonian and Oxford PEP graduate – characterised by privilege and a distant connection to Royalty – was in one sense a return to the vintage Tory captain so typical of his party's history. He enjoyed additional advantages; being handsome, vibrant, happily married to the pretty daughter of a Baronet with a young family, and had earlier served an apprenticeship as a ministerial adviser to Norman Lamont, before later "cutting his teeth" in the City. Significantly, his political antecedents were firmly on the right, and though seeking power, he did not indulge ideological adventures that risked alienating Tory voters. Most importantly, Cameron was fresh, and untainted by previous associations with the Thatcher or Major governments; the latter's sleaze records having been widely blamed for three consecutive electoral defeats in 1997, 2001 and 2005 respectively. That electoral malaise had not lifted by early 2006, and indeed the party seemed condemned to lengthy opposition.

Yet in another way, Cameron proved a very different kind of leader to those preceding him, and one whose primary task was to halt the seemingly inevitable decline plaguing the Conservative Party over the previous decade. He produced an agenda for change that embraced a targeted electorate exceeding traditional Tory parameters – to include high powered women and ethnics, prominent homosexuals, social liberals, small as well as large entrepreneurs, creative artistes and other previous backers of Tony Blair's 'Cool Britannia'. It was a strategy that reaped dividends, but in the short term generated proliferating numbers of Asian and female candidates contesting winnable parliamentary seats as Conservatives in 2010 and 2015.

Otherwise, having been elected from a position on the political right, the earlier Cameron was deemed sufficiently credible by an assortment of rightist voices to articulate the Conservative Party's innate distrust of the European Union. All the more was Cameron's resistance to further European integration applauded by a mainstream of colleagues, with the exception of the Europhile tendency based around Ken Clark and the Tory Reform Group. Tory withdrawal from the Christian Democrat grouping at Strasbourg, on Cameron's initiative, was endorsed back in London, while his general Euro-sceptical line was welcomed by many Tories who suspected the "…creeping tentacles of Brussels..." that they believed were undermining British sovereignty.

Yet for all his modernising and inclusiveness, there were definite limits to Cameron's agenda, and inevitably he was not going to please everybody, most especially on the Conservative hard right. For one thing, in the manner of a new leader, there was a clear-out of non-cooperative figures at Conservative Central Office, a process that was neither painless nor trouble-free. Most fire occurred over the subsequent appointment of Australian election campaign strategist, Lynton Cosby, whose methods were resented by many as unproven and risky. The dominant influence of Shadow Chancellor, George Osbourne, caused annoyance among the many MPs and Central Office staff who saw the Cameron-Osbourne axis, along with Boris Johnson, as a collection of Old Etonians bringing their 'toffs' agenda to bear on the party.

Without doubt, Cameron wanted to improve the effectiveness of a creaking Conservative organisation, both at central level and around the country.*(1) He also believed that to win another election, the Conservatives needed to update their whole programme with the aim of charting new causes and finding new voters among ethnics, 'gays', women and social rights campaigners, even if that meant offending traditionalists. Finally, he desired a settlement of the divisive European question for party and country. Those key issues of free markets and economic growth had to be reconciled with delegated powers to an institution that by its very nature, affronted national sovereignty and was resented by so many Tories.*(2) It was to prove a most daunting challenge, and one – as records show – that finally defeated the Tory leader's best efforts undertaken over a decade in opposition and office.*(3)

Yet David Cameron's 10½ years at the Tory helm must not be seen as a grim era in the history of his party. Quite the opposite! For one thing, under Cameron the Conservatives electoral decline was halted, and over the initial four years the party began recovering much ground and some seats previously lost to New Labour and the Liberal Democrats. Secondly, under Cameron, the Conservatives managed to see off the challenge of UKIP. Although the anti-EU party scored heavily in

European elections of 2009 and 2014, while making gains in local elections, in fact the actual damage done to party strength at Westminster was minimal – amounting to two by-election losses of Tory defectors and a single seat in the general election of 2015. Third, contrary to what was reported as his greatest nightmare, the September 2015 Scottish independence referendum delivered a 55% majority vote for staying in the United Kingdom. While Cameron cannot claim exclusive credit for this result, especially given the prominence of Labour and Liberal Democrat figures like Alasdair Darling, Gordon Brown and Menzies Campbell in the campaign, still he pitched in with other pro-Union voices to defend the constitutional status quo.

Fourth, most importantly, Cameron restored the Conservative Party to government – a task eluding his three immediate predecessors – initially in coalition with the Liberal Democrats 2010-2015, and then winning an outright majority for his party. To the extent that the Conservatives came through two consecutive elections, 2010 and 2015, with enhanced strength reflects credibly on the party leader, as did the overall success of the five year coalition with the Liberal Democrats under Nick Clegg. Yet Seldon and Snowdon also noted that while working with the Liberal Democrats in government, in fact Cameron was preparing to truncate Liberal Democrat pockets of support such as would cost his coalition allies dearly in the 2015 general election.*(4) This exercise was directed by Conservative election strategist, Lynton Crosby, operating from Central Office. Moreover, the campaign was achieved with ruthless efficiency in a manner that left little affection among his erstwhile Coalition partners, but delighted right wing back benchers and Tory grass roots.

Overall, the Cameron years marked a watershed. British Conservatism was modernised and secularised; new elements were added to the pool of supporters and participants, while electoral appeal was targeted at sections of the electorate previously outside the Tory realm, and variously indifferent and hostile to the party. Simultaneously, out-dated and extreme remnants of the former Conservative nation (Andrew Gamble's thesis)*(5) such as imperial defenders, 'white' racial campaigners and even former church and state moral campaigners were either formally discarded or rendered obsolete by changing political tides. A key objective of this final substantive chapter is to assess the extent to which Cameron had effected the displacement of traditional boundaries within the Conservative Party, replacing it with something new and different. Equally, given the nature of party culture, the leadership agenda was precisely what generated a response from the members and parliamentarians, specifically through organised campaigning groups and the ideological tendencies that were their voices. It is to be considered here just how far this process evolved in the general thrust of Cameron's leadership and programme, and whether the leader himself was the progenitor of a new Conservatism that witnessed an awakening of new traits and types in his ever-evolving party.

Conclusive answers remain some years off, but at this stage tentative indications must serve to guide this author. Moreover, evaluations of Cameron must encompass the sober realities of his failures as much as successes.

2.   Conservatives in search of a return to Government

In their biographical assessment, Elliot and Hanning have emphasised the absolute determination of Cameron to lead his party back to office.*(6) After all, in a movement that consciously asserts itself to be the natural party of government, recent history shows British Conservatives to hold scarce tolerance for electoral losers – a lesson painfully highlighted by the adverse experiences of most Tory leaders since the era of Edward Heath. Hailing from the same social class that supplied so many Tory leaders, Cameron felt confidently equipped to refashion the party for government, and on an agenda apparently chiming with the mood of millennium Tories.

In any case, so dismal was the electoral record of recent Tory leaders that the party's very future as a governing force was in question. Such conditions placed the new leader under strain, but also allowed him scope for setting fresh direction. If to return to government the Conservatives needed to ditch outdated baggage and embrace unlikely new friends, so be it. Cameron was aware of his priorities and also the limited time available for attaining them.

His principal characteristics included a fundamental reform of Central Office and the party organisation, with efficiency and discipline being key goals. A hard line was taken against Tory 'gravy train travellers', meaning those MPs (e.g. Derek Conway, Julie Kirkbride and Andrew Mackay) benefiting from excessive and/or fraudulent expenses claims, most of whom were forced to resign or at the very least required to repay excess allowances as a condition of retaining the Conservative whip. Others like Lord Taylor of Warwick (jailed for expenses fraud) were driven from the party in a credibility renaissance.

The subsequent introduction of Australian election strategist, Lynton Crosby, proved most crucial for the Conservatives plans to win the 2015 election, but the foundations for a professional approach to electioneering were laid from the beginning. So also were the policy unit, initiatives and political advertising prerogatives of Central Office placed under Cameron's own direct authority.

As previously mentioned, in a bid to popularise the Tories in hitherto hostile sections, Cameron purposely welcomed a stream of 'power women' like Karren Brady (created a Tory peer) and others from industry, fashion and the popular entertainment worlds to party ranks.*(7) So also did he embrace ethnic figures like Pritti Patel (a future minister) and Dr Nadhim Zahawi as parliamentarians, along with Sayeeda Warsi (a future Tory peer and minister), and 'gay' figures like Alan Duncan and Ruth Davison as "...valued colleagues..." in a party which he committed to legalising same-sex marriage.

The pro-'gay' programme certainly did not appeal to all Tory MPs or grass roots activists, as Cameron was to later discover. However, with a sympathetic media profile and, after 2010, a vigorously supportive Liberal Democrat coalition partner, he was able to garner enough support to withstand critics and force through changes to the marriage laws. Another lobby to whom Cameron made a pitch was the environmentalists, remembering that the Green Party had earlier won much support among younger middle class females, who tended to be green conscious. Embracing Zac Goldsmith, a prominent environmental campaigner, as Conservative candidate and later MP for Wimbledon, was geared to winning back Green voters to the party.*(8)

Aside from a socially inclusive and equal opportunities agenda, Cameron's policy agenda was cautious. Being broadly of the Right, Cameron's focus was primarily on economic austerity, balanced budgets, a pro-Union constitutional policy, solid defences with the renewal of the Polaris nuclear submarine fleet, and a robust assertion of British sovereignty within the European Union. This preference for orthodoxy reflected Cameron's desire for achieving party unity as a priority so as to boost electoral appeal. He was also anxious to test Conservative appeal to younger, gay, female and ethnic voters, anticipating that therewith lay new sources of social support for the Conservative Party.

For the first 20 months of his term, Cameron counterpoised the New Labour administration of Tony Blair, which was then in its final stages of life. Following Blair's retirement in July 2007, Cameron confronted the succeeding administration of Gordon Brown. A particular challenge occurred with the financial crisis involving banks and building societies that erupted over 2007 and 2008. Another challenge occurring over 2009 was the MPs expenses scandal, initiated by investigative reports published by the *Daily Telegraph*. Conservative MPs and peers were confronted with evidence of impropriety in similar fashion to Labour and, to a lesser degree, the Liberal Democrats. Cameron's response was unyielding, and he very publicly demanded of his colleagues that excesses be swiftly repaid, while serious offenders were denied re-selection as Conservative parliamentary candidates. Those two crises dragged out until the general election of May 2010, when there was a sense of three-party competition involving Cameron, Brown and the Liberal Democrat force headed by Nick Clegg, his party's third leader in three years.

While over the period opinion polls, local elections and European elections all pointed to a modest recovery for Cameron, in no way had the Conservative leader achieved an unassailable advantage over his rivals by the start of the general election campaign in Spring 2010. Public debates favoured the Tories on economic management – especially for managing depleted public finances, while hearkening to Tory Euro-sceptical sabre rattling – but was less warm on the party's foreign affairs conduct and managing the NHS and social services. Accordingly, by the time of the election campaign things had reached the point where the contest was as much Labour's to lose as a potential prize for the Conservatives and/or Liberal Democrats. In any case, Labour under Gordon Brown was seeking an unprecedented fourth term having been in office for the previous 13 years. The stakes were indeed high!

3.   Group and Campaigner Activity

The Cameron era was not especially noteworthy for a proliferation of unofficial group or campaigning activity. There were two reasons for this trend.

First, the party having turned to a fresh young leader in 2005, showed its desperation to regain office. Conversely, factional activity was believed by many to be divisive and highlighting divisions in Conservative ranks; a trait deemed at best unhelpful towards securing a mandate from the public. Second, there was a sense of giving the new leader fresh opportunity to establish his authority and preferred direction. Again, factionalism was widely deemed to risk confrontation, which might have destabilised the party. For those reasons, factional politics were kept low key and of a type that professed overt loyalty to the leader and his regime as a credibility litmus test.

There was no place for the Monday Club or other hard right vehicles in Cameron's party, and certainly none of the latter's bellicose rhetoric from days of old. Other organisations like the anti-Communist Western Goals Institute while remaining on the fringes, nonetheless kept a low and cooperative profile, avoiding previous antagonisms and polemics.*(9) Others like Olga Maitland's Women and Families for Defence and the Conservative-leaning Peace Through NATO had either petered out, amalgamated or simply wound up. There was also the pro-nationalist Traditional Britain Group, with Lord Sudeley as its president and veteran right winger, Gregory Lauder-Frost, as its administrative key figure. Actually, TBG's minor numbers belied a prominent profile in right wing tabloids.*(10) The same was equally true of mainstream centre right groups like the Thatcherist Conservative Way Forward, Bruges Group and No Turning Back, all of whom had put their profiles on 'silent mode' or were no longer active. Even the centrist Tory Reform Group, with its influential magazine, *Tory Reformer*, and an array of leading Westminster patrons centred on Ken Clarke and Michael Heseltine provided a cooperative tone and profile, such as would make the Cameron reforms and direction so much smoother in their impact on the party. It was not that battlers from either Right or Left had lost their zeal or sense of purpose, but rather pressing was the need to support the new leader as he sought to bring his party out of the electoral doldrums, into which it had slipped over the previous 12 years.

Cameron's zest for further secularisation, specifically gay marriage rights, did encounter considerable opposition from the Conservative Family Campaign and, after 2012, a vigorous campaigning body called Grass roots Conservatives. The latter – led by an Oxfordshire Anglican cleric, Rev. Chris Sugden – took their opposition to same-sex marriages to the form of an open challenge on air and in the press, and were intense in their efforts.*(11) With Cameron being a man of modest spirituality, and with his wife Samantha openly espousing libertarian ideas on sexuality, gender and family issues – consistent with her background as an Art graduate – the winding down of the Conservatives erstwhile image as an ally of the Church of England proved to be straightforward and relatively painless.*(12) Yet the process drove a wedge between Cameron and traditional Tories on the Right, many of whom came to view him with grave suspicion.*(13) This perception did not endear his pleadings for remaining in Europe during the referendum or indeed the propriety of his continued leadership after defeat. Indeed remaining elements of the Christian Right proved just as hostile to Cameron in his hour of loss as other fellow travellers.

In the Opposition years prior to 2010, when Cameron was pleading for unity and a combined effort to achieve a return to power, the Conservative Conference and organisation generally proved cooperative. There were no displays of open dissent and no major media campaigns that might have undermined the leader. Some disquiet did emerge among back benchers and among rank and file over Cameron's social liberalism, especially in such areas as ethnic relations and a pro-gay sexual agenda. However, more generally, the party threw its weight behind its youthful leader as he battled with the Labour Premier, Gordon Brown, in a bid to gain public confidence. Although the Liberal Democrats under Nick Clegg had etched out a place on the public rostrum, right up until the election of 2010 that delivered a hung parliament, there was no preparation for any kind of pact between Cameron and Clegg. Nor is it likely that such a prospect would have been welcomed by the grass roots or back benches of either party. That a coalition happened was a consequence of responses to the inconclusive election result, and nothing else.

4.   Election 2010 and Coalition to follow!

The general election of 6th May 2010 witnessed a substantial Tory recovery.

Conservatives: 307 seats (+97) with 36.1% of vote.

Labour: 258 seats (-91)   with 29.0% of vote.

Liberal Democrats   57 seats (-5) with 23.0%   of vote.

SNP 6   Plaid Cymru 3   Greens 1   DUP 8   Sinn Fein 5   SDLP 3
Independents 2 --- combined 12% of vote.

Yet the reality was that notwithstanding the Labour government's clear defeat after 13 years, Conservatives, though the largest party, were lacking an overall majority. The choice was between a minority government or coalition. In the event, with Labour a defeated force, the Liberal Democrat leader, Nick Clegg, did not feel able to credibly support a coalition with Gordon Brown's defeated party, and opted instead for a pact with David Cameron's Conservatives.*(14) The choice of coalition did not prove universally popular in either of the two parties, and received a cool response on the Tory back benches as well as among Liberal Democrat rank and file.*(15) Yet that was the way in which both parties proceeded, claiming the national interest as prime justification.

5.   Coalition Government 2010-2015

Britain's first-ever peace time coalition government was headed by David Cameron as Premier, Nick Clegg as Deputy Premier and a Conservative-dominated cabinet whose ranks also included five Liberal Democrat ministers. There followed a mixed legacy of stable government, austere finances, modest constitutional innovations, cautious domestic social reforms, a generally Euro-sceptical foreign policy and the successful defence of the Anglo-Scottish Union against a sustained SNP referendum campaign for Scottish independence. Like all coalitions, there were robust policy debates, with compromises required of both parties which in turn aggravated relations with their respective grass roots (e.g. university fees with the Liberal Democrats, European relations with the Tories), but for the duration of its term the Coalition generally worked.

In its economic policy, Conservative Chancellor, George Osbourne, assisted by the Liberal Treasury Chief Secretary, Danny Alexander, raised VAT to 20%, curtailed a raft of public spending programmes and squeezed savings from all public services, including the armed forces. The austerity programme was aimed at restoring sound finances and curbing a huge government debt inherited from the previous Labour administration. In education, university fees were raised against a major campaign of opposition waged by the National Union of Students, but in the primary schools sector free school meals were universally agreed, along with a boosting of health support and intervention options. Elsewhere, under Liberal stewardship, an environmental audit was applied to all government departments (with silent chaffing from Tory back benchers over costs), while in domestic affairs contentious 'same-sex' marriage legislation – which split both the Tory party and the country – was successfully steered through Westminster in 2014 after a fierce debate.

In constitutional affairs, the record was decidedly modest with the passage of a bill for Fixed Term Parliaments, normally of five years duration. However, Clegg's attempt at securing voting reform proved less successful. Against a background of near-universal Tory opposition, Clegg managed to get a bill through Cabinet and the Commons putting an option of the Alternative Vote up for a referendum poll in May 2011 – barely 12 months into the Coalition. This failed miserably by a substantial majority, with most Conservative ministers, plus their Labour counterparts, openly opposing the proposal.*(16)

Overseas affairs were conducted on a largely Euro-sceptical basis under William Hague at the Foreign Office. With a series of retirements, deaths and occasional defections (documented in previous chapters) at Westminster, and the prevalence of a strong anti-European strain in constituency associations, Europhiles in the Conservative Party had diminished down to a handful of MPs centred on Ken Clarke and his Tory Reform Commons group. At the same time, despite the prevailing policy echoed by Cameron, Hague and Osbourne, there were several occasions during their term that the government was accused by Conservative right wingers of capitulating to Liberal Europhiles. This strain escalated in the final twelve months of the Coalition as both parties prepared their ground for the forthcoming general election.

Otherwise the Right was kept firmly at bay. An example of the latter was the government's Irish policy. Aside from committing to the 1998 Good Friday Agreement and continuing its predecessor administration's support for devolved power-sharing in Belfast, Cameron broke new ground in three other areas. First, in July 2010 was a disarming Commons admission and apology for the Bloody Sunday outrage in Derry (when paratroopers shot dead 14 unarmed Civil Rights demonstrators, 30th January 1972) – coming on the back of the Saville Report. This gesture did much to win good will from Irish nationalist quarters, which made for a more effective relationship between London, Belfast and Dublin. Second, was the loan extended by Cameron's government to a financially beleaguered Dublin government in 2012, which alongside European Union aid, helped the new Taoiseach, Enda Kenny, work his way out of the straitjacket posed by a near-collapsing economy. It says much for the neutered capacity of the Conservative Right – never nationalist Ireland's natural friend – that both those measures aroused scarcely a whimper from that quarter. Third, was an historic and government-sponsored first visit by the Queen to the Irish Republic in May 2011; itself highly successful and swiftly followed by an inclusive Royal visit to Northern Ireland in 2012. Cameron's talent for identifying advantageous diplomatic and political ground proved an effective weapon for garnering coalition appeal.

The greatest battle waged by Cameron's government was to counter a move by the SNP-led Edinburgh administration, headed by talented First Minister, Alex Salmond, to secure a referendum mandate for Scottish independence. This poll had been long in coming, and though resolved in favour of the Union in a referendum held on 14th September 2014, the margin of victory was slim (10%), enough to give nationalists heart for a second poll soon afterwards. What was particularly significant was that though losing the vote, actually the SNP consolidated their strength in the ensuing general election of May 2015, taking 56 of Scotland's 59 Westminster seats. Although the 2017 snap election saw Scottish Conservatives regain much ground, including 13 seats for 28.6% of votes, the reality is that the Nationalists remain Scotland's governing party in the Holyrood administration, and also the country's majority party with 35 Westminster MPs for 37% of the Scottish national vote. For a committed Unionist as Cameron, the legacy amounted to a rather tenuous hold on the Union, and then only attained through interventions by pro-Union Labour and Liberal figures like former premier, Gordon Brown, and Menzies Campbell.

Otherwise, as the Coalition progressed to the end of its five year term, the European question gradually escalated to the predominant issue of the day. This situation was accentuated when the Prime Minister let be known a plan to renegotiate UK membership terms with the EU in a second term, and would be putting those directly to the British electorate in a referendum. As much as anything else, Cameron was seeking to ward off support for the rival UKIP, to whom two Conservative MPs defected and subsequently won by-elections. He had also become concerned by UKIP's premier showing in the 2014 Strasbourg elections when UKIP with 26.7% of votes took 24 seats – topping the UK poll. As the Westminster election loomed, Cameron feared the risk of a high UK vote cutting into Conservative support such as might deny him a victory. As events turned out, he need not have worried because UKIP's performance though formidable, resulted only in one MP and not its leader Nigel Farage.

6.   Factional Politics during Coalition years

Interestingly, all of the major ideological group protagonists – including Tory Reform Group, Conservative Way Forward, No Turning Back Group and Bow Group – offered little in the way of formal opposition to the Coalition. From the beginning, their journals and newsletters all seemed to adopt the stance of 'wait and see – give the Coalition a chance to prove its worth'.*(17)

Among mainstream Conservatives at both Westminster and among rank and file there was evident relief that the party was now back in office, albeit depending on Liberal Democrat support and with a proportional share of Cabinet positions going to Liberal Democrats. This view was also reflected in editorials of the Daily Telegraph over the same period, June to Christmas 2010, and indeed for several months thereafter. So also did other right wing papers like the Mail, Express and Spectator accept the reality of the Coalition, albeit pleading publicly that it was a temporary expedience and born of necessity rather than desire. There was a feeling at all levels of the Conservative Party that this was a price worth paying for restoring national finances and efficient public administration, and the party would draw long term rewards.

Significantly, it seemed to be recognised among a cross stream of Tories that policy compromises would be necessary in order to keep the Liberal Democrats on board, who in turn would be expected to make manifesto sacrifices of their own. The latter process caused serious vexation to both parties. Tories disliked Liberal Euro-zeal and constitutional reform plans, while the Liberals agonised about increased university fees, in direct contravention of a manifesto pledge.

Only among hard right groups like the estranged Monday Club, Western Goals Institute and other nationalist lobbies was there open dissension with the Coalition. Predictably, the Conservative Family Campaign and Grass Roots Conservatives pitched hard on behalf of what they viewed as the inappropriate abandonment by Cameron of remaining Christian heritage in response to the militant secularists strains of Liberal Democrats.*(18) So too did the European Foundation and an array of Euro-sceptics voice concern at the pact between a Conservative party that was pro-sovereignty and a Liberal Democrat force that unashamedly professed faith in the European Union, and sought an extension of European-government in UK affairs. This tendency became more marked as time progressed, election time beckoned and ideological strains opened.

At the same time, none of those organisations abounded with influence or Westminster connections. Their membership was relatively small, numbering less than 400 in each case and lacking the disciplined cadres of former days in the case of the Monday Club. Additionally, all were concentrated in the South of England, thereby lacking much of a hand at the grass roots or across the country. Equally significantly, while showing a presence on the fringe of Conservative Conference, for the greater part all were bereft of Westminster sponsors. Moreover, Central Office did not encourage applications from their activists to join the Approved Parliamentary Candidates Panel. In that sense, the rightist fringe groups proved to be little more than publicists for causes that had really had their day and were quite irrelevant to Coalition conditions.

Only the ever-recurrent wave of 'brains trusts' and/or Conservative-leaning think-tanks, most of them previously listed, offered any serious contribution to debates on party direction. Of those bodies, the more prominent voices were those of the long established and free-market-orientated Centre for Policy Studies, Institute for Economic Affairs and Adam Smith Institute, all with London offices and staff, funded by sympathetic business sources and continuing to produce pamphlets and booklets for the thinking public and party faithful. They had each been around since the last days of Edward Heath's leadership, had helped ferment the Thatcher policy "revolution", and had proved to be solid Thatcher supporters. However, among the newer bodies, there was the Conservative Home website, whose lead figure, Tim Montgomery, had become a recognisable voice on-line and on air, and whose views were channelled via the cyber-highway to tens of thousands of Conservatives lead figures, rank and file members and voters every week.

Also, Iain Duncan Smith's (Work and Pensions Secretary 2010-16) Centre for Social Justice remained pro-active with its plans for curbing the benefits culture. Working alongside a sister body, Social Justice Policy Group, from an office at Artillery Row, London (with IDS as Chairman of both bodies), CSJ/SJPG had earlier produced a substantial report which won the approval of David Cameron, and had informed much of the Coalition's approach to work and pensions for some five years.*(19) It continued to support IDS with further recommendations during his term in office, while also acting as a publicist and defender of government social policy during the Coalition and thereafter.

Otherwise, two factors militated against the prevalence of factionalism during the Coalition years. First, there was a need for Cameron to steer the Coalition successfully through its term as smoothly and efficiently as was possible in the circumstances. Hostile factionalism would inevitably have drawn negative media attention, which would in turn have rebounded on party and Prime Minister to the detriment of the Conservative electoral image. Such divisive conduct – as it would have been viewed by most party colleagues – would not have been welcomed by the party establishment, who in turn would likely have imposed some retribution. Second, over the last 18 months of Coalition government, most efforts among dissidents and loyalists alike were directed towards preparing for the European Union debate and referendum that had been promised for a second Conservative term. Other causes seemed to be marginal in importance compared to settling the uncertainties over Europe.

As for the Coalition, the prospect of its continuation drew a blank from both parties. Liberals, drawing on local, European and occasional by-election results and opinion polls ratings, knew their electoral prospects to be poor. Yet they talked up likely expectations – foolishly as events showed – to 25-30 Commons seats, and defined a radical agenda for forcing the main parties to contemplate coalition.*(20) As for Conservatives, according to Seldon and Snowdon, there was no desire to revive the Coalition after the election. Instead Tories applied the Lynton Cosby strategy for defeating the greater number of sitting Liberal Democrats in rural and suburban seats, hence the intensity of local campaigns and voter engagement.*(21) Set against those conditions, internal factional politics had little place, but external sabre rattling thrived.

7.   Election 2015: Cameron's Triumph!

Conservatives	331 seats (+24)	36.9% of vote.
Labour	232 (-26)	30.4 %
Liberal Democrats	8 (-50)	7.9%
UKIP	1(+)	12.6%
Greens	1(+1)	3.8%
Scottish Nationalists	56 (+49)	
Plaid Cymru	3 (0)	
Ulster Democratic Unionists	8 (0)	
Ulster Unionists Party	2 (+2)	
Sinn Fein	4 (-1)	
N.I. SDLP	3 (0)	
Independent Ulster Unionist	1(I) *(22)	

Overall result: with a combined UK voter turnout of 66.2%, David Cameron's Conservative Party had won an outright Commons majority of 12 seats.

Equally significant was the fact that the Liberal Democrats, Cameron's former Coalition partners in the outgoing parliament, had been reduced to a rump of just 8 seats. With the exception of the Scottish seats, most other Liberal Democrat losses had been to Conservatives who had campaigned vigorously in Twickenham, Torbay, Yeovil and the West Country, all to the detriment of sitting Coalition MPs, including Ministers like Dr Vincent Cable and David Laws.

In winning a full mandate, Cameron appeared to have secured a personal triumph over not just external foes, but also the Conservative Right, sections of whom had muttered aloud over both concessions made to the Liberals and also Brussels. Now Cameron was back on his own terms …. or so it seemed!

8.   Countdown to European Referendum, May 2015 - June 2017

In normal circumstances, a victorious prime minister could reasonably expect enhanced personal authority and a recognised mandate for key policies. Such are the legitimate fruits of electoral success and in the immediate aftermath of his victory, David Cameron's position looked wholly vindicated.

Yet less than 14 months later it was all over for the Prime Minister. In the intervening period, Cameron had sought direct endorsement from the British public for a renegotiated treaty of UK membership of the European Union, but failed to get predominant support from either his Cabinet, parliamentary party, Conservative grass roots or, most crucially, the British people. The broad 10% margin that separated the Remain option from Brexit in the referendum result of 23rd June, 2016 proved to be the Achilles heel which ended Cameron's premiership and the tenure of his government. So too did it bring down the curtain on Britain's 45 year membership of the European Union, and in the process unleashed a most bitter and protracted round of Brexit negotiations that at this time of writing (i.e. 10th October 2017) are still ongoing.

To a degree, Cameron was the architect of his own fall from high office. He had sanctioned a 2015 manifesto commitment for a referendum over the basic question of EU membership within two years of the ensuing parliament. This pledge was in itself necessary in order to keep the Conservative Right aboard, most of whom were at best Euro-sceptical while others wanted straight UK withdrawal. Yet with the Liberal Democrats gone, Cameron's second Cabinet lacked a firm check on his Euro-sceptical colleagues, and indeed found himself unable to maintain a consensus on the EU question either in Cabinet or the party. He might have been better counselled to delay a referendum for the longest time possible, i.e. 2017, so as to argue the case and build support. Also, it would have been better had Cameron immediately suspended collective support rules among Cabinet members instead of having to concede the latter during the campaign, by which time he had lost the long serving pro-Brexit IDS.

In the event, that 13 months period between election 2015 and the 2016 referendum was dominated by the European debate and little else. It was, as Owen Bennett's published account graphically catalogues, the issue that drove key debates, forced alignments, generated activists' energies and underpinned factional activities within the Conservative Party. Furthermore, the campaign produced a series of cross alignments and liaisons between Tory campaigners – Remain and Brexit – and others on the outside, in Labour, UKIP and the Ulster Democratic Unionists. It also needs to be understood that because this was a referendum, it was subject to specific regulations about funding, broadcasting, participation by party leaders etc. on both sides of the debate, and overseen by the Electoral Commission.*(23) This check certainly imposed constraints on the groups involved, but did not prevent the outbreak of hyper factionalism in the Conservative Party as a result. Nor did it enable the Prime Minister to control the debate or result in a way that he might have hoped.*(24)

Cameron's position was fatally undermined by two failings at the beginning of 2016. First, at the EU summit held in January, though making solid progress on the thorny questions of EU immigrants rights of employment and access to the social services, nevertheless the proposed revised Treaty of Membership failed to give the government entitlements for deporting undesirables or limiting numbers. This proved unsatisfactory to a large number of back bench Tory MPs, 8 Cabinet and 12 junior ministers, thereby generating an image of a government in disarray. That image got further compounded by leading Brexit advocates – Boris Johnson, IDS and Michael Gove – assailing the Premier. Second, Cameron announced a referendum for June 2016 when he could quite legitimately have delayed the poll until the following year. Evidently, a desire to bring closure and still riding on the expectation that what was effectively a public confidence mandate would go his way drove the Premier. The latter seemed justified by polls, which until the final three weeks of the campaign signalled a steady if modest lead for the Cameron's Remain campaign.

In the end, Cameron's confidence proved misplaced on the outcome, along with his judgement on the timing of the poll.

This leaves only one remaining area of enquiry relevant to this study: notably how did the Tory factional protagonists align in the crucial European debate?

Bennett noted one of the main strains within each umbrella organisation to be between different figures competing within for a platform and influence over the direction of both Brexit and Remain campaigns.*(25) He further cited the added complication about the referendum statutory guidelines recognising and funding just one campaigning organisation on either side of the debate. The broadcasters were also expected to endorse the "official" bodies with debates and allocated slots for respective spokesmen. There was no ban on the use of spokesmen from organisations outside the umbrella groups, but only the official bodies were eligible for funding and allotted air time. Also, determinations of which campaigns were appointed was a subjective business and did involve choices being made between rival bidders.*(26)

Recognition matters did not generate problems for the Remain campaign, who united largely behind a cross section of Conservative, Liberal Democrat, Labour and other spokesmen. However, from the beginning there were rival Brexit campaigns, namely the official 'Vote-Leave' and unofficial 'Leave.EU'.*(27) The principal difference was between those Brexit people campaigning under a primarily Conservative aegis, and other Conservatives, along with Labour colleagues (e.g. Kate Hoey and Gisela Stewart), and Ulster Unionists in the unofficial organisation prepared to work with Nigel Farage and his UKIP activists. There was a hangover feeling from the previous year's election that it was dangerous to provide a platform for Farage, something Johnson, IDS, Teresa Villiers, Gove and other front bench Brexit Tories would have none of.

As for Conservative factions, none assumed control of the party debate or indeed the wider public debate. Instead those organisations provided extra profile for the campaigns. For the Remain lobby, there was explicit support from the Tory Reform Group and its sister bodies, Conservative Group for Europe, and Conservative Mainstream. The latter included front line Westminster speakers, vigorous campaigners and campaign volunteers within the party. The *Tory Reformer* proved a redoubtable voice for Europe, and its profile was helped due to this being a campaign where Tories took the lead while a divided Labour Party languished on the margins.*(28)

Conversely, the Right, virtually to a man, backed the Brexit campaign and so it followed with the established rightist groups. Both Leave umbrella groups benefited from the energies of the organised Conservative Right, including Conservative Way Forward, No Turning Back Group and Bill Cash's European Foundation. So also did the Conservative associations experience the weight of the Right's Brexit message, and between rival Conservative and UKIP activists there was a grudging level of cooperation to achieve Brexit.*(29) As far as the grass roots was concerned, the appeal and sustained efforts waged by the Leave campaign enjoyed greater impact to that of the Prime Minister. In part, this was due to the ground teams of right wing activists whose efforts were encouraged by groups from within the party, and partly due to Cameron's ill-judged effort at imposing a discipline on pro-Brexit MPs and party officials. The whole exercise imploded with maximum embarrassment on the Premier.*(30)

9.   Referendum Defeat and Resignation

Result of the UK European Referendum held 23ʳᵈ June 2016:

Remain: 16,141,241 (48.1%)   Leave: 17,410,742 (51.9%)
Turn-out: 72.2% *(31)

On 24th June, mid-morning, David Cameron made a televised speech from the steps of his official residence at Downing Street, acknowledging the result but announcing his resignation from prime ministerial office.

10.   Analysis

David Cameron's leadership term – lasting some 10.½ years – was momentous for Conservatives in more than one way and thus leaves a durable legacy.

First, Cameron made his party electable as an organ of government. Given the enormous setbacks emanating from those three consecutive election defeats 1997, 2001 and 2005, plus all the carping from critics in the media and the enforced resignation of IDS in 2003, this was no small attainment. Cameron was the leader to halt the slide and restore Tories to office. Moreover, he did it on his own terms, making policy choices and utilising his own key people.

Second, Cameron redefined Conservatism for his day and generation in terms of secularisation, social inclusiveness, national sovereignty and a thrusting free market. In so doing he carried much but not all of his party, and along the way shed many key allies whose combined weight was to force him from office.

Third, it was the party's democratic constitution with its provisions for regular and free internal elections, accountability of public representatives and leaders, and input by grass roots to policy making that eventually proved the undoing of Cameron. In days gone by, there would have been no such checks on the Leader's freedom of movement and action and only the election results would have delivered the final verdict. However, Cameron was unable to use his Leader's office for foisting his line on the party, and having failed to win his case on Europe by debate, he had to accept the reality of leading a divided party in what turned out to be a most divisive European referendum.

Looking back at David Cameron's years at the helm, the contra -dynamics of a democratic party constitution and internal democratic culture were the forces that both made and ultimately broke Cameron. Given that his departure also signalled the opening of a long-running and it would seem, torturous process for his successor called 'Brexit', then maybe closure for him was providential in both timing and essence? That is a story for another day and a later enquiry!

FOOTNOTES and REFERENCES

1. See Timothy Bale The Conservatives since 1945; Drivers of Party Change (OUP, 2012); Chaps 3 & 4. Bale examines critically the role of party organisation in the wider Conservative electoral appeal. Whether by accident or design, Cameron appeared to have subscribed to this thesis.

2. Elliot & Hanning (2009); Chaps 16-17.

3. As became apparent later, the growing assortment of rightist malcontents included among their quarrels Cameron's rapid promotion of homosexuality, same sex marriage and free-market feminism as alienating the party's core voters. Those same campaigners tended towards a rightist position on Euro-Brexit, immigration and the defence "core British values". See subsequent series of interviews with rightist groups and figures, not least Rev. Chris Sugden, Secretary, Grassroots Conservatives, 4th August, 2017.

4. Seldon & Snowdon (2015); Chap. 39, pp 493-505.

5. Gamble (1975); Introduction.

6. The Right's attitude towards Cameron was characterised less by ideological hostility as more distrust of his "..modernising agenda..", which seemed at odds with so many of their own basic instincts and policy presumptions. This rift rumbled on through the Coalition years and was apparent to Conservative Party observers, though not the voters, throughout the 2015 election campaign. The discontent boiled over the in the thirteen crucial months following the election victory of May 2015 and underpinning the European Union referendum campaign that finally resulted in a vote by the British electorate to quit the EU (2009) on 23rd June, 2016. See - Elliot and Hanning (2009), Chaps. 16 & 17; Seldon and Snowdon (2015), Epilogue pp 527-545; Owen Bennet The Brexit Club (Biteback, 2016).

7. Although Brady established herself as Chief Executive at first Birmingham City FC and, more recently, West Ham FC, the plain

fact is that that both positions were conferred by the head of the parent company, David Sullivan, and his associate, David Gold. Sullivan was founding proprietor of the pornographic-leaning Daily Sport, and Brady, herself an attractive female, worked closely with him over the years. See - Wikipedia profile.

8. Zac Goldsmith was son of the right-wing publisher, financier and late Thatcher supporter, as well as bank-roller of the 1997 short-lived Referendum Party, Sir James Goldsmith. In May 2010, the younger Goldsmith was elected Conservative MP for Richmond Park, and in 2016 ran unsuccessfully as Conservative candidate for London Mayor. After resigning his Commons seat in Autumn 2016, in protest against the third Heathrow Airport runway, he failed to get to get re-elected in a December by-election. By Spring 2017 Mr Goldsmith reconciled with the Tories, and regained his former West London seat from the Liberal Democrats in the snap general election held that year.

9. Western Goals Institute - a well-funded and rightist anti-Communist campaigning organisation, formally independent of the Conservative Party but campaigning on its fringes. Its leading figure was Greg Lauder -Frost, a man with a long history of campaigning on the Tory Right who was effectively disavowed by the Tory establishment. Ref. Discussions with Mrs Eila Bannister and former MP, Mr John Townsend. Also - WGI newsletters and publications .

10. By 2016, the Traditional Britain Group had become a united platform for three right wing nationalist groups, all based around London and the 'Home' Counties; namely Monarchist League, Western Goals Institute and Monday Club. - Ref. Discussions with former Monday Club activist, Mr J. Farquhar.

11. (i) See Grass roots Conservatives website, stating aims and values, along with campaign reports. (ii) Discussions between GRC Hon Secretary, Rev. Chris Sugden, and author, 4th August, 2017.

12. In Spring 2010, just weeks before the election campaign, pictures of a younger Samantha Cameron, scantily-clad and in bohemian company, appeared in the Sunday Times front page. While not scandalous, nevertheless it generated unwelcome attention on the

Opposition Leader's wife, her own judgement and sense of decorum, along with predictable questions about drug use while a student. Such estimations inevitably shifted the focus to her husband.

13. Rightist suspicions of Cameron were very cogently communicated by Rev. Chris Sugden in discussions with author. Also, see GRC website.

14. Nick Clegg   Politics between the Extremes (Bodley Head, 2016), Chap. 1, pp 21-27.

15. (i) Bennett (2016), Chap 15, pp 125-130. (ii) Seldon & Snowdon (2015), Chaps 10, 39 & 40. (iii) Discussions with Coventry Tory activists, Mr David Sandy and Cllr Kevin Foster (since May 2015 Conservative MP for Torbay). (iv) The author also recalls the stage management of a special Liberal Democrat conference held in Birmingham, 23rd May, 2010, to ratify the Coalition. Anti-Coalition speakers from Liberal grass roots were blatantly vetoed and minimised at the direction of the party leadership.

16. In reality, Clegg stood little chance with the AV proposal. It did not satisfy many electoral reformers, including elements within his own party, with the result that campaigning was half-hearted. Also, to be successful a proposal for constitutional change needs time for an informed debate, and a coalition of cross party and non-party supporters. Clegg had neither of the latter, and barely six months to persuade the electorate, none of which were achieved. That he agreed to the referendum so soon into the Coalition's lifetime says much about the Liberal leader's poor judgement.

17. See Summer and Autumn 2010 issues of Tory Reformer and Crossbow, none of which displayed any antagonism or fundamental objections to the Coalition.

18. Interview - Rev Chris Sugden with author. Also, see GRC website.

19. 'Breakthrough Britain: Ending the costs of social breakdown - Policy recommendations to the Conservative Party'. Published July 2007, Social Justice Policy Group. - This author records his sincere appreciation to Right Hon. Iain Duncan Smith, MP and his former Westminster secretary, Miss Olivia Kybett, for the excellent co-operation so kindly extended him for research and enquiries.

20. Clegg (2016), Chap 6, pp 152-158 - where he discusses electoral politics and options for his party.

21. Seldon & Snowdon (2015) - Chaps 23, 31, 39 & 40.

22. Election 2015 figures drawn from BBC website. This author does not consider it useful to record Celtic parties (ie. SNP, Plaid Cymru, SDLP, Sinn Fein or Unionists) share of UK-wide vote as their pitch is only to the national electorates of Scotland, Wales and Northern Ireland respectively. The same rule applies when assessing the performances of Scottish and Welsh Labour, Conservatives and Liberal Democrats.

23. See Bennett (2016); Chaps 6, 8,9 & 11.

24. Bennett (2016); Chaps 12, 29 & 30.

25. Ibid.

26. Bennett - general.

27. See Times and Guardian reports of referendum campaign - 2nd June, 2016. Also, Sunday Times reports/analysis 5th June, 2016.

28. See Tory Reformer, issue Spring 2016.

29. (i) Discussions with a Conservative peer with right wing affiliations who requested anonymity. (ii) See Bennett; Chap 24.

30. (i) Bennett; Chap. 28.   (ii) See leaders in Observer and Sunday Telegraph, 19th June, 2016.

31. Official figures published by Electoral Commission.

CHAPTER 11

CONCLUSIONS

1. Monolith with Diverse Tendencies?

We now return to Richard Rose's view (first enunciated some 53 years ago) that while Labour was a party of factions, the Conservative Party was more characterised by political tendencies.*(1)

Available evidence shows Rose's evaluation to have been bland, indeed misplaced, but not totally. Notwithstanding clear signs by 1963 of an evolving Tory intra-pluralism, coupled with back bench demands for a say in leadership choice and policymaking, in fact the party was still then a force of compliant infantry centred on an autocratic leadership.*(2) Conservative annual conference amounted to a sounding board for the grass roots with no legislative or mandating powers; constituency associations were essentially supine infantry battalions led by local officials, and in many cases influenced by Central Office. As for central organisation and the parliamentary party, this also fell under the leader's writ, with only electoral results putting the leader under any kind of accountability. In those conditions, only ideological tendencies could function, e.g. One Nation Group, East of Suez Group, Pressure for Social and Economic Toryism, etc. To that extent, Rose's model bears some relevance to the party led by Churchill, Eden and Macmillan.

Frankly speaking, the party bequeathed by Harold Macmillan to Earl Home in October 1963 rather resembled an historic remnant (not unlike Home himself!) from the days of landed gentry, squires and common folk. Minimal in its democratic workings, confident in its upper middle class – even upper class – social moorings, British Conservatives of those times never demurred from a presumption of superior capacity and entitlement to govern. So too were they led by a class of self-appointed and self perpetuating oligarchs.*(3)

After 1963, the picture changed fundamentally; a pattern documented by material appearing in Chaps 5-10.

Over the past half century since the mid-1960s, Conservatives experienced an internal democratic changeover, although some writers, e.g. Seyd, Whiteley & Richardson, question the Tory "conversion" to democracy.*(4) Additionally, there are campaigning Tories demanding further progress in democratising the party.*(5) Be that as it may, the plain fact is that those pan-democratic tides permeating the world of British, West European, North American and Australasian liberal democracy in the post-1960s impacted on British Conservatives like other major parties. Such is particularly true of governing parties, a category where Tories have long ticked the boxes.

2. Change

The facts of that 'conversion' make for clear reading. Over the past half century, British Conservatives have initiated the following changes:

- Introduced a reformed system with a place for grass roots participation in the selection and reselection of MPs, parliamentary candidates and local councillors.
- Reformed the method for choosing the party leader, initially to a full ballot of all Tory MPs, and, since 1999, extending the choice between two final runners to a postal ballot of the full party membership.
- Approved in 1999, a formal party constitution defining offices with titles, powers and expectations, as well as putting membership on a proper footing and ensuring accountability devices for removing unsatisfactory holders of office.
- Allowed the annual conference a practical acknowledgement of its role in relaying rank and file sentiment to the leadership.
- Encouraged the emergence of a professional political class to manage and, ultimately, lead the party in the post-millennium era.
- Recognised the legitimate place of informal party groups, campaigning bodies and ideological tendencies in contributing to policy and leadership debates.
- Facilitated the emergence of independent research institutes and commentary bodies, all of them occupying an increasingly prominent profile in party affairs, e.g. 1970/80s Freedom Association, Conservative Home website and a plethora of free market 'brains trusts', most either self funded or financed by friendly business sources.

While it might be premature to talk of a Conservative democratic revolution, nevertheless the party of old that embodied a privileged elite rooted in the English and Scottish upper classes has been swept away in favour of something more meritocratic and professionalised. Such reforms have chimed with post-1945 democratic tides and are electorally credible with the society emerging from the post-war and post-millennium years. While ever-committed to core Tory causes, e.g. constitution, monarchy, parliamentary sovereignty, free enterprise, a strong nation and defence of heritage etc, Conservatives have adapted to changing political and social tides. Even the social safety net which Conservatives have long boasted as their prime inheritance from Disraeli and Shaftesbury, has had to be updated to an acceptance and willingness to manage the welfare state, albeit with their emphasis on selective benefits and caution over universal fare. It has also meant embracing multi-cultural and secular Britain with its agenda of 'gay' rights, feminist empowerment and equal opportunities, as well as phasing out remaining ties to organised Christianity, especially the Church of England.

For the Conservatives, the primary goal has long been their own survival and the successful adaptation of their interests to an ever-evolving society of post-war and, more recently, post-millennium Britain.

3. Political Democracy

The slow growth of intra-democracy over the post-1960s years forced Conservatives to accommodate a plurality of ideas and groups in their party. Such changes were forced on the Tories by the course of external reforms on the outside. Amongst the latter were those laws empowering young people such as the 1969 Representation of the Peoples Act, trade unionists achieving the right to strike ballots and internal elections for all major offices, along with increased use of constitutional referenda in all parts of the UK from the early 1970s onwards. There was also the variable extension of popular democracy in the centre right parties of other West European countries, e.g. the German Christian Democrats and French Gaullists, and even the Conservatives' sister party in Belfast, the Ulster Unionists.

It would have looked untenable for a party that so championed select aspects of popular democracy for trade unions and as a device for defeating Celtic nationalists to be denying the same rights to its own membership.*(6) In any case, as was shown by this study, from the 1960s onwards there were active campaign groups – not all of them featuring leftist Tory Reformers – seeking extended participation by members of middle rank and grass roots in key party affairs. The latter campaigns are ongoing, but whether as a result of their lobbying or in spite of the latter actually democratic culture has made an awkward entry to the modern Conservative internal structures.

Now, in 2016/17, the contemporary Conservative movement embraces a broad mantle of campaigning groups, ideological tendencies and even a body of organised and disciplined factions all operating within and beyond the party fringe. They include all the main ideological elements thereby testifying to a fractured and at times non-harmonious Conservative history, i.e. Imperialists, free enterprise defenders, supporters of church and state, rabid anti-Communists, One Nationites, Europhiles, Euro-sceptics, British sovereignty campaigners, New Right economic liberals, Irish, Welsh and Scottish unionists, British nationalists, social libertarians and many other bedfellows. Some are officially registered, while others operate independently, but all are committed to a Conservative election victory and a government pursuing the Conservative political cause. Such is their common theme.*(7)

At the same time, while free to pursue their campaigns nevertheless groups and their spokesmen/women are expected to conform to a code of conduct sanctioned by the party constitution which prioritises loyalty and discipline. To pursue an agenda directly hostile to the party risks withdrawal of official recognition and concomitant loss of Westminster patrons, in turn rendering the group irrelevant. The experiences of the Monday Club in 2002 and later the Western Goals Institute serves to illustrate that the risk of leadership opprobrium is by itself enough to drive dissenter groups out of the party. This ever-recurring trait of MP/peer-dominated organisations has ensured that what are supposed to be autonomous groups are in fact led by those with a base at Westminster, and having a pre-disposition for putting the organisation at the service of the party's Westminster political masters.

4. Conservative Groups

Actually, the previous script abounds with evidence of many such compliant organisations. To the extent that MPs and peers continue to dominate the group fringe, this aspect of Conservative politics remains every bit as durable from the days of Sir Waldron Smithers, MP and his reactionary bedfellows in the National League for Freedom operating in the 1940s up to the campaigns of Europhiles and Eurosceptics, right and leftist ideological tendencies, and Tory Gays, Greens and Family lobbies of the present.*(8)

This study found nothing especially sinister about Conservative factions or the ideological alignments that they epitomised over the past seven decades. There was no secret pot of cash or live resources ready to be utilised for some extra-constitutional machination by forces of the Right or action against leftist activists in the unions, universities or elsewhere. Nor, with the exceptions of the Monday Club and Freedom Association – and even then only to a modest extent – was there evidence of Conservative groups either initiating or collaborating with right wing extra party movements such as might have undermined democratic institutions or punished radical opponents. Although from the early years of the twentieth century, individual Tories had aligned with various imperial, anti-Communist and militant free market campaigns, plus the alliance with Ulster Unionists resisting Irish Home Rule, conversely little of the kind was forthcoming from party groups in the post-1945 years. Indeed to a greater extent, most Conservative groups of both left and right proved to be models of democratic propriety whose activities, however tendentious, were entirely legitimate without trace of subversion.

Another function of Conservative groups across the board during the last seven decades was to act as refuges for political dissenters of the prevailing leadership regime. The Monday Club's origins as a right wing policy crusader in the 1960s One Nation era of Macmillan and Heath, as well as a platform for rightist dissenters like Enoch Powell and leading Ulster Unionist, William Craig, was an example in point. Equally relevant from the other side was the revitalised Tory Reform Group headed by Peter Walker, Ken Clarke and Ian Gilmour, whose principal role during the Thatcher years and later Major era was to accommodate One Nationites and Europhiles.*(9) Though the Monday Club did engage in some organised action with the aim of unseating one or two centrist Conservative MPs in the re-selection process, in fact it and TRG, along with other ideological groups like Conservative Way Forward, European Foundation and Grass Roots Conservatives acted primarily as publicists for their respective causes, publishing their own journals and literature, and running meetings addressed by sympathetic Westminster patrons.

The tactic of power-politicking – working for the selection of "their people" as Council, Westminster and Strasbourg candidates – as briefly practised by certain Labour factions in the 1970s and '80s never really took off in the Conservative Party with the degree of organisational discipline practised by activists of the Militant Tendency and Campaign groups.*(10) Where the occasion arose, when factions appeared to be gaining a hold on either a constituency association like Surbiton in the1960s (Monday Club) or the disrupted Federation of Conservative Students conference in 1986 (Libertarian Alliance), there occurred a leadership intervention unusually to curb the group. In fact the Monday Club found itself marginalised, and Norman Tebbit in 1986 disbanded the FCS, thereby reasserting central control. For sure, Conservatives drew clear limits to the scope open to factions, especially where challenging leadership or disrupting the party was concerned.

Beyond those roles listed, Conservative groups acted as harbingers of ideas and publicists of rival causes, frequently offering platforms to leading spokespersons on all the major causes of the day. In that sense, they could credibly be said to be contributing to the plurality of values, ideas and causes of their party, and whether as dissenters or supporters of leadership, they have long checked the policy monolith that British Conservatives once oozed.

Given the fractious state of the party in the wake of David Cameron's Euro-referendum failure in June 2016 and his successor, Theresa May's spectacular failure to achieve a clear mandate in the snap general election of May 2017, confused direction, Mrs May's captaincy and Brexit are realities with which the Conservatives are currently dealing. Whether those questions will reignite a proliferation in factionalism and lasting fragmentation is a scenario about which there is yet no clear light. All that can be deduced is that since 1945 the British Conservative Party has had to grapple with each crisis arising in a manner appropriate to its time and the demands of a society where the party has long claimed the empirical wisdom and skills of state craft to manage better than opponents. Whether such claims will continue to show merit or rank as empty bombast from a party out of step and time is a question where only time and events hold the answers.

FOOTNOTES and REFERENCES

1. Richard Rose Political Studies (1963).

2. After the disputed leadership selection (using the old 'emergence' method) of 1963, Conservatives opted to elect their leader by an MPs ballot. This mechanism remained in force until William Hague's 2003 constitution introduced the direct full membership ballot.

3. Of all literature available on the evolving post-Home Conservative Party, Andrew Gamble's 1974 book, Conservative Nation, and 1979 essay (Drucker eds.) offers the greatest clarity and candidness, in this author's view. Highly recommended to students and party observers!

4. P. Seyd, P. Whiteley & J. Richardson Chap. 1, True Blues (OUP, 1994).

5. For example - the Tory Charter Movement and Conservative Campaign for Democracy.

6. See Seyd, Whiteley & Richardson (1994), Concluding chapter.

7. See McKee essays on Conservative Factionalism, Contemporary Record, (Sep.1989) and Politics Review (April 1996).

8. Encyclopedia of British and Irish Political Organisations: Parties, Goups and Movements of the Twentieth Century: - Eds. Barberis, McHugh & Tyldesley (2000) - p. 326 (1136).

9. Ironically, after his departure from executive office John Major went on to become an open sympathiser with Tory Reform, and at the time of writing is President of the Tory Reform Group.

10. See Seyd's article on the Monday Club, Government and Opposition (1972).

SELECT BIBLIOGRAPHY

1. Publications - Books and individual chapters

Aitken J.   Margaret Thatcher: Power and Personality (Bloomsbury, London, 2013).

Alexander A. & Watkins A.   The Making of the Prime Minister 1970 (Macdonald Unit 75, London, 1970).

Anderson B.   John Major: The Making of the Prime Minister (Fourth Estate, London, 1991).

Bale T.   The Conservatives since 1945: The Drivers of Party Change (Oxford University Press, Oxford, 2012).

Ball S.   The Conservative Party since 1945 (Manchester University Press/ St Martin's Press, Manchester & New York, 1998)

Banton M. (Eds.)   Political Systems and the Distribution of Power (Tavistock Publications, UK, 1965).

Barr J.   On the Make: The Bow Group, 1950-2000 (Politicos, London, 2001)

Behrens R. The Conservative Party from Edward Heath to Margaret Thatcher (Saxon House, London, 1980).

Belloni F.P. & Beller D.C. (Eds.)   Faction Politics (ABC-CIO Press, USA, 1978)

Bennett O.   The Brexit Club: The Inside Story of the Leave Campaign's Shock Victory (Biteback, London, 2016).

Bew P.   Churchill and Ireland (OUP, Oxford, 2016)

Blake R.   The Conservative Party from Peel to Thatcher (Fontana, London, 1985).

Blondel J.   Voters, Parties and Leaders: The Social Fabric of British Politics (Penguin Books, Harmondsworth, 1974).

Bradford S.   Disraeli (Phoenix/Orion, London, 1989).

309

Butler D. & Pinto-Duschinsky M. The British General Election of 1970 (Macmillan, London, 1971).

Butler R.A. The Art of the Possible: The Memoirs of Lord Butler (Hamish Hamilton, London, 1971).

Carrington P.A.R. Reflect on Things Past: The Memoirs of Lord Carrington (Collins, London, 1988).

Carlton D. Anthony Eden: A Biography (Allan & Unwin, London, 1981).

Chambers W.N. Political Parties in a New Nation: The American Experience, 1776-1809 (OUP, Oxford, 1963).

Charmley J. A History of Conservative Politics, 1900-1996 (Macmillan, London, 1998).

Churchill W. Great Contemporaries (Fontana, London, 1937).

Clark A. The Tories: Conservatives and the Nation State, 1922-1997 (Weidenfeld & Nicolson, London, 1998)

Alan Clark Diaries (Weidenfeld & Nicolson, London, 1993).

Alan Clark: The Last Diaries: In and Out of the Wilderness; Edited by Ion Trewin (Weidenfeld & Nicolson, London, 2002).

Clarke K. Ken Clarke, Kind of Blue: A Political Memoir (Macmillan, London 2016).

Clegg N. Politics Between the Extremes (Bodley Head, London, 2016)

Cole J. As it Seemed to Me: Political Memoirs (Weidenfeld & Nicolson, London, 1995).

Cosgrave P. The Lives of Enoch Powell (Bodley Head, London, 1989).

Critchley J.   Heseltine: The Unauthorised Biography (Andre-Deutsch, London, 1987).

Crosland C.A.R.   The Future of Socialism (J.Cape, London, 1956).

Davies A.J.   We, The Nation: The Conservative Party and the Pursuit of Power (Little, Brown and Co, London, 1995).

Derbyshire J.D. & Derbyshire I.   Politics in Britain from Callaghan to Thatcher (Chambers, London, 1988).

Dunleavy P., Gamble A., Heffernan R. and Peele G.   Developments in British Politics (Palgrave/Macmillan, Basingstoke, 2003).

Eccleshall R.   English Conservatism since the Restoration (Routledge, London 2002).

Eden A.   Memoirs - Anthony Eden: The Reckoning (Cassell, London, 1965).

Elliot F. & Hanning J.   Cameron: The Rise of the New Conservative (Harper-Perennial, London/New York, 2007).

Fisher N.   Iain Macleod (Andre Deutsch, London, 1973).

Gamble A.   The Free Economy and the Strong State: The Politics of Thatcherism (Macmillan, London, 1989)

   The Conservative Nation (Routledge and Kegan Paul, London, 1974)

   The Conservative Party, Chap 1, Multi-Party Britain, H.M. Drucker Eds., (Macmillan, London, 1979)

Garner R. & Kelly R.   British Political Parties Today, Second Ed., (MUP, Manchester, 1998).

Gilbert M.   Churchill: A Biography (Park Lane Press, London, 1979)

Gilmour I.   Inside Right (Hutchinson, London, 1977)

   The Body Politic (Hutchinson, London, 1969)

Dancing with Dogma: Britain under Thatcherism (Simon
& Schuster, London & New York, 1992).

Gilmour I. and Garnett M. Whatever Happened to the Tories?-The
Conservatives since 1945 (Fourth Estate, London, 1997)

Godson D. Himself Alone: David Trimble and the Ordeal of Ulster
Unionism (Harper-Collins, London, 2004)

Gorman T. with Kirby H. The Bastards: Dirty Tricks and the
Challenge to Europe (Pan Books, London, 1993)

Gray J. & Willets D. Is Conservatism Dead? (Profile Books,
London, 1997)

Halsey A.H. (Eds.) Trends in British Society since 1900 (Macmillan,
London 1972).

Halsey A.H., Heath A.F. & Ridge J.M. Origins and Destinations;
Family, Class and Education in Modern Britain (OUP, Oxford, 1980).

Hanson A.H. & Walles M. Governing Britain (Fontana/Collins,
London, 1970).

Harbinson J.F. The Ulster Unionist Party, 1882-1973 (Blackstaff,
Belfast, 1974).

Hastings M. Max Hastings; Editor: An Inside Story of Newspapers
(Macmillan, London/Basingstoke and Oxford, 2002).

Heath E. Autobiography of Edward Heath: The Course of my Life
(Hodder & Stoughton, London, 1998).

Hennessy P. Never Again: retain 1945-51 (J. Cape, London, 1992).

Having it so Good: Britain in the 1950s (Penguin,
London, 2007).

Heseltine M. Life in the Jungle: My Autobiography (Hodder &
Stoughton, London, 2000).

Hill B.W. Eds.   Edmund Burke on Government, Politics and Society (Fontana, London, 1975).

Hoffman J.D.   The Conservative Party in Opposition, 1945-51 (MacGibbon & Kee, London, 1964).

Hogg Q.   The Case for Conservatism (Penguin Books, London, 1947).

Howard A.   RAB: The Life of R.A. Butler (J. Cape, London, 1987).

Howe G.   Geoffrey Howe: Conflict of Loyalty (Pan, London, 1994).

Howell D.   British Social Democracy (Croom Helm, London, 1976).

Hurd D.   Douglas Hurd: Memoirs (Little Brown, London, 2003).

Ingham B.   Kill the Messenger (Fontana, London, 1991).

Jarvis M.   Conservative Governments: Morality and Social Change in Affluent Britain, 1957-64 (Manchester University Press, Manchester, 2005)

Jenkin J. & Moncrieff C. (Eds.)   John Major: Prime Minister (PA/Bloomsbury, London, 1990)

Jenkins P.   Mrs Thatcher's Revolution: The Ending of the Socialist Era (J. Cape, London, 1987).

Jenkins R. H.   Churchill (Pan, London, Basingstoke and Oxford, 2002).

Katz R.S. & Mair P. (Eds)   How Parties Organise: Change and Adaptation in Party Organisations in Western Democracies (Sage, London/California, 1994).

Kavanagh D. & Seldon A. (Eds.)   The Thatcher Effect: A Decade of Change (Oxford University Press, Oxford, 1989).

Kavanagh D. & Morris (Eds.)   Consensus Politics from Attlee to Thatcher (ICBH/Basil Blackwell, Oxford, 1989).

Kavanagh D.   Thatcher and British Politics: An End to Consensus (OUP, Oxford, 1987).

Kee R.   1945: The World We Fought For (Hamish Hamilton, London, 1985)

King A. & Crewe I.   The Birth, Life and Death of the Social Democratic Party (OUP, Oxford, 1995)

Kirk R.   The Conservative Mind (Faber & Faber, London, 1956)

Kogan D. & Kogan M.   The Battle for the Labour Party (Kogan Page, London, 1982)

Laing M.   Edward Heath: Prime Minister (Sidgwick and Jackson, London, 1972)

La-Palombara J. & Weiner M. (Eds.)   Political Parties and Political Development (Princeton University Press, USA, 1966)

Layton-Henry Z. (Eds.)   Conservative Party Politics (Macmillan, London/Basingstoke, 1980).

Leach R.   British Political Ideologies, Second Ed., (Harvester-Wheatsheaf & Prentice Hall, London and New York, 1996).

Lynch P.   The Politics of Nationhood: Sovereignty, Britishness and Conservative Politics (Macmillan, Basingstoke/London, 1999).

MacFarlane L.J.   British Politics 1918-64 (Pergamon, Oxford, 1965).

Macmillan H.   Memoirs: At the End of the Day (final volume - Macmillan, London, 1973).

Major J.   The Autobiography (Harper-Collins, London, 1999).

Mallie E. & Maloney E.   The Road to Peace in N. Ireland (Pan Books, London, 1998).

Maloney E. & Pollak A.   Paisley (Poolbeg, Belfast, 1986).

Marquand D.   The Unprincipled Society: New Demands and Old Politics (J. Cape, London, 1998)

Marsland D.   Real Welfare: Self Reliance or State-dependence? (Libertarian Alliance Publications, London, 2003).

McAllister I. & Rose R.   The Nationwide Competition for Votes: The 1983 British Election (Pinter, London/New York, 1984).

McAlpine A.   Memoirs: Once a Jolly Bagman (Weidenfeld & Nicolson, London, 1997).

McKenzie R.T.   British Political Parties (Heinemann, London, 1963).

Michels R. (Introduction by S. Lipset)   Political Parties (Collier Books, London, 1962).

Maudling R.   Reginald Maudling: Memoirs (Sidgwick & Jackson, London, 1978)

O'Neill T.   The Autobiography of Terence O'Neill: Prime Minister of Northern Ireland, 1963-1969 (Rupert Hart-Davis, London, 1972).

Patten J.   Things to Come: The Tories in the 21st Century (Sinclair Stevenson, London, 1995).

Parry R.   Scottish Political Facts (T. & T. Clark, Edinburgh, 1998).

Pelling H.   Winston Churchill (Macmillan, London, 1974).

Pimlott B.   The Queen: A Biography of Elizabeth II (Harper-Collins, London, 1997).

Powell J. Enoch   'The Conservative Party'; Chap. 5, Kavanagh & Seldon Eds., 1989.

Prior J.   A Balance of Power (Hamish Hamilton, London, 1986).

Ramsden J.   An Appetite for Power: A History of the Conservative Party since 1830 (Harper-Collins, London, 1998).

Rhodes Boyson J. (Eds.)   1985: An Escape from Orwell's 1984: A Conservative Path to Freedom (Churchill Press, Enfield, Middlesex, 1975).

Ribbins P. & Sherratt B.   Radical Educational Policies and Conservative Secretaries of State (Cassell, London, 1997).

Rifkind M.   Power and Pragmatism: The Memories of Malcolm Rifkind (Biteback, London, 2016).

Roberts A.   Eminent Churchillians (Phoenix, London, 1995).

Rose R.   The Problem of Party Government (Penguin Books, London, 1974).

Rose R. (Eds.)   Studies in British Politics, Third Ed., (Macmillan, London, 1975)

Ross T.   Why the Tories Won: The Inside Story of the 2015 Election (Biteback, London, 2015)

Sampson A.   Macmillan: A Study in Ambiguity (Penguin, Harmondsworth, 1967)

                    Anatomy of Britain Today (Hodder & Stoughton, London, 1965)

Sarberis P., McHugh J. and Tyldesley M. - with Helen Pendry Encyclopedia of British and Irish Political Organisations: Parties, Groups and Movements of the Twentieth Century (Pinter, London/New York, 2000)

Sartori G.   Parties and the Party System (Cambridge University Press, Cambridge, 1978)

Seldon A. with Lewis Baston   Major: A Political Life (Phoenix, London, 1997)

Seldon A. & Snowdon P.   Cameron at 10: The Inside Story, 2010-2015 (Collins, London, 2015)

Seldon A. & Ball S.   The Conservative Century (OUP, Oxford, 1994)

Seldon A. (Eds.)   How Tory Governments Fall: The Tory Party in Power since 1783 (Fontana/Harper-Collins, London 1996)

UK Political Parties since 1945 (Philip Allan, London, 1990).

Sewell D.   Catholics: Britain's Largest Minority (Penguin, London, 2001).

Shepherd R.   Enoch Powell: A Biography (Hutchinson, London, 1996).

Sked A. & Cook C.   Post-War Britain: A Political History Second Edition (Pelican Books, London, 1988).

Skidelsky R. (Eds.)   Thatcherism (Basil Blackwell, Oxford, 1989).

Stevenson J.   Third Party Politics since 1945 (Blackwell/ICBH, Oxford, 1993).

British Society, 1914-45 (Penguin,Harmondsworth, Middlesex, 1984).

Tebbit N.   Upwardly Mobile: An Autobiography (Weidenfeld & Nicolson, London, 1988).

Thatcher M. Margaret Thatcher: Path to Power (Harper-Collins, London, 1995)

The Downing Street Years (Harper-Collins, London, 1993).

Thompson E.P.   The Making of the English Working Class (Pelican, London, 1979).

Walters S.   Tory Wars: Conservatives in Crisis (Politicos, London, 2001).

Ward G.   Fort Grunwick (Maurice Temple, London, 1977).

Warner. G.   The Scottish Tory Party: A History (Weidenfeld & Nicolson, London and Edinburgh, 1988).

Watkin E.I.   The Catholic Centre (Catholic Book Club, London, 1943).

Watkins A.   A Conservative Coup: The Fall of Margaret Thatcher (Duckworth, London, 1991).

Whitelaw W.   The Whitelaw Memoirs (Aurum Press, London, 1989).

Whiteley P., Seyd P. & Richardson J.   True Blues: The Politics of Conservative Party Membership (OUP, Oxford, 1994).

Wood A.   Great Britain 1900-1965 (Longman, London 1978).

Young G.M.   Stanley Baldwin (Rupert Hart Davis, London, 1952)

Young H.   One of Us (Macmillan, London, 1989)

2.   Journal Articles, Chapters and Published Papers

Ashford N.   *'The New American Right';* Social Studies Review, Nov. 1987.

'The European Economic Community'; Chap 5, Eds. Zig Layton-Henry (Macmillan, 1980).

Belloni F. P. & Beller D.   *'The Study of Party Factions as Competitive Political Organisations';* Western Political Commentary (USA, 1976).

Brand J.   *'Faction in the British Parliament, 1945-1986';* Parliamentary Affairs, (UK, Vol. 42, 2, 1989).

Eccleshall R.   *'English Conservatism as Ideology';* Political Studies (25, 2006).

Foot M.   *'A Miscellany of Crossbreeds'; - essay on Enoch Powell –* Loyalists and Loners, pp 185-193, (Collins, London, 1986).

Garvin T.   *'The Growth of Faction in the Fianna Fail Party, 1966-80';* Parliamentary Affairs (Vol. 4, 24, 1981).

Hine D.   *'Factionalism in West European Parties: A   Framework for Analysis';* Journal of West European Studies (UK, N. America and Western Europe, Vol. 5, January 1982)

Joseph K.   *'Reversing the Trend'* (Barry Rose, 1975) and *'Stranded on the Middle Ground'* (Centre for Policy Studies, 1976) – Published keynote speeches of Sir Keith Joseph.

Kellas J.   *The Scottish Political System';* Social Studies Review, May 1988.

Layton-Henry Z.   *'Race, Electoral Strategy and the Major Parties';* Parliamentary Affairs (xxxi, 3, 1978).

McKee V.   *'Conservative Factions';* Contemporary Record (UK, Vol. 3, 1, Autumn 1989)

> 'Factions and Tendencies in the Conservative Party since 1945'; Politics Review (UK, Vol. 5, 4, April 1996)
>
> *'Factionalism in the SDP, 1981-87'*; Parliamentary Affairs (Vol. 42, 2, 1989)
>
> *'Fragmentation on the Labour Right';* Politics (Vol. 11, 1, 1991)
>
> *'Factionalism among the Liberal Democrats';* Chap 7, The Liberal Democrats' Eds. D.J. Maciver (Harvester-Wheatsheaf, London, 1996).
>
> *'Politics of Post-War British Conservatism',* Ad Veritatem, Journal of the Graduate School, University of Santo Tomas, Manila, Philippines (Vol. 4, 2, March 2005)

Minogue K.   'Europe in Hubris: The Tempting of Modern Conservatism' – (Centre for Policy Studies, 1992)

Ramsden J.   *'A Party for Owners or a Party for Earners? How far did the British Conservative Party really change in Opposition?'* – Transactions of the Royal Historical Society (London, 1987)

Rose R.   *'Parties, Factions and Tendencies in Britain'*; Political Studies (Vol xii, I, 1964).

   'The Bow Group's Role In British Politics'; Western Political Quarterly (UK/ Ireland/N. America, 1961)

Seyd P.   *'Factionalism in the 1970s'*, Chap. 10, Conservative Party Politics, Eds. Zig Layton-Henry (Macmillan, London, 1980).

   'Factionalism within the Conservative Party: The Monday Club'; Government and Opposition (UK, Vol. 7, 4, 1972)

3.   Primary Research Materials - Unpublished

Ashford N.   'The Conservative Party and European Integration'; Unpublished Ph.D. thesis, University of Warwick, 1983.

Barnes J.   'Ideology and Factions'; Chap. 8, in A. Seldon & Stuart Ball (eds.), Conservative Century: The Conservative Party since 1900 (OUP, Oxford, 2000).

Behrens R.   'The One Nation Group 1951-59'; Paper presented to the UK Political Studies Association Conference, 1988, Portsmouth.

O'Brien M.   Margaret Thatcher and Northern Ireland (Unpublished M. Soc. Sciences thesis, Queens University, Belfast, 1993) - Awarded QUB's esteemed 1993 Montgomery Medal in recognition of its academic excellence.

Grant L.   'Clear Blue Water: Secrets from the Deep: A Study of the '92 Club within the Conservative Party'; Unpublished M.A. Dissertation, University of Hull, 1999.

McKee V.   Right wing Factionalism in the British Labour Party, 1977-87 (Unpublished M.Phil. thesis, CNAA/Birmingham Polytechnic, 1988)

British Social Democratic Factionalism: Case Studies of the SDP 1981-88 and Liberal Democrats 1988-96 (Unpublished Ph.D. thesis, London Guildhall/Metropolitan University, 1996)

4. Primary Documents

  (i)   Tory Charter Movement - Statement of Aims

  (ii)   Selective correspondence, Libertarian Alliance; Coventry, Warwick University and St Andrews groups.

  (iii) Occasional correspondence, Friends of the Union.

  (iv)   Correspondence - National Life and Conservative Life Group; courtesy of former Life Political Officer, Mr Peter Garret.

  (v)   Correspondence and mailings, 1984-1988, Peace Through NATO and the Conservative Party; courtesy of Mr Ken Aldred, Director, and Mrs Caroline Macleod (nee-Flynn), Youth Officer.

  (vi)   Correspondence and select internal documents, Tory Reform Group.

  (vii) Monday Club, Statement of Aims (1976).

  (viii) Monday Club pamphlet on House of Lords defence - John Stokes MP.

  (ix)   Monday Club, Minutes of Executive Council, 11th February, 1991 - supplied on a confidential basis by a former officer who wished to remain anonymous.

(x)   Monday Club Newsletter, all issues 1990-1993; kindly supplied by Mrs Eila Bannister.

(xi)   Correspondence from Mr Gerald Hartup, Secretary - Freedom Association (London) to Mr Martin O'Brien, Editor, Irish News (Belfast), 5th May, 1984 threatening legal action for a critical article on the organisation run by the newspaper.

(xii) Internal correspondence on strategy and campaigns (1987-98), Freedom Association, supplied by a former middle ranking officer who requested anonymity.

(xiii) Selsdon Group - Statement of Aims.

(xiv) Briefing papers 1996-98, Friends of the Union, prepared and dispersed by Miss Patricia Campbell, full-time Director.

(xv) Bruges Group - Statement of Aims, plus accompanying briefing papers, kindly supplied by anonymous internal source.

(xvi) 'Breakthrough Britain: Ending the costs of Social Breakdown: - Policy Recommendations to the Conservative Party'; Jointly published in July 2007 by Centre for Social Justice and Social Justice Policy Group, both headed by Iain Duncan Smith, MP.

5. Newspapers, Magazines and Newsletters.

Specific titles and issues referred to in each chapter's Footnotes.

(i) Secular Press: Guardian, Observer, Times, Sunday Times, Daily Telegraph, Daily Express, Independent, London Evening Standard, Northern Echo, Manchester Evening News, Western Mail, Scotsman, Glasgow Herald, Birmingham Post and Mail, Coventry Telegraph, Warwick Boar, National Student, Irish News (Belfast), Belfast Newsletter, Belfast Telegraph.

(ii) Pro-Conservative Magazines - official and unofficial:
Conservative Newsline, Spectator, Now (long defunct!), Monday

World, Salisbury Review, Tory Reformer, Free World, Bow Group News, European Foundation Journal.

(iii) Religious Press: Church Times, Church of England Newspaper, Life and Work (Church of Scotland), Tablet, Catholic Herald, Universe, Catholic Times, Presbyterian Gazette, Protestant Telegraph, Methodist Recorder, Jewish News and Jewish Chronicle.

(iv) Pro-Conservative Group leaflets, websites and occasional material: Conservative Gays, Conservative Life Group, Conservative Family Campaign, Conservative Environmental Campaign, Conservative Women, Grass Roots Conservatives, Thistle Group, Conservatives for Europe, No-Turning Back Group, Conservative Mainstream, Bruges Group, Conservative Way Forward, Ulster Unionist Newsletter, Friends of the Union Newsletter, Conservative Campaign for Party Democracy newsletter, Tory Charter Group occasional campaigning leaflets, Charter News, True Blues Newsletter, Coalition for Peace and Security newsletter and occasional leaflets, Women for Families and Defence newsletter, Western Goals Institute, Monarchist Group, Tory Action, League of St George, Libertarian Alliance, League of Empire Loyalists, Federation of Conservative Students, Conservative Lawyers, Women and Trade Unionists, plus the rival literature from both camps in the European referendum debates of 1975 and 2016.

(v) Specialist Policy Publications: Author examined a variable set of policy publications from following 'Think-Tanks' and campaigning groups, not all pro-Conservative: Centre for Policy Studies, Adam Smith Group, Bow Group, Centre For Social Justice, Selsdon Group, Thistle Group, European Foundation, Freedom Association, One Nation Group, Friends of the Union, Tory Reform Group, Peace Through NATO, Coalition for Peace and Security, Conservative Campaign for Electoral Reform, National Viewers and Listeners Association, Society for the Protection of Unborn Children and LIFE-UK.

(vi) Eric Chalker   'The Stalinist Tories need Purging'; Independent, 25th June, 1997.

(vii)   Vincent McKee   'The American and British Right: Comparisons of Tactics and Impact'; Church Times, 15th October 2007.

Series on Catholic Politics in Modern Britain, Catholic Life, 2002-2003.

McKee's Profile of Iain Duncan Smith in Catholic Herald and Irish Catholic, both Spring 2006.

6. Recorded Interviews with Specialist Witnesses

Notes:

(a) All interviews took place with the author.

(b) Except where indicated 'Unrecorded', all other interviews were recorded.

Mr (now Lord) Peter Temple-Morris, MP - at House of Commons, 24th October, 2000.

Mr James Barr, author -Bow Group History, at House of Commons, 13th March, 2000.

Rt. Hon. (Lord) Michael Heseltine - at his residence, Thenford, Northamptonshire- 21st May, 2004.

Rt. Hon. (Lord) Norman Tebbit at House of Lords, London - 9th July, 2001

Rt. Hon Iain Duncan Smith, MP - at Westminster, 1st December, 2005

Sir William Cash, MP - at Commons, Westminster, 21st November, 2000.

Mr John Strafford, Secretary, Campaign for Conservative Party Democracy, at his residence, Gerard's Cross, Greater London, 4th January 2003.

Mrs Theresa Gorman, MP (since deceased) at House of Commons, Westminster - 21st October, 2000.

Mr Giles Marshall, Secretary - Tory Reform Group, Coventry, 25th March, 2000.

Cllr Francis Lancaster, at Worcestershire hotel, 20th November 1999.

Mr Justin Powell-Tuck, Conservative campaigning activist, at his Central London office, 23rd February, 2000

Mr John Townsend (retired right wing MP), at his business office, Hull, 26th October, 2001.

Rt. Hon. Stephen (now Lord) Dorrell, MP at the House of Commons, Westminster, 13th July, 2000.

Mr Eric Chalker, Secretary, Tory Charter Movement, at his business offices, Surrey, 23rd February, 2000.

Rt. Hon. Sir (later Lord) Reginald Prentice, MP - at his residence, Surrey, 10th September 1986.

Mr William McDowell, former Parliamentary research aide to the late Ulster Unionist MP for Bannside, Mr Harold McCusker, Central Methodist Hall, Westminster, 29th October, 1988.(Unrecorded)

Mr Bernard Capel, activist with Libertarian Alliance, Coventry, 29th October, 1999.

Mr Peter Garret, Political Officer, National Life, and Co-ordinator of Conservative Life Group; 30th June, 2003, and 28th November 2003. Both discussions took place at a Coventry restaurant.

Mr Ken Aldred, Director PTN, Portsmouth, and several preceding informal discussions at PTN London office and offices of the English-Speaking Union, London, 1985 - 1987. (Unrecorded)

General discussions with Professor J.J. and Mrs Nuala Scarisbrick, National Chairman and Administrator respectively of Life-UK throughout 1980s, and with the late Mrs Phyllis Bowman, Director, Society for the Protection of Unborn Children. Invariably, discussions focused on pro-Life political campaigns being mounted by both groups. (Unrecorded)

General discussions in 1980s about campaigns and patrons with officials of the National Viewers and Listeners Association, including its distinguished lead figure, the late Mrs Mary Whitehouse. (Unrecorded)

Discussions and correspondence with the late Professor David Regan, University of Nottingham; an ardent NATO campaigner and leading Conservative academic, 1985-88.

Mrs Eila Bannister, Monday Club activist, Greater London Area. Discussions on 23rd October and 10th December, 1993, and 3rd January, 1998 at Mrs Bannister's North London residence.

Mr Gordon Whiting MBE (deceased), Professional Agent - Coventry Area Conservatives, at party office, Coventry, 23rd October, 1983.

Mr George Ward, Managing Director- Grunwicks, at his London office, 3rd February, 2003.

Un-named national figure in Libertarian Alliance, University of Warwick, 16 May 1998. (Unrecorded)

Un-named former middle-ranking officer, Freedom Association, 9th October, 1998. (Unrecorded)

Un-named official of Coventry South West Conservative Association, 6th June, 1998.

Discussions (by telephone) with Lord David Alton, 23rd February, 2010. (Unrecorded)

Un-named official of Bruges Group, London, 15th July 1997.

Private discussions with Iain Dale, Conservative activist and Manager of Politicos, July 1998 and February 1999. (Unrecorded)

Discussions with J. Farquhar, a former Monday Club activist, 1st October, 2003, London.

Discussions with Rev. Chris Sugden, Secretary of Grass Roots Conservatives - 28th July, 4th August and 26th August, 2017.

Forty Shades of Blue

328

INDEX

Index

Thatcher M. (Mrs) - 2, 11, 14, 17, 23, 26, 38, 90, 103, 119, 154, 162, 167, 187, 191, 203, 228, 260, 262, 284.

Tendencies - 34, 46, 47, 48, 301, 306.

Tory Action - 165

Tory Campaign for Gay Rights - 242, 248

Tory Charter Movement - 19, 47, 48, 50, 51, 78, 132, 163, 188, 220, 242, 256, 258.

Tory Progressives - 13, 23, 59, 62, 64, 65, 66, 67, 68, 69, 70, 71, 72, 74, 75, 76, 77, 85, 86, 87, 88, 89, 91, 93, 99, 101, 103, 117, 123, 138, 161, 221, 251.

Tory Reform Committee - 65, 76, 78, 86, 129, 138

Tory Reform/ Tory Reform Group - (xvii), 7, 28, 45, 47, 76, 78, 85, 89, 90, 105, 173, 175, 189, 241, 255, 258, 264, 265, 276, 285, 287, 306, 308.

Tory Reformer (magazine) - 177, 199, 237, 255, 258

Tory rank and file - 23, 25, 103

Townsend J. - 134, 247

Trimble D. - 43, 44

Ulster Unionists (OUP/UUP) - 18, 70, 100, 102, 102, 123, 164, 165, 174, 193, 194, 225, 231, 255, 290, 303, 306.

   Ulster Democratic Unionists (DUP) - 42, 255, 290, 292

   Friends of the Union (i.e. Ulster/GB) - 194, 214, 215

United Kingdom Independence Party - 235, 287, 292

Union Flag Group (Scotland) - 172

Van Strubenzee W. - 211

Walker P. - 91, 139, 161, 173, 305.

Walters S. - 27, 32, 253, 258.

Ward George (Mr) - 168

Western Goals Institute - (xvii), 171, 193, , 288, 304.

337